THE
NEGOTIATION
CHALLENGE

Remigiusz **Smolinski**
James B. **Downs**

THE
NEGOTIATION
CHALLENGE

How to Win
Negotiation Competitions

ISBN: 978-83-950029-0-8 (ebook)
ISBN: 978-83-950029-2-2 (paperback)

The Negotiation Challenge
www.thenegotiationchallenge.org

Table of Contents

List of Tables

List of Figures

1
INTRODUCTION

Blessed are the peacemakers,
for they will be called children of God.
Matthew. 5:9

Negotiation is our passion and we love sharing it with others. Through our research, we have spent decades trying to understand its complexity. We have used what we have learned in teaching generations of students and business executives across the world how to produce wise and sustainable agreements. As part of these efforts, we have also initiated an annual international negotiation competition for graduate students called *The Negotiation Challenge* (www.thenegotiationchallenge.org). It offers participants a unique opportunity to compare their negotiation skills, live their passion and network with like-minded colleagues from around the world. The Negotiation Challenge has been an amazing opportunity for us to observe and interact with some of the best student negotiators in the world and analyze the secrets of their superior performance.

The Negotiation Challenge, the competition as well as this book, has its origins in our desire to help our students, the leaders of tomorrow, become better negotiators. Since conflicts are an inherent and inescapable part of our lives, we must learn how to manage and resolve them. Indeed, now more than ever, our world needs skilled negotiators who understand not only how to navigate difficult negotiation situations, but also how to engineer value and craft smart and sustainable agreements. However, teaching these skills is a great pedagogical challenge. For example, how do we optimize our classroom teaching to generate the best possible results or how can we help our students become the best negotiators they can be? In addition, although comparing students' negotiation skills before and after a negotiation class delivers valuable insights concerning the efficiency of our teaching methods, this environment lacks the revealing dynamic that a real-world situation has. That is, do the skills they have learned also work outside of the classroom setting? Thus, letting students compete at The Negotiation Challenge puts their negotiation and our pedagogical skills to the ultimate test and helps us answer these questions by seeing how our best students perform when faced with world's best student negotiators.

During the last decade of running our competition, the participating students, as well as their coaches and professors, have regularly asked us for our advice and guidance concerning the most effective preparation for The Negotiation Challenge. Although we have openly shared our observations with them, many have also encouraged us to publish the negotiation simulations we have written for The Negotiation Challenge to make them available for those considering participating in the competition. Thus, although this book has been long overdue, we are very happy to finally satisfy these requests.

The remainder of this book is structured as follows. Chapter 2 describes The Negotiation Challenge as a competition. It explains how and why it started. It also describes its structure and discusses the evaluation criteria that we use in an attempt to capture and measure what we term negotiation intelligence. In this part of the book, we also give details on the competition's admissions criteria that applicants need to fulfill to compete in The Negotiation Challenge. We conclude this chapter with facts and figures from past competitions including the list of hosting institutions and

the winning teams. Chapter 3 then addresses four key types of negotiation, each as an independent section. These include distributive negotiation with value claiming strategies and tactics, integrative negotiation with value creation strategies and tactics, complex
multi-issue negotiations, and multi-party negotiations. Importantly,
each of these sections includes four supporting roleplay simulations, which negotiators can use to develop and reinforce their skills
in preparation for The Negotiation Challenge or other negotiation
competitions. These 16 roleplays are carefully selected role simulations that were written for and used during previous Negotiation
Challenge competitions. Chapter 4 concludes this book with our
advice and recommendations for potential participants of negotiation competitions to consider. We do hope that our suggestions will
both improve the chances of admission for applicants and enhance
their performance during the competition.

We acknowledge that there are already many great negotiation textbooks available on the market that systematically reveal
important research findings about negotiation and in turn help us
understand its complex nature. Based on solid research foundations, these textbooks present well-structured empirical insights,
derive useful theories, and present pragmatic tools and frame-
works. However, what is missing in this collection of literature
is a resource that helps one apply and practice these lessons.
The goal of this book is to fill this gap. As firm believers in expe-
riential learning, we wrote this book to offer students or anyone
ready to be a better negotiator an immediate opportunity to apply and reinforce their negotiation knowledge through roleplay
simulations. As such, we hope that The Negotiation Challenge with
its carefully selected practical exercises offers readers an opportunity to improve their negotiations skills. In turn, we hope it
helps them to negotiate smarter agreements and, even if a little at
a time, make our world a better more peaceful place.

2
THE **NEGOTIATION** **CHALLENGE** COMPETITION

Most negotiation scholars and practitioners would probably agree that negotiation should be classified as a skill. Solid confirmation of this widespread belief is that most business and law schools include negotiation courses in their curricula. Indeed, some of them even go a step further and offer entire graduate programs focused on negotiation. Moreover, since negotiation is also recognized in the corporate world as a key managerial skill, many companies routinely conduct specialized negotiation training programs.

Fortunately, unlike talent (aptitude), which is inborn, skills can be learned. In this sense, negotiating is similar to driving, playing sports or a musical instrument like a piano. Through repetition, complemented by structured feedback, the vast majority of us can learn any of these skills. Indeed, the role that this dynamic plays cannot be underestimated, even for the most talented among us. For example, consider the following: Wolfgang Amadeus Mozart, despite his great talent, would not have been able to produce his great works, had he not spent hours practicing his piano and violin. Lionel Messi, regardless how talented he was already as a child, would never have become one of the world's best soccer players without the thousands of hours spent on the pitch practicing his ball skills. Nor would Sebastian Vettel ever have become a multiple Formula 1 world champion without the countless hours spent on the racetrack.

Therefore, if we accept that negotiation is a skill, we must also agree that it is possible to measure and compare it. After all, this is the spirit behind competitions as the International Chopin Piano Competition, the soccer World Cup and Formula 1 for racecar drivers. In this regard, it must also be possible to set up a championship competition for negotiators. By doing so, we can learn how to become better negotiators and what it takes to become a negotiation champion.

Curious to address this issue, in the spring of 2007, we organized the first edition of The Negotiation Challenge with the vision to attract the world's smartest student negotiators and create an environment in which they could share their passion and compare their negotiation skills.

2.1 The structure

Encouraged by the enthusiastic feedback that we have received over the years from participants and their coaches, we have built a competition format that challenges participants to demonstrate the full spectrum of their negotiation skills in a way that is also captured and compared through a set of fair evaluation criteria.

We believe that the best negotiators understand the importance of preparation, have a broad repertoire of negotiation methods at their disposal, can correctly recognize the type of the negotiation situation they are facing and use the appropriate method in the right situation. We called the sum of these skills their **negotiation intelligence**. The Negotiation Challenge is designed to systematically measure and compare this negotiation intelligence by exposing the participants to various communication modes and a variety of negotiation types. For each combination, we have developed a set of evaluation criteria that best captures the negotiators' performance.

These negotiation types are simulated by roleplays that have been especially developed for our competition. Included among the skills for which these simulations test are the ability to claim value in distributive negotiations, the ability to engineer value both in scoreable and non-scoreable negotiations, and also relationship building. To be thorough, we also split the teams and evaluate the negotiation skills of their individual team members.

Since its inaugural event, The Negotiation Challenge has evolved dynamically through different formats. However, it currently begins with four qualification rounds. The first round typically takes place online prior to the main onsite event. This round can occur either in a synchronous (e.g., video or audio call, instant messenger) or an asynchronous format (e.g., email). Sometimes we leave this decision completely up to the participants, which often ends up as their first negotiation issue. During the main onsite event, we conduct an additional three face-to-face rounds. The best two teams from these qualification rounds advance to the championship final negotiation which is held publically in front of all participants and other interested spectators.

2.2   Searching for negotiation champions

It is often difficult to evaluate and compare negotiators' performance. A primary reason for this is that only an academic setting (classroom and laboratory) allows us to set up and conduct multiple identical negotiations holding all variables constant except only the negotiators themselves. Only in such an environment could we isolate their negotiation skills as the main factor shaping the negotiation process and its outcome. Secondly, even if we could do so, we would still be challenged since we do not have a clear understanding of which and to what extent specific aspects of their negotiation skills contribute to shaping the process and improve its outcome. Unfortunately, this knowledge is one of the main prerequisites for the systematic development of negotiation skills and at the same time an important shortcoming of negotiation pedagogy.

In contrast, negotiation competitions are exactly about comparing negotiation performance. Importantly, this comparison takes place under the critical eyes of the participants themselves, who optimally want a fair evaluation of their performance. Indeed, our experience is that participants are very serious with this point. It is important for them that their evaluations are conducted in a well-ordered, fair and convincing manner. Therefore, a transparent evaluation is needed in negotiation competitions, which is based on convincing principles. Thus, after having intensive discussion and deliberation on this point throughout the history of The Negotiation Challenge, we have agreed on an evaluation methodology, which has been broadly accepted by its participants.

The first and arguably most important evaluation criterion of success is, of course, the **outcome** of the negotiation. After all, the genuine purpose of negotiations is to achieve the best possible outcome. Yet, a precondition for using the outcome to rank negotiators is the ability to measure it. For many negotiation scenarios, such as who gets a better price, a better salary or better delivery conditions this is easy to measure. However, for other scenarios, the outcome of a negotiation includes another dimension, which is beyond the substance of the negotiation. This dimension is the **relationship** between the parties. For example, how trustworthy were the negotiators? Did the parties act fairly during the process? Did one of the parties (or both) lose face? Did

negotiators feel fortified or lost in the negotiation? What is the relationship between the negotiators after the negotiation? These
issues are involved in every negotiation and are a genuine part of
the outcome. This is reflected in the general distinction between
people and substance in negotiation research that is included in
the first principle of the Harvard Method: "Separate the people
from the problem" (Fisher et al., 1982).

Let us explore this point more deeply. Most people would
agree that despite a good result, if it is achieved based on mistrust or one of the parties feeling cheated, the negotiation is
certainly not as good as if this was not the case. For this reason,
a comprehensive ranking should not only be based on the substantive outcome, but it also has to consider also the relational
outcome. Thus, to consider this, one must better define what
the relational outcome is so that it can be more accurately measured. Seemingly, it is more complex than just trust and fairness.
It has various dimensions. One tool that can be used in this regard
is the "Subjective Value Inventory (SVI)" that Curhan & Elfenbein
proposed in 2007. It is a scale capturing various dimensions of
negotiation outcome using sixteen questions spread across four
categories (see *Table 1*). Based on the SVI, the relational outcome
can indeed be measured and compared. Still, despite its useful-
ness, the SVI has certain limitations that are inherent to every
questionnaire-based measurement of a complex phenomenon.
The first is that since it is based on subjective (cross-) evaluations,
is only a proxy for the objective reality.

Instrumental outcome

1. How satisfied are you with your own outcome—i.e., the extent to which the terms of your agreement (or lack of agreement) benefit you?

2. How satisfied are you with the balance between your own outcome and your counterpart(s)'s outcome(s)?

3. Did you feel like you forfeited or "lost" in this negotiation?

4. Do you think the terms of your agreement are consistent with principles of legitimacy or objective criteria (e.g., common standards of fairness, precedent, industry practice, legality, etc.)?

Self

5. Did you "lose face" (i.e., damage your sense of pride) in the negotiation?

6. Did this negotiation make you feel more or less competent as a negotiator?

7. Did you behave according to your own principles and values?

8. Did this negotiation positively or negatively impact your self-image or your impression of yourself?

Process

9. Do you feel your counterpart(s) listened to your concerns?

10. Would you characterize the negotiation process as fair?

11. How satisfied are you with the ease (or difficulty) of reaching an agreement?

12. Did your counterpart(s) consider your wishes, opinions, or needs?

Relationship

13. What kind of "overall" impression did your counterpart(s) make on you?

14. How satisfied are you with your relationship with your counterpart(s) as a result of this negotiation?

15. Did the negotiation make you trust your counterpart(s)?

16. Did the negotiation build a good foundation for a future relationship with your counterpart(s)?

Table 1. The Subjective Value Inventory (Curhan & Elfenbein, 2007)

Next, the measurement of the relational outcome of the negotiation is structurally independent of the substantial outcome. For example, how important is the relationship with my suppliers compared with the deals that I can negotiate with them? The solution on how to link them to each other is very situational and often unclear.

Lastly, evaluating the negotiation performance exclusively based on the (substantial and relational) outcome does not encompass the element of chance in every negotiation: With some luck, even a beginning negotiator can achieve a good deal; weak negotiators perform well if the counterpart is even weaker. In such cases, the link between negotiation performance and outcome can be distorted.

To mitigate these limitations, it is useful to include the negotiation process itself into the performance evaluation. This is intuitive since performance is an attribute of the process and the outcome only a result of that. A good negotiator is doing good things to get a good result. Conceptually then, the process drives the outcome. Thus, based on the research insights of negotiation success drivers, which link process and outcome in negotiations, in negotiation competitions we use judges who evaluate these drivers as they observe the negotiations being conducted. Though we readily admit that a subjective element certainly exists to using judges, the complexity and the qualitative nature of the process does not allow otherwise for objective (numerical) procedures. Indeed, human judgment is needed to assess such important dynamics as fairness, the subtle interactions within and between the teams or their ability to listen actively and to contribute to a joint understanding of the case. For the competitions, we implement this process evaluation, in condensed form, through four categories (see *Table 2*): overall handling; communication; contribution to a joint understanding of the case and contribution to a wise and efficient agreement.

The first evaluation category is the overall handling of the negotiation. These criteria address the completeness of the negotiation and the balance between its main parts. In their assessment, the judges try to capture the first and last impression the negotiators made on each other and evaluate the dynamics of the information sharing process. Despite the seemingly formalistic nature of this category, it is important since it can have an impact on the whole negotiation process and outcome.

The second category is communication skills. Roger Fisher et al. (1982, xvii) defined negotiation "as back and forth communication designed to reach an agreement." According to this definition, negotiation is a specific type of communication used with an intention to settle a dispute or facilitate a transaction. This definition also implies the vital role communication plays in negotiation. The quality of the negotiators' communication skills is one of the strongest determinants of the negotiators' performance. Thus, in this category, the judges try to capture how well the teams are able to "communicate actively and speak clearly" both with their negotiation partners as well as within their team.

The third evaluation category is the contribution made to a joint understanding of the case. Here, the judges look into the specific negotiation tasks of the negotiation. First, we evaluate whether all tasks have been recognized and discussed appropriately. Secondly, we look into the level and dynamics of information exchange and the joint understanding of the different tasks. Does this reflect the problem setting accurately? How do the different parties contribute to the joint understanding of the different tasks? An essential element of this evaluation category is the parties' ability to communicate their own interests and to understand the interests of the negotiation partners. The parties need to develop an accurate understanding of the negotiating issues and the preferences they have concerning them. This is a prerequisite for value creation, exhausting the whole potential of the negotiation situation and reaching an efficient outcome.

The Negotiation Challenge Competition

The last category is the parties' contribution to a wise and efficient agreement. It includes the ability to both create and to claim value. Here, the judges observe how well the negotiators are able to combine both skills to exhaust the full potential of the deal and at the same time claim a significant portion for themselves. For value creating, the judges focus on its two main aspects: capitalizing on the differences in interests between the parties and the creativity in generating value-adding options. At the same time, judges must be on the lookout for teams ignoring value claiming as they attempt to create an impression of being strong value creators by appearing to be overly cooperative. As important as both abilities are individually, to win The Negotiation Challenge, the participating teams must be able to combine both while at the same time sustaining a positive relationship with their partners. During our competition, the judges look for exactly this combination of skills.

Finally, it is important to note that the total score given to the teams on the evaluation form does not necessarily have to be the arithmetic average of the four evaluation categories. Rather, the detailed evaluation criteria should only guide the judging process and be used to help each judge justify their impression and evaluation of performance. In fact, after the negotiation, the judges gather and use these forms to compare and calibrate their individual evaluations with each other and then agree on and compose the final team rankings for each of the roles. This is a very important step in the evaluation process, which typically results in long and intensive discussions due to the fact that different standards and reference points may be used while assessing the negotiators' performance. However, it ultimately leads to a consensual ranking supported by all involved judges.

Although non-scoreable complex negotiation rounds evaluated by the judges have become an integral part of The Negotiation Challenge, performing well in them is not enough to win the competition. That is, to prevail in The Negotiation Challenge, the best teams need to perform and rank well in every round.

Underperformance in any of the rounds radically reduces the chances of making it to the final. The Great Negotiators are complete negotiators.

Evaluation Criteria	Team representing Party A:	Team representing Party B:
Overall handling of the case • Introduction of the case • Strategic information exchange • Closing of the case		
Communication skills • Active listening • Persuasive argumentation • Communication within the team		
Contribution to identifying issues and understanding the interests • Identifying issues and their importance • Understanding linkages between issues • Communicating interests • Understanding interests and their importance		
Contribution to a wise and efficient agreement: • Ability to create AND to claim value! • Have all interests of all parties been considered? • Have the parties been able to invent options for mutual gain, and find creative solutions? • Trust and relationship after the negotiation • Success in value creations • Success in value claiming		
Total score (not necessarily the average)		

1 – very poor; **2** – poor; **3** – fairly poor; **4** – adequate; **5** – fairly good; **6** – good; **7** – very good

Table 2. Judge's evaluation sheet

2.3 Becoming negotiation champions

Competing in teams of three, participants of The Negotiation Challenge are primarily graduate students from top business and law schools around the world. Besides a passion for negotiation, individual participants are expected to possess both a theoretical background and a level of practical experience in negotiation that includes various types of negotiation situations. Moreover, since the competition is conducted exclusively in English, participants are expected to have a strong command of the language.

We particularly appreciate when participating teams are selected and endorsed by their respective academic institutions. This is especially valuable when the endorsement is preceded by an internal competition designed to select the best-qualified applicants. Because it significantly raises the quality of competition, we also strongly encourage coaching by university faculty prior to the competition and for these coaches to attend the competition. Although teams satisfying these criteria are generally given priority, we most certainly encourage anyone to apply. They will be given a fair opportunity to demonstrate their knowledge and experience through their application letter.

Applying to participate in The Negotiation Challenge consists of submitting one curriculum vitae (CV) per team member, a motivation letter and sometimes an essay on one of multiple specified topics. The CVs and motivation letter should demonstrate the team members' interest, knowledge, and experience in the field of negotiation. It should also demonstrate the academic institutions' overall reputation and its specialization in the field of negotiations (e.g., as evidenced by relevant international rankings). This is particularly relevant when the application is endorsed by the institution. If the team is expected to receive specialized coaching in preparation for the competition the coach's name and position in the institution should be included. Needless to say, the application should clearly demonstrate all team applicants' individual fluency in the English language.

Selection criteria generally consider the following:
- quality of the team as evidenced by the application;
- whether or not there has been an internal selection procedure and endorsement of the application by the team's academic institution;
- the institution's international reputation;
- whether or not the teams have or are expected to receive subsequent coaching by a faculty member; and
- geographical and cultural diversification.

The admissions committee selects the participating teams with the best interests of The Negotiation Challenge in mind and its decisions, which typically are reached approximately two weeks after the application deadline, are final.

2.4 Facts and figures

The Negotiation Challenge started in 2007 at the HHL Leipzig Graduate School of Management in Leipzig, Germany. After five successful years, we decided to experiment with other locations, which led us in 2017 to conduct the competition outside of Europe for the first time. Below is the complete list of locations and hosting institutions of The Negotiation Challenge to date:
- TNC 2018 in San Francisco, USA
- TNC 2017 in Bogota, Columbia at the University of Los Andes
- TNC 2016 in Vienna, Austria at the University of Vienna and Vienna University of Technology
- TNC 2015 in Munich, Germany at Technische Universität München

- TNC 2014 in Reykjavik, Iceland at Reykjavik University
- TNC 2013 in Athens, Greece at ALBA Graduate Business School
- TNC 2012 in Paris, France at IESEG School of Management
- TNC 2007-2011 in Leipzig, Germany at HHL Leipzig Graduate School of Management

Moreover, encouraged by the positive reception of each of the hosting institutions and participants over these years, our current goal is to expand the global nature of the event and organize future events on different continents each year.

In terms of the size of the competition, participation interest in The Negotiation Challenge has grown tremendously since the inaugural edition, which started with only ten teams. However, due to organizational and budgetary reasons, from the 80 applications that we now receive on average each year, unfortunately, we can invite only 18 teams to participate in the competition. Although we are very happy to see that so many students share our passion, rejecting highly qualified applicants is always a very difficult and painful decision.

However, for those teams that get invited, The Negotiation Challenge is as close as it gets to competing in the World Championship of Negotiation. Competing here means competing against some of the world's best academic institutions. Indeed, as confirmation of this, here is the list of the previous winning teams, which have received the title of The Great Negotiators. The list includes some of the world's best negotiation minds:

- TNC 2018 – American University, Washington College of Law, USA
- TNC 2017 – IPADE Business School, Mexico
- TNC 2016 – American University, Washington College of Law, USA
- TNC 2015 – HHL Leipzig Graduate School of Management, Germany

- TNC 2014 – Warsaw School of Economics, Poland
- TNC 2013 – Reykjavik University, Iceland
- TNC 2012 – ESSEC Business School, France
- TNC 2011 – Warsaw School of Economics, Poland
- TNC 2010 – University of California, Hastings College of the Law, USA
- TNC 2009 – HHL Leipzig Graduate School of Management, Germany
- TNC 2008 – Harvard Law School and University of California, Hastings College of the Law, USA
- TNC 2007 – Harvard Law School, USA

As a final word for this chapter, this list of The Great Negotiators and the top places in the final rankings regularly include the names of teams representing schools known for their negotiation programs. This is additional supporting evidence that doing well or winning a negotiation competition is not just a coincidence but rather a product of well-designed negotiation curricula, inspiring instructors and structured preparation.

3
MASTERING
THE NEGOTIATION
CHALLENGE

This chapter includes a selection of the best role simulations that have been written for The Negotiation Challenge. They are divided into categories, which reflect the types of negotiations encountered in the competition itself. The first section addresses distributive negotiations. It is followed by sections on scoreable and then non-scoreable integrative negotiation. The final section concludes by addressing three-party negotiations. Furthermore, just like the competition itself, the level of complexity of the role simulations increases with each section and with exercise. However, although the structure of this book was meant to mimic that of the completion, readers should feel free to use these simulations individually, or in any order they consider appropriate.

Prior to using our roleplay simulations during The Negotiation Challenge, they were extensively tested and received positive feedback from the negotiators. Because these simulations have been successfully used in actual competition, we chose to publish them to help potential candidates prepare for The Negotiation Challenge and other similar negotiation competitions organized across the world. Indeed, having access to such simulations and their results can help applicants calibrate their expectations against past results, develop best practices, and improve their negotiation intelligence.

In addition to competition preparation, our roleplay simulations can also be used as classroom exercises, during corporate training seminars or simply as a form of social entertainment among friends. In all these cases, they will generate the pedagogical effects described in the debriefings and lots of fun while using them.

To help the reader decide on which simulations to choose, we have prefaced each roleplay with summary reference information. This preface consists of a brief description of the scenario, its pedagogical focus, the number of parties, the preparation and negotiation time that are necessary to complete the exercise and its complexity level. We hope this information helps with the preliminary evaluation of the simulations' suitability for the readers' purposes.

Following the preface, the roleplay simulations in this book typically start with general instructions, which are the same for all negotiating parties, since they convey the common knowledge shared by them. After the general instructions come each party's confidential instructions, which describe their preferences and other private information and reflect the information asymmetry between the parties. During the preparation phase for each negotiation, parties are expected to read their general and confidential instructions and prepare their negotiation strategy. When the parties are ready to proceed, the negotiation can start.

Lastly, we have also included a debriefing section. The purpose of the debriefing is to reveal informative and instructional information. This includes the simulation's full structure, a discussion on the potential and optimal results, our experience-based educational insight gained from using the simulations during actual competitions, and actual results obtained in the simulations used in The Negotiation Challenge. As mentioned above, this information should help negotiators grow their skills by having a reference by which to reflect and calibrate their results. In addition, instructors using our simulations for educational purposes might find them helpful to prepare their own post-negotiation debriefings. Indeed, these debriefings have an indicative character and can be flexibly adjusted to the instructors' needs. However, it is important to note that due to the revealing nature of these debriefings, the information included in them **must not be distributed to the students before the negotiation.**

One final legal statement: Together with the purchase of the book, the owner obtains a **perpetual and unlimited license** to use all teaching material included in this book **for educational purposes.** To obtain reproducible copies of the roleplay instructions and to inform the authors about the intention to use them, potential users are kindly requested to visit **http://thenegotiationchallenge.org** and contact the authors at: **book@thenegotiationchallenge.org.** We also kindly welcome all feedback and comments.

3.1 Distributive Negotiation

The first type of negotiation that we model during The Negotiation Challenge is distributive negotiation. Negotiation scholars and practitioners use various terms for describing this type of negotiation: competitive, zero-sum (fixed sum) bargaining, win-lose negotiation or distributive bargaining. In this type of negotiation, the pool of resources to be divided between the parties is fixed and limited and the underlying objective of each party is to claim their biggest share. Therefore, the goals of the parties are in fundamental, direct conflict with each other. This creates a highly competitive environment as each party attempts to maximize their own benefits and convince their counterparts to agree to the proposed distribution of the available resources. Moreover, in purely distributive negotiations, each party will have a hard time identifying and pursuing value-generating options because their interests in and valuations of the negotiated issues are identical. This means that what one party ends up with is what the other will not have. If not managed properly, this competition for available resources can trigger aggressive behavior and foster conflict.

When facing such a type of negotiation, there are various value claiming strategies and tactics designed to maximize one's share of available resources. The origins of such strategies and tactics lie in the strategic use of information, in managing the other party's perception and in the overall negotiation process itself. Also, despite the inherent conflict of interest in distributive negotiations, the application of value claiming strategies and tactics often need to be combined with relationship building measures. For example, this is the case when the results of a distributive negotiation determine whether the parties will enter a long-term relationship or when such a negotiation takes place in an already existing relationship. In all such cases, the negotiators need to find a balance between their own benefits and the benefits of the relationship with their negotiation partners.

Therefore, as mentioned above, while evaluating the negotiators' performance in the distributive rounds of The Negotiation Challenge, we focus on the substantive outcome, and when justified, we also combine it with the relational outcome measured by the Subjective Value Inventory survey questionnaire.

The ability to master distributive negotiations is an important skill in the repertoire of The Great Negotiators. First, this is because many situations are distributive in their nature (e.g., selling a house or buying a car). Secondly, even the most integrative negotiations include distributive phases during which the parties need to focus their efforts on value claiming.

This section includes four selected negotiation roleplay simulations written for and used during The Negotiation Challenge. They were designed to test the negotiators' ability to claim value and when necessary, to combine it with building sustainable relationships. They can be used to practice these skills while preparing for negotiation competitions.

Livery Collar

Author: **Remigiusz Smolinski**

Number of parties:	Preparation time:	Negotiation time:	Complexity level:
2	**15-30** minutes	**30-45** minutes	**low**

Pedagogical focus

reservation point, BATNA, information exchange,
value claiming strategies and tactics, strategies of the first offer,
anchoring, objective criteria, fairness, distributive negotiation

Short description

Livery Collar is a roleplay simulation concerning a two-party distributive negotiation for the reacquisition of an important piece of property. It is based on the story of the lost livery collar originally belonging to the HHL Leipzig Graduate School of Management, one of the oldest business schools in Germany. Following the turmoil of the end of the Second World War, the livery collar was unaccountably lost, only to turn up in South America many years later in the hands of a wealthy former German immigrant to Argentina. In 2006, this immigrant commissioned the help of a law firm to help him anonymously return the piece to HHL. This law firm is now faced with the task of negotiating the terms of the exchange in a way that helps them cover their costs and fees. HHL, in turn, after searching for it in vain for years, is excited that the livery collar has reappeared and that they have an opportunity to reacquire it. Unfortunately, funds to pay for it are limited, and thus they will have to be clever negotiators.

Confidential Instructions
for **Meyer and Associates Representatives**

As a founding partner at Meyer and Associates, it has been one of the most peculiar engagements Jonathan Meyer has ever experienced in his long and successful career as a lawyer. One of his best long-term clients, Antonio Heinze, a CEO of Heinze International, called him last week to ask a huge but unorthodox favor. "Jonathan, I need your help." His voice sounded almost like an order and whatever his response might be, saying "No" was not an option.

Antonio was the oldest son of Hans Heinze, who in 1945 founded a small shipping company on the outskirts of Buenos Aires and over the decades, has grown it to become the largest shipping company in South America and the fifth largest in the world. Before moving to Argentina, Hans grew up in Leipzig, Germany in a wealthy merchant family. However, shortly before the start of the Second World War the family had to leave their beloved city and emigrated first to Zurich and then to Buenos Aires.

"My father has something that does not belong to him and wants it returned to its lawful owners", continued Antonio. Later that day, Jonathan entered the spacious, classically decorated living room of Antonio's impressive residence. Antonio welcomed him warmly and led him to a glass cabinet filled with old books, albums, and pictures illustrating the history of the Heinze family. "Here it is," said Antonio solemnly, while taking out a glazed wooden box from the cabinet. He continued, "This is the original livery collar which was made for the deans of the oldest business school in Germany, HHL Leipzig Graduate School of Management."

A livery collar or chain of office is a heavy chain, usually of gold, worn as an insignia of office in Europe from the Middle Ages onwards. There are not many areas where livery collars are worn today, but one of them is certainly academia. Over the centuries, livery collars have become symbols of status and dignity and were proudly worn by the most distinguished leaders of prestigious academic institutions around the world.

Although HHL was established in 1898 as one of the world's first business schools, it was not until a quarter of a century later, in March 1925, that the Saxonian Ministry of Economics approved the order for a livery collar for the future deans of HHL. With a total budget of 4,000 Reichsmarks,[1] its construction was commissioned to master goldsmith Johannes Eckert, a famous Dresden goldsmith who was often compared to Johann Melchior Dinglinger, one of Europe's greatest goldsmiths of the 17th-18th century and the court jeweler of August II King of Saxony. Intended as a prestigious symbol of status, the whole livery collar was to be made of pure 24-carat gold. Meister Eckert's work exceeded the expectations of his clients and in 1926, the new livery collar was delivered to HHL's Dean, Professor Grossmann by Director Klien from the Saxonian Ministry of Economics.

Five years later in the spring of 1931, because the collar was poorly visible by the audience during the official ceremonies when it was used (it kept hiding under the Dean's jacket lapel), it was returned to Master Eckert's workshop for improvements. With a total budget of 1,500 Reichsmarks donated by the famous Leipzig publisher Edgar Herfurth, Master Eckert mounted four additional links on both sides of the medallion and added four light green tourmalines and four Japanese Akoya pearls. Together with these changes, HHL's livery collar was a masterpiece of its time. It was presented at numerous art exhibitions around the world as an extraordinary example of the modern

---

[1] Reichsmark was the currency in Germany from 1924 to June 20, 1948. According to German Federal Statistical Office, the purchasing power of a Reichsmark in the 1920s and 1930s corresponds to ca. 3-4 Euro at the time the events described in this role play took place.

German goldsmith school. For such events, HHL consequently insured the piece for 6,000 Reichsmarks.

For almost two decades, HHL's livery collar served its purpose by decorating the distinguished chests of six consecutive deans. However, sometime afterwards it mysteriously disappeared. The last time it was traceably mentioned in historical sources was in June 1943 when it was listed in a catalog of valuable objects prepared for Lieutenant Schmidt, the head of Leipzig's air defense.

However, in 1974, Hans Heinze was contacted by an anonymous seller who claimed to have "a precious souvenir" from Leipzig, Hans' hometown. Though he did not know who this mysterious seller was nor how he came into possession of the livery collar, he suspected the story was rather suspicious. Despite this, his interest in the object was intense enough to have the object at least examined for authenticity. After experts confirmed its originality, Hans Heinze transferred an equivalent of 125,000 Euro[2] to a bank account in the Cayman Islands. Two days later, he became the new owner of HHL's livery collar.

"How much is it worth today?", asked Jonathan, expecting that this would be a central issue given that the object may soon change owners. Apparently, Antonio was very well prepared for this question. According to historical sources, the value of HHL's livery collar in the 1920s and 1930s was about 6,000 Reichsmarks. This amount would equate to about 24,000 Euro today. However, the livery collar was made of 24-carat gold. Since the 1920s, the price of gold has increased over 21 times from around 20 US dollars per ounce in 1926 to almost 445 US dollars in 2006. This would imply a value of around half a million Euro. However, considering its historical and artistic value, Antonio estimated that the price of HHL's livery collar today might be even 20-30% higher.

"Is this how much you would like me to sell it for?", asked Jonathan. Antonio paused with a smile and then replied, "We are

---

[2]   125,000 is the 2006 value of the amount paid by Hans Heinze in 1973.

ready to give it back for free. The price you manage to negotiate should cover your costs and fees. Whatever you get is yours." The Heinze family has been very prosperous in the last decades and indeed could afford such a gesture. Antonio then added, "There is one condition, however. The Family Heinze must not be publically associated with this transaction. We want to remain anonymous and need your absolute discretion." Jonathan dutifully replied, "Consider it done."

On Tuesday, February 14, 2006, Jonathan Meyer phoned the HHL's dean's office and requested a meeting concerning HHL's potential reacquisition of its lost insignia. Six weeks later, on March 31, HHL's dean, Professor Hans Wiesmeth received an official envelope sent from the Meyer and Associates office in Buenos Aires, which included six high-quality photos of HHL's old insignia and a newly issued certificate confirming its originality. A face-to-face meeting was then arranged for December, which gave both sides sufficient time to make the necessary preparations.

You are about to meet the HHL Dean, Prof. Dr. Hans Wiesmeth, HHL Chancellor, Dr. Judith Marquardt and the President of the Association of HHL Friends, Prof. Dr. Hans Göschel. Your objectives for the upcoming negotiation are:

- Make sure HHL's **livery collar returns to its lawful owner**
- Negotiate the **best possible price** for the transfer of HHL's livery collar. Ultimately, whatever you get is your direct revenue.
- Remember Hans and Antonio Heinze want to remain **anonymous**.
- Make sure the final agreement does not contain any additional monetary or non-monetary, fixed or variable components and/or does not depend on conditional clauses.

Confidential Instructions
for **HHL Representatives**

It was evident to everyone that the upcoming meeting would be very special. It would not be just another trivial negotiation like so many in the past. This time the stakes are very high. They could be facing the only opportunity to regain what they have been looking for since their search began almost a decade ago. Therefore, by a unanimous decision of HHL's executive management, its most prominent representatives were designated to this negotiation. HHL's Dean, Prof. Dr. Hans Wiesmeth, Chancellor, Dr. Judith Marquardt and the President of the Association of HHL Friends, Prof. Dr. Hans Göschel were about to meet the legal counsel of an anonymous person, who claimed to possess the long-lost HHL ceremonial livery collar.

A livery collar or chain of office is a heavy chain, usually of gold, worn as an insignia of office in Europe from the Middle Ages onwards. There are not many areas where livery collars are worn today, but one of them is certainly academia. Over the centuries, livery collars have become symbols of status and dignity and were proudly worn by the most distinguished leaders of prestigious academic institutions.

Although HHL was established in 1898 as one of the world's first business schools, it was not until a quarter of a century later, in March 1925, that the Saxonian Ministry of Economics approved the order of a livery collar for the future deans of HHL. With a total budget of 4,000 Reichsmarks,[3] its construction was commissioned to master goldsmith Johannes Eckert, a famous

---

[3] Reichsmark was the currency in Germany from 1924 until June 20, 1948. According to Federal Statistical Office purchasing power of a Reichsmark in 1920s and 1930s correspond to ca. 3-4 Euro at the time the events described in this role play took place.

Dresden goldsmith who was often compared to Johann Melchior Dinglinger, one of Europe's greatest goldsmiths of the 17th-18th century and the court jeweler of August II King of Saxony. Intended as a prestigious symbol of status, the entire livery collar was to be made of pure 24-carat gold. Meister Eckert's work exceeded the expectations of his clients, and in 1926 a new livery collar was delivered to HHL's Dean Professor Grossmann by Director Klien from the Saxonian Ministry of Economics.

Five years later in the spring of 1931, because the collar was poorly visible by the audience during the official occasions when it was used (it kept hiding under the Dean's jacket lapel), it was returned to Master Eckert's workshop for improvements. With a total budget of 1,500 Reichsmarks donated by the famous Leipzig publisher Edgar Herfurth, Master Eckert mounted four additional links on both sides of the medallion and added four light green tourmalines and four Japanese Akoya pearls. Together with these changes, HHL's livery collar was a masterpiece of its time. It was presented at numerous art exhibitions around the world as an extraordinary example of the modern German goldsmith school. For such events, HHL insured its insignia for 6,000 Reichsmarks.

For almost two decades, HHL's livery collar served its purpose by decorating the distinguished chests of six consecutive deans. However, sometimes afterward it mysteriously disappeared. The last time it was traceably mentioned in historical sources was in June 1943 when it was listed in a catalog of valuable objects prepared for Lieutenant Schmidt, the head of Leipzig air defense. Only in the 1990s, following the turmoil of both the post-war period and the reintegration of Germany, was an investigation launched by Professor Göschel, an expert in HHL history, to discover what happened to it. His efforts revealed that originally the insignia was supposed to be transported to and stored safely at the Central Bank in Berlin. Unfortunately, no official records confirming the delivery were ever found. Professor Göschel speculated that it was probably lost during the major air bombing of Leipzig on December 4, 1943, which completely destroyed HHL's old campus in the Ritterstrasse. Unfortunately, despite further considerable efforts by HHL and the State of Saxony to locate its whereabouts, no further evidence was ever uncovered about its fate or location.

That is, until Tuesday, February 14, 2006, when Professor Hans Wiesmeth received an unexpected call. The person calling introduced himself as Jonathan Meyer, a law partner at Meyer and Associates in Buenos Aires, Argentina. On behalf of his client, a South American resident wishing to remain anonymous, he requested a meeting concerning HHL's potential reacquisition of its lost insignia. Intrigued by this proposition, Professor Wiesmeth kindly explained that before any meeting concerning such a serious issue could take place, HHL would need a confirmation that the livery collar is indeed authentic and in the possession of Mr. Meyer's client. Mr. Meyer promised to deliver the requested confirmation within the following two months, and he kept his word. On Friday, March 31, Professor Wiesmeth received an official envelope sent from the Meyer and Associates office, which included six high-quality photos of HHL's old insignia and a newly issued certificate confirming its originality. Following this, a face-to-face meeting was then arranged for December, which gave both sides sufficient time to make the necessary preparations.

As part of these preparations, the first step was to estimate how much HHL's livery collar was worth in today's value. According to historical sources, its value in the 1920s and 1930s was about 6,000 Reichsmarks. This amount would equate to about 24,000 Euro today. However, the livery collar was made of 24-carat gold, and since the 1920s, the gold price has increased over 21 times from around 20 US dollars per ounce in 1926 to almost 445 US dollars in 2006. This would imply a value of around half a million Euro.

In further preparation, HHL ordered three independent appraisals of the current value of its insignia. The experts were not unanimous, but considering its historical and artistic value, they estimated it to vary from slightly over 600,000 Euro up to nearly 750,000 Euro. Each of them, however, clearly mentioned that there are not many potential buyers in the world who would be willing to pay such prices.

For HHL, however, its historical livery collar is priceless. Therefore, it recently held a fundraising event that helped it raise almost 250,000 Euro that it can use toward the reacquisition of its historical insignia. Although this amount exceeded the organizers' expectations, it, unfortunately, was much less than the experts' appraisals. Nevertheless, HHL's executive management decided that it would proceed with the negotiation but with the limitation that the raised 250,000 Euro will be the absolute maximum that they will pay for the lost livery collar. However, if this turned into a problem, HHL was also prepared to offer the naming of one of its classrooms after the anonymous owner, assuming of course that he or she would be ready to give up that anonymity. Indeed, comparable offers are usually extended to supporters of HHL for donations of 250,000 Euro or more. Although including this option in the final agreement has certain opportunity costs, it would be strongly preferred by HHL's executives since it solves the cash shortage issue.

Whatever happens, HHL cannot afford to miss this chance. Its livery collar has to return to Leipzig.

Summarizing, your objectives for the upcoming negotiation are:

- Reacquire HHL's **livery collar from the anonymous owner**.
- Negotiate the **lowest possible price** for HHL's livery collar. Remember you must not spend more than 250,000 Euro.
- If possible, try to **offset the final price with a non-monetary service** by naming one of HHL classrooms after your transaction partner.
- Make sure the final agreement does not contain any additional monetary or non-monetary, fixed or variable components and/or does not depend on conditional clauses.

Debriefing

Livery Collar is a distributive negotiation roleplay simulation written for The Negotiation Challenge 2011 in Leipzig, Germany. It was held at HHL Leipzig Graduate School of Management following a speech from the HHL Dean wearing this historic livery collar.

The main issue in the negotiation between the representatives of HHL and the attorneys from Meyer and Associates is the price of HHL's historic livery collar. The roleplay simulation includes various reference points that might be used by each party to both calibrate their respective expectations and develop their strategies. They are summarized in the following overview:

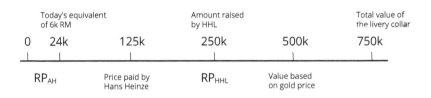

Figure 1. The structure of the Livery Collar roleplay simulation

HHL's reservation point (RP) is at 250,000 Euro, which they raised for the reacquisition of the livery collar. Although the Heinze family is ready to donate the insignia for free, it has empowered Jonathan Meyer with the liberty to negotiate any price that he considers appropriate. This results in a huge Zone of Possible Agreement (ZOPA) of 250,000 Euro. Additionally, the instructions offer many other reference points that might help the parties to support their case.

As the two parties will most likely never interact with each other again, the importance of the relationship between them is diminished. Therefore, it is not considered in the evaluation of the negotiator's performance. The evaluation focuses solely on the price to which they agree.

The highest price obtained during The Negotiation Challenge 2011 was 250,000 Euro, the lowest was 200,000 Euro with a few teams ending up without an agreement. The source of controversial and heated debates between the participating teams was the fact that some reference points, for instance, the value of the livery collar being based on the development of the gold price, were much higher than what HHL could afford to pay for it. Some teams used the implied values of 500,000-750,000 Euro to shape their expectations and aspirations. As such, they found it difficult or even impossible to accept that the highest end of the ZOPA is significantly smaller.

Livery Collar is a roleplay simulation well suited for introducing the topic of distributive negotiation and can be used for analyzing the efficiency of first offer strategies.

Benedict Basso

Author: **Remigiusz Smolinski**

Number of parties:	Preparation time:	Negotiation time:	Complexity level:
2	**15-30** minutes	**30-45** minutes	**inter-mediate**

Pedagogical focus

reservation point, BATNA, information exchange, value claiming strategies and tactics, combining them with trust creation and sustaining good working relationships, strategies of the first offer, anchoring, objective criteria, fairness, distributive negotiation

Short description

Benedict Basso is a two-party distributive negotiation simulation concerning the conditions of an employment contract. It includes Benedict Basso, a rising opera star during the late 18th century in the Leipzig Opera, one of the oldest opera venues in Europe. In addition to coming from a strong musical family and having a unique and talented voice, he has worked very hard to pursue his dream of becoming an opera performer. He is very proud of this. Now he finds himself with a key opportunity to sing the title role in a popular opera that could significantly help his career. That is, if he can successfully conclude the contract details with the opera's production company and its famous impresario director, Pasquale Bondini. Pasquale Bondini, an experienced opera singer himself, is also a talented, highly experienced and politically well-connected director. He knows what it takes to put on a successful and profitable production and therefore must consider multiple issues to make it happen. He will push hard for an equitable deal with Benedict.

Confidential Instructions
for **Benedict and his Advisors**

Benedict Basso is a rising star of the Leipzig Opera. Established in the year 1693, it is the third oldest opera venue in Europe after La Fenice (Venice, Italy) and the Hamburg State Opera (Hamburg, Germany).

Benedict possesses a unique type of voice called basso cantante, which means "singing bass." Basso cantante is a high lyrical voice typical for Italian opera singers. It is also characterized by a faster vibrato than its closest equivalent, the bass-baritone. Benedict grew up surrounded by musicians and artists. His father played in the concert society known as the "Grand Concert" which later became the world famous Gewandhaus Orchestra. His mother sang as a soprano. As an exceptionally talented child, Benedict was admitted to the elite St. Thomas School and throughout his studies sang in the famous St. Thomas Choir. However, his passion has always been the opera. Indeed, he practiced hard. He also attended every performance at the opera, admired the greatest singers and wanted to be like them. With such dedication and focus, it was not long before he was given a chance. At the age of 18, he sang his first aria on the stage of the Leipzig Opera. The audience loved him. Although he was still a teenager, he could already sing much better than many of the more experienced opera singers. Indeed, the Leipziger Zeitungen[4], the Leipzig daily newspaper, compared him even to Francesco Benucci – one of the best opera singers of his time – and added that Benedict's voice had a unique characteristic – "it could touch people's hearts."

The fame of this wonderful bass from Leipzig soon reached Pasquale Bondini, an Italian impresario who since 1777 has been

---

[4]   Daily newspaper, successor of Einkommenden Zeitungen, which first published in 1650, is considered the first daily newspaper in the world.

the director of the King of Saxony's small but highly regarded and very popular opera company in Dresden. Two years ago, his company decided to also expand into Leipzig and perform in front of its wealthy merchant-dominated audience. However, since he and his personnel were already heavily engaged in numerous projects in Dresden, he had to engage new artists. Operas performed by this company mainly included works of leading Italian composers. Therefore, hiring Benedict to sing in the company's Leipzig performances initially seemed to be a reasonable solution.

Benedict and Pasquale met in Dresden to get to know each other and discuss Benedict's potential engagement with Pasquale's opera company. The meeting lasted only for 20 minutes and unfortunately ended angrily. Benedict simply could not believe his ears. He thought they were meeting to discuss the financial conditions of his engagement. Instead, he only heard Pasquale boasting about how busy and successful he and his company were and that Benedict's lack of experience might put his whole expansion plan at risk. When he added that Leipzig was still culturally underdeveloped and that to become a real virtuoso one would have to be Italian like him, Benedict stood up and left. This was simply too much for him. Pasquale's superiority complex, his arrogance and lack of respect for Benedict's skills and recent performance success convinced him that he was not interested in working at the Pasquale Bondini Opera Company.

A year later, in December 1786, the Pasquale Bondini Opera Company produced *The Marriage of Figaro* in Prague. This was a comic opera written by Wolfgang Amadeus Mozart, with its text (libretto) written by Lorenzo Da Ponte. It premiered only six months earlier at the Burg Theater in Vienna with the first two performances directed by Mozart himself. For this, Mozart supposedly received 450 florins (Austro-Hungarian Gulden) from the Imperial Italian Opera Company for his work on it. This was three times more than his annual salary in 1773–1777 when he was employed as a court musician by the ruler of Salzburg, Prince-Archbishop Hieronymus

Colloredo. Da Ponte was paid 200 florins. However, despite brilliant music and the casting of the celebrated Italian bass Francesco Benucci in the title role, Figaro was not well received in Vienna.

In contrast, Pasquale Bondini's Prague production with lead singer Giovanni Bellotti, an Italian bass, who until recently was the leading buffo singer in Venice, turned it into a tremendous success. Indeed, the newspaper, Prager Oberpostamtszeitung called the work "*a masterpiece,*" and said, "*no piece has ever caused such a sensation.*"[5] Invited by local music lovers, Mozart visited Prague and listened to the production. He was impressed by what he saw and even spontaneously decided to conduct it himself.

Attracted by the great success of *Figaro* in Prague, a prominent merchant and opera connoisseur, Johannes von Reichenbach, invited Pasquale Bondini to perform it on the stage of the Leipzig Opera for the celebrations of his 70th birthday. Supposedly, Mr. von Reichenbach offered him a fortune but set one condition: the title role be sung instead by his favorite opera singer, Leipzig's wonderful bass, Benedict Basso.

The number of job openings for opera soloists are generally very limited. Therefore, they welcome each new opportunity with great interests. Singing for Pasquale's opera company has helped many young artists promote their name. Many of them were even able to sign lucrative contracts afterward. These reasons persuaded Benedict to give Pasquale another chance despite an extremely negative first impression he had made at their last meeting.

Generally, opera soloists can make from 5 florins per performance up to 200 florins per performance for the most elite singers. The market average is probably close to 20 florins per performance. It is not clear how much lead singer Giovanni Bellotti is currently earning but supposedly, Pasquale is paying his artists rather well. He was probably earning significantly more than the market average. Benedict is currently paid 30 florins per

---

[5] Source: Deutsch, Otto Erich. Mozart: A Documentary Biography. Stanford University Press, p. 281.

performance at the Leipzig Opera. He believes that this is an appropriate salary for someone his age and experience and would never accept singing for less at Pasquale's company. His advisors recommended demanding a significant premium for the lead role in Pasquale's *Figaro*. They pointed out that even 80 florins or more would not be unreasonable for such a role.

Benedict perceives the upcoming negotiation as an opportunity and not a necessity. Singing with Pasquale's stars would give him a chance to prove that he is more than just a provincial singer and that his talent can shine just as brightly as theirs. Even if this negotiation fails, for opera connoisseurs in Leipzig he will still remain their Benedict – someone for whom it's worth to go to the opera. He would, however, prefer not to disappoint Mr. von Reichenbach and his guests.

Benedict and his advisors will meet with the representatives of Pasquale Bondini Opera Company today. During their last encounter, Benedict perceived him as a very arrogant and self-centered person who showed no respect for anyone other than himself. Singing Figaro, however, might open a new chapter in Benedict's career. It is a unique opportunity, which might take him to the "top" where he feels he undoubtedly belongs. It would be very unwise not to seize the opportunity.

Summarizing, your objectives for the upcoming negotiation are:
- Make sure Benedict **signs a contract** with Pasquale Bondini Opera Company and performs the title role in *The Marriage of Figaro*;
- Negotiate the **highest possible remuneration** for Benedict;
- Make sure Benedict's salary does not contain additional monetary or non-monetary, fixed or variable components and/or does not depend on conditional clauses;
- If you reach an agreement, Benedict and Pasquale will have to work closely together. Make sure you **repair their damaged relationship**.

Confidential Instructions
for **Pasquale Bondini Opera Company**

This has been an extraordinary season for Pasquale Bondini, an Italian impresario who, since 1777, has been the director of the King of Saxony's small but highly regarded and very popular opera company in Dresden. Not many experts believed that his decision to produce *The Marriage of Figaro* in December 1786 in Prague would lead to an artistic and commercial success but once again, Pasquale's intuition was right. People loved Figaro, they loved Pasquale and they loved his opera company.

The Marriage of Figaro is a comic opera written by Wolfgang Amadeus Mozart, with its text (libretto) written by Lorenzo Da Ponte. It premiered six months earlier in May 1786 at the Burg Theater in Vienna. Mozart supposedly received 450 florins (Austro-Hungarian Gulden) from the Imperial Italian Opera Company for his work on it. This was three times more than his annual salary in 1773–1777 when he was employed as a court musician by the ruler of Salzburg, Prince-Archbishop Hieronymus Colloredo. Da Ponte was paid 200 florins. However, despite brilliant music and the casting of the celebrated Italian bass Francesco Benucci in the title role, Figaro was not well received in Vienna.

In contrast, Pasquale Bondini's Prague production with lead singer Giovanni Bellotti, an Italian bass who until recently was the leading buffo singer in Venice, turned it into a tremendous success. Indeed, the newspaper, Prager Oberpostamtszeitung called the work *"a masterpiece,"* and said, *"no piece has ever caused such a sensation."*[6] Invited by local music lovers, Mozart visited Prague

---

[6]   Source: Deutsch, Otto Erich. Mozart: A Documentary Biography. Stanford University Press, p. 281.

and listened to the production. He was impressed by what he saw and even spontaneously decided even to conduct it himself.

Attracted by the great success of *Figaro* in Prague, a prominent merchant and opera connoisseur, Johannes von Reichenbach, invited Pasquale Bondini to perform it on the stage of the Leipzig Opera for the celebrations of his 70th birthday. Mr. von Reichenbach offered him a fortune but set one condition. The title role had to be sung instead by his favorite opera singer, Leipzig's wonderful bass, Benedict Basso.

Benedict Basso is a rising star of the Leipzig Opera. He possesses a unique type of voice called basso cantante, which means "singing bass." Basso cantante is a high lyrical voice typical for Italian opera singers. It is also characterized by a faster vibrato than its closest equivalent, the bass-baritone. As an exceptionally talented child, Benedict was admitted to the elite St. Thomas School and throughout his studies also sang in the famous St. Thomas Choir. At the age of 18, he sang his first aria on the stage of the Leipzig Opera and the audience loved him. He was still a teenager but could already sing much better than many of the more experienced opera singers. The *Leipziger Zeitungen*,[7] Leipzig's daily newspaper, compared him even to Francesco Benucci – one of the best opera singers of his time – and added that Benedict's voice had a very unique characteristic – "it could touch people's hearts."

Two years ago, the fame of this wonderful bass from Leipzig reached Pasquale Bondini, when his company decided to expand to Leipzig and perform in front of its wealthy, merchant-dominated audience. However, since he and his personnel were already heavily engaged in numerous projects in Dresden, Bondini had to employ new artists. Therefore, hiring a known talent like Benedict to sing in the company's Leipzig performances seemed to be a reasonable solution.

---

[7] Daily newspaper, successor of Einkommenden Zeitungen, which first published in 1650, is considered the first daily newspaper in the world.

Benedict and Pasquale met in Dresden to get to know each other and discuss Benedict's potential engagement with Pasquale's opera company. Unfortunately, the meeting lasted only for 20 minutes and ended angrily. Pasquale simply could not believe his ears. He thought that they would start their meeting with getting to know each other. Instead, he felt that Benedict was focused only on money. Pasquale wanted to introduce himself and his opera company. He wanted to give Benedict an impression how much he had done for young artists and how much he could do for him. However, instead of excitement and appreciation, he felt Benedict responded with impatience and greed. When he mentioned that eventually leaving Leipzig and moving to Italy would be a requirement to become a real opera star, Benedict just stood up and left.

This was simply too much for Pasquale. Benedict's arrogance and lack of respect for Pasquale's achievements and status convinced him not to hire Benedict at that point. However, with the amount of money now offered by Mr. von Reichenbach, Pasquale is persuaded to give Benedict another chance.

Generally, opera soloists can make from 5 florins per performance up to 200 florins per performance for the most elite singers. Market average is probably close to 20 florins per performance. Pasquale is paying his artists rather well and Giovanni Bellotti, at 80 florins per performance is one of his best-paid soloists. It is not clear how much Benedict is currently earning at the Leipzig Opera. Pasquale suspects, however, that it is probably not much more than the market average. He is ready to pay him a certain premium for staring in his production, especially since involving Benedict was an explicit wish of Mr. von Reichenbach. However, to pay the salaries for all his artists, cover all other costs and guarantee an acceptable profit margin, Pasquale cannot afford to offer Benedict more than 150 florins. This would be the highest salary he has ever paid to a singer. Only a very few virtuosi in the world are earning more. Therefore, Pasquale would strongly prefer to keep Benedict's salary at the amount he is currently paying to Giovanni for playing Figaro. Benedict would have to have very good reasons to convince Pasquale to offer him more.

The representatives of Pasquale Bondini Opera Company will meet with Benedict and his advisors today. During their last encounter, Pasquale perceived him as a very arrogant and money oriented person who showed no respect for his achievements and status. Hiring Benedict is Mr. von Reichenbach's hard precondition for involving Pasquale's Opera Company in the celebrations of his 70th birthday. It is also a great business opportunity and it would be very unwise not to seize it.

Summarizing, your objectives for the upcoming negotiation are:

- Make sure Benedict **signs a contract** with Pasquale Bondini Opera Company and performs the title role in The Marriage of Figaro;
- **Stay within your budget** saving as much of it as you can; remember, the higher Benedict's salary, the lower your profit margin;
- Make sure Benedict's salary does not contain additional monetary or non-monetary, fixed or variable components and/or does not depend on conditional clauses;
- If you reach an agreement, Pasquale and Benedict will have to work closely together. Make sure you **repair their damaged relationship**.

Debriefing

Benedict Basso is a distributive negotiation roleplay simulation written for The Negotiation Challenge 2010 in Leipzig, Germany. This negotiation took place at the Leipzig Opera House and was preceded by a private concert for the competition participants.

The main issue in the negotiation between Benedict Basso and his advisors and the Pasquale Bondini Opera Company is his future salary for performing the title role in Mozart's *The Marriage of Figaro*. Both roles include various reference points that might be used to both calibrate their respective expectations and to develop their strategies. They are summarized in the following overview:

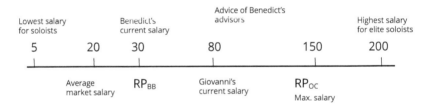

Figure 2. The structure of the Benedict Basso roleplay

Benedict Basso's reservation point is his current salary at the Leipzig Opera of 30 florins per performance, whereas Pasquale Bondini Opera Company cannot offer him more than 150 florins per performance. This results in a Zone of Possible Agreement (ZOPA) of 120 florins per performance. Additionally, the instructions offer multiple secondary reference points that help each party to support their case.

The complexity of this negotiation lies in the fact that a potential agreement is only the beginning of a working relationship between the parties. That is, focusing solely on obtaining the highest/lowest salary at the expense of damaging an already impaired relationship would be a less than optimal outcome. Therefore, value claiming strategies and tactics applied in the negotiation must be weighed carefully and combined with relationship building measures.

Therefore, to evaluate the performance of the negotiators in The Negotiation Challenge we combined the substantive outcome (salary) that the parties agreed to with the relational outcome from the Subjective Value Inventory (SVI) score obtained from their negotiation partners. However, as each of these variables is expressed in different units, we needed to normalize them and convert them to statistical z-scores. Both z-scores for the substantive and relational outcome were then added together. Although it could make sense to assign different weights to each partial z-scores, for this particular evaluation, we weighed them both equally since it best reflects the parties' objectives to maximize both salary and relationship outcomes. The final score approximates the relative performance of each team compared to the performance of all participating teams.

For the benefit of reference, the highest salary obtained during The Negotiation Challenge 2010 was 100 florins, the lowest 66 florins and the average was 89.40 florins. The results obtained by the participating teams covered 28% of the ZOPA with the average salary nearly splitting it in half. Interestingly, the highest salary was accompanied by the lowest SVI evaluation, which ultimately resulted in a below average total outcome. The lowest salary was accompanied by an average SVI evaluation, which produced the best total result among the Opera Companies. The best total outcome among the teams representing Benedict Basso consisted of the second highest salary and the best SVI evaluation.

The main challenge that we observed for the negotiating teams was finding the balance between the effectiveness of their value claiming strategies and relationship management. The results clearly showed that the substantive and relational outcomes do not have to negatively correlate with each other. The best performing Benedict Basso team was a strong example that even in distributive negotiation obtaining a good substantive outcome does not have to take place at the cost of damaging a relationship.

Benedict Basso is a negotiation roleplay simulation suitable for introducing the topic of distributive negotiation. It can also be used for analyzing the efficiency of first offer strategies and their potential impact on the relationships between negotiating parties.

John Kicker II

Author: **Remigiusz Smolinski**

Number of parties:	Preparation time:	Negotiation time:	Complexity level:
2	**15-30** minutes	**30-45** minutes	**inter-mediate**

Pedagogical focus

reservation point, BATNA, information exchange,
value claiming strategies and tactics, combining them
with trust creation and sustaining good working relationships,
strategies of the first offer, anchoring, objective criteria,
fairness, distributive negotiation

Short description

John Kicker II is a two-party distributive negotiation roleplay simulation over the terms of a sports employment contract. It includes John Kicker, an outstanding European soccer star who, after a career-ending knee injury, finds himself with an opportunity to transition into a career as General Manager of his former team, the Rocks. With the help of his agent, he will be negotiating the terms of this employment with the Rock's current president, Mr. Busman.

Confidential Instructions
for **John and his Agents**

You are partners in a firm that manages and acts as an agent for athletes and celebrities. Five years ago, you represented John Kicker and helped him sign his second contract with the Rocks, a successful European football team. John was very pleased with the outcome of your work and recommended your agency to other players. Thanks to John's recommendation you have since successfully expanded your business in the field of professional soccer.

John originally started his professional career with the Rocks back in the early 1980s. Back then, coaches, sports experts and the press unanimously agreed that John Kicker had exceptional talent and could become one of the best defenders this game has ever seen. Therefore, it came as no surprise to anyone when he received a nomination to play on the national team.

Following a series of brilliant games with the national team during the World Cup, John took advantage of his popularity and left the Rocks to sign a three-year contract with the Champs, then and still now one of the most successful clubs in the world. Indeed, they have won the League 31 times and hold over a dozen international cup titles, including winning the prestigious Champions League a record nine times.

Playing for the Champs had always been John's dream and so he jumped at the opportunity. However, after signing, although he demonstrated outstanding performance at the beginning, for the majority of the season his time was disappointingly spent either on the bench or playing with their second team. Based on local press reporting, many suspected the reason to be motivational and behavioral problems that led to trust and confidence issues with the coach. This lack of play gave Champ's fans very few occasions to admire John's legendary skills and as a result, his popularity declined. Despite this, the Champs maintained John's contract and even rejected offers from other clubs to acquire him. Indeed, the Champ's public spokesperson repeatedly reported that John was "not for sale" and that the Champ's coach, Coach Meister, saw a great future for him in the club.

When his contract did eventually expire, no one was really sure whether John could still play as well as he used to. Although everybody still remembered his extraordinary skills, none of the big clubs in the League were interested in taking the risk. As a result, John ended up with the Contenders, a second league club which, though well organized, could not compare with the Champs.

Unfortunately, he did not adjust well with the Contenders. The local press reported on motivational and behavioral problems and how this led to relationship issues with the coach. As a result, after an outstanding performance at the beginning of the season, for the remainder of the season, John again watched his colleagues from the bench.

You bumped into John at a New Year's celebration event five years ago. During your chat, John told you that he has been confidentially approached by the Rocks. They are interested in signing him again and he was looking for someone to represent him in this upcoming negotiation. By the end of the party, John had become your client.

Indeed, though you know that the Rocks have never been as successful as the Champs, each season they did deliver a very solid performance, winning on average over half (50-60%) of their 38 games in the League. Moreover, you knew that Franz Irons, the coach for the Rocks, believes that success in modern European football starts with a solid defense and that he has developed the Rocks into probably the best defensive team in the League. In this regard, although John was ready to play almost for nothing just to get a chance to show the world that he was still one of the best defenders around, you knew that John would be a strong fit for this team.

With your strong negotiation with the Rocks' General Manager, Mr. Spodir, The Rocks offered John a two-year contract, replacing Bob Wall, a very talented young player whose serious health problems suddenly interrupted a very promising career. They hoped that, supported by Coach Irons, John would regain his once famous past form. In addition to John, the Rocks also acquired several other good players with the goal of having a successful season.

As the season played out, the Rock's decision paid off as John played probably the greatest season of his whole career. Indeed, the Rocks won more games in the League than ever before. Moreover, although the experts were giving the Rocks no chance of winning a single game against their international level competitors, they surprisingly even qualified for the playoff phase of the European Cup. The fans were ecstatic over this incredible performance and attributed it primarily to the comeback of John Kicker. As a natural leader, John became the team's captain and an inspiring role model for the younger players. John was a star again and the fans loved him! Unfortunately, at the end of the second season with the Rocks, after Mr. Spodir had publicly announced the club's intention to extend his contract, John sustained a severe knee injury, which put an end to his remarkable professional career.

You met John yesterday to check on him after a recent knee surgery and congratulate him on his 38th birthday. During this visit, he mentioned the courses he has taken recently at a prestigious business school well known for their excellent program in sports management. He also mentioned that he received an interesting job offer from the Rocks management. Specifically, the Rocks want him to become their new General Manager responsible for acquiring the rights to players, negotiating their contracts, and selling them to other teams. He wants you to represent him. With his playing career ended due to the knee injury, this is exactly what John was hoping for. Due to his history with them, he has a very strong emotional bond with the Rocks. He also feels deeply indebted to the Rocks for believing in him and giving him a second chance. He would be very honored to replace the retiring Mr. Spodir and become their new General Manager.

Throughout his successful career, John has earned enough money to retire. Therefore, money is not necessarily the most important issue in this negotiation. He feels indebted to the Rocks for giving him the chance and is ready to work for whatever salary you are able to negotiate for him. Mr. Spodir, who is about to retire after having worked for the Rocks for over 20 years was probably earning a salary considerably higher than the current market average of 100,000 SMUs (Soccer Monetary Units). Although he was a seasoned manager with a great sport's intuition and judge of character, his salary certainly did not even come close to what he would earn in a similar position at the Champs. Rumor has it that their current General Manager is earning about 200,000 SMUs. Smaller teams in the League, however, are paying their Managers much less, about 60,000 SMUs per year.

John told you he would accept any salary, which you consider fair regarding his status, experience and the current market conditions. He suspects that the Rocks are probably slowly running out of ideas of how to replace Mr. Spodir before the upcoming transfer window next week. John understands that working as a General Manager would be something he has never done before, but he believes he is well prepared for it and is looking forward to taking on the challenge.

Becoming the new General Manager of the Rocks, however, is not the only opportunity he can pursue. Recently, he has also received a call from the Champs who were looking for an experienced scout that is well connected in John's home region. Although no amounts were mentioned during the call, remuneration for such jobs usually consists of a relatively low base salary and a commission based on the number of talented athletes spotted by the scout. With his experience, contacts and popularity in the soccer world, John would probably make about 80,000 SMUs per year in the beginning. Although the Champs are a wealthy and successful club, John is simply not sure whether working for them again is such a great idea. He is concerned that they are implicitly asking him to "steal" young talents from the Rocks. This seriously worries him.

However, a much more interesting offer was the one John recently received from the Contenders. They asked whether he would be interested in coaching their junior team. The Contenders are still playing in the second league, and their financial resources are significantly smaller than the Champs. The 40,000 SMUs that John would probably earn per year is not much but becoming a coach would be a fun and rewarding job he would certainly enjoy.

Today, you will meet with Mr. Busman, the Rocks' president and his team. During your last encounter five years ago, Mr. Busman appeared to you as a very honorable and genuine person for whom people are much more important than money. It is no wonder that you were able to develop a good personal relationship very quickly and you have kept in touch with him ever since. Therefore, you are fully confident that together you will find the best possible solution for all involved parties.

Summarizing, your objectives are:
- make sure **John signs a contract** with the Rocks
- negotiate the **highest possible remuneration** for John
- John likes clear and simple arrangements so make sure John's salary does not contain any variable components and/or conditional clauses

If you reach an agreement, John and Mr. Busman will need to work closely together. Make sure you sustain a **good relationship** with him.

Confidential Instructions
for **Mr. Busman's Team**

This has been your fifth season as the president of the Rocks – a solid traditional European football club playing in the prestigious League. Under your leadership, they have delivered a strong performance record, winning on average almost 60% of their 38 games in the League each season. Franz Irons, the coach of the Rocks, believes that success in modern soccer starts with a strong defense. He has followed this belief throughout his career with the Rocks and has built probably the best defense in the League.

Generally, things have been going rather well since you joined the club, both in terms of the athletic as well as the financial performance. Three weeks ago, however, your colleague Mr. Spodir, the current General Manager of the Rocks, informed the club about his intention to retire at the earliest convenient date. Mr. Spodir's son, daughter and four grandkids are all living overseas and he has decided to move closer to them. Although he had repeatedly mentioned this on various occasions, no one believed it would ever happen. Your first thought was that his assistant, Mr. Secondski, would succeed him at least for some time. However, he has accepted a lucrative job offer from the Champs and therefore will also be leaving the Rocks. The transfer window is opening next week, and the Rocks urgently need to sign up a new General Manager who can prepare and coordinate all of their transfers and take care of other ongoing organizational issues.

In your last meeting with Mr. Spodir, he suggested offering this position to John Kicker, a former player of the Rocks and an idol of many fans. John played a pivotal role in the Rocks' recent success. He even started his professional career with the Rocks back in the early 1980s. Back then, the coaches, football experts and the press unanimously agreed that John Kicker had exceptional talent and could become one of the best defenders this game has ever seen. Therefore, it came as no surprise to anyone when he received a nomination to play on the national team.

Following a series of brilliant games with the national team during the World Cup, John took advantage of his popularity and left the Rocks to sign a three-year contract with the Champs, one of the most successful football clubs in the world. Indeed, they have won the League 31 times and hold over a dozen international cup titles, including winning the prestigious Champions League a record nine times.

After signing, however, most of his time with the Champs was spent either on the bench or playing with their second team. Rumors began to circulate that tensions within the team were the cause. However, the club's spokesperson addressed these speculations stating that there were no issues with John or between him and the Champs coach, Coach Meister. However, because Champs' fans had so few occasions to admire John's legendary skills his popularity began to decline. Despite this, the Champs maintained John's contract and even rejected all offers by other clubs interested in acquiring him. Their public spokesperson repeatedly reported that John was "not for sale" and that Coach Meister saw a great future for John and the Champs.

When his contract did eventually expire, no one was really sure whether John could still play as well as he used to. Although everybody still remembered his extraordinary skills, none of the big clubs in the League were interested in taking the risk. As a result, John ended up with the Contenders, a second league club which, though well organized, could not compare with the Champs.

Unfortunately, he did not adjust well with the Contenders. The local press reported on motivational and behavioral problems and how this led to relationship issues with the coach. As a result, after an outstanding performance at the beginning of the season, for the remainder of the season, John again watched his colleagues from the bench.

Mr. Spodir spotted this as an opportunity to reacquire John for the Rocks and replace Bob Wall, a very talented young player whose serious health problems left a vacancy on the Rocks' team. A contract was signed. John was ready to play for almost nothing just to get a chance to show everybody that he was still one of the best defenders in the country. Playing for nothing, however, turned out to be unnecessary. The Rocks were pleased to give him a second chance and generously offered him a two-year contract. They really hoped that under the direction of Coach Irons, John would regain his historically great form.

As the season played out, the Rock's decision paid off as John played probably the greatest season of his whole career. The Rocks won more games in the League than ever before, and although the experts were giving the Rocks no chance of winning a single game, they surprisingly qualified for the playoff phase of the European Cup. The fans were ecstatic over this incredible performance and attributed it primarily to the comeback of John Kicker. As a natural leader, John became the team's captain and an inspiring role model for the younger players. John was a star again and the fans loved him! Unfortunately, at the end of the second season with the Rocks, after Mr. Spodir had publicly announced the club's intention to extend his contract, John sustained a severe knee injury, which put an end to his remarkable professional career.

You realize that John is probably not an ideal candidate to take over Mr. Spodir's legacy. Although he was a great defender and played many great games for the Rocks, he has absolutely no experience in managing sports clubs. It is simply unclear whether he would be able to perform the job. The truth is, however, that the Rocks have no real alternative at the moment. The transfer window is opening next week and Mr. Spodir and his wife are leaving the country on the weekend. As President of the Rocks, you could temporarily take over some of the most urgent tasks, but due to your other responsibilities, you will definitely not be able to devote the time this job requires.

After over 20 years with the Rocks, Mr. Spodir was earning 120,000 SMUs (Soccer Monetary Units) which is about 20% more than current market average. Although he was a seasoned manager with a great sport's intuition and judge of character, his salary certainly did not even come close to what he would earn in a similar position at the Champs. Rumor has it that their current General Manager is earning about 200,000 SMUs. Smaller teams in the League, however, are paying their Managers much less, about 60,000 SMUs per year.

You are rather hesitant whether you should offer John more than what Mr. Spodir was earning as it would certainly be too much for someone who knows so little about the business of managing a team. On the other hand, going into the transfer period without a general manager might turn out to be disastrous for the next year's budget and the team's performance. So, in view of the emergency situation, you have decided to offer John up to 150,000 SMUs if necessary. If John asks for more than that, the Rocks will just have to postpone some of the transfers until the next window.

You will meet with John and his agents today. During your last encounter five years ago, they appeared to you as very knowledgeable and cooperative individuals. You were able to develop a good personal relationship very quickly and have kept in touch with the agents since. Therefore, you are fully confident that you will find the best possible solution for all involved parties.

Summarizing, your objectives are:
- make sure **John signs a contract** with The Rocks
- **stay within your budget** saving as much of it as you can
- make sure John's salary does not contain any variable components and/or conditional clauses

If you reach an agreement, you and John will start working closely together. Make sure you develop a **good relationship** with him.

Debriefing

John Kicker II is a continuation of a negotiation roleplay simulation originally written for the first edition of The Negotiation Challenge in 2007, in which John negotiated the terms of his second contract with The Rocks. It was a part of The Negotiation Challenge 2010 and was negotiated in the luxury boxes of the Leipzig Central Stadium, today known as the Red Bull Arena.

In this simulation, John and his agents negotiate with The Rocks' President, Mr. Busman, and his team the conditions of his potential employment contract as a General Manager. Both roles include various reference points that might be used to both calibrate their respective expectations and to develop their strategies. They are summarized in the following overview:

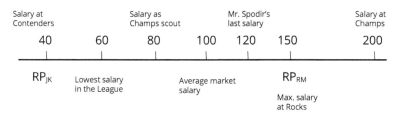

Figure 3. The structure of the John Kicker II simulation

John Kicker's reservation point is at 40,000 SMUs, which is the salary he could earn as a coach working for The Contenders in the second league. The management of The Rocks, however, can offer him up to 150,000 SMUs. This results in a Zone of Possible Agreement (ZOPA) of 110,000 SMUs. Additionally, the instructions offer many other reference points that help the parties to support their case.

As in the Benedict Basso simulation, the complexity of this negotiation lies in the fact that a potential agreement is only the beginning of a working relationship between the parties. That is, focusing solely on obtaining the highest/lowest salary at the expense of damaging a future working relationship would be a less than optimal outcome. Therefore, value claiming strategies and tactics applied in the negotiation must be weighed carefully and combined with relationship building measures.

Therefore, to evaluate the performance of the negotiators in The Negotiation Challenge, we combined the substantive outcome (salary) that the parties agreed to with the relational outcome from the Subjective Value Inventory (SVI) score obtained from their negotiation partners. However, as each of these variables is expressed in different units, we needed to normalize them and convert them to z-scores. Both z-scores for the substantive and relational outcome were then added together. Although it could make sense to assign different weights to each partial z-scores, for this particular evaluation, we weighed them both equally since it best reflects both parties' objectives to maximize both salary and relationship outcomes. The final score approximates the relative performance of each team compared to the performance of all participating teams.

For the benefit of reference, the highest salary obtained during The Negotiation Challenge 2010 was 175,000 SMUs, the lowest 60,000 SMUs and the average was 112,250 SMUs. The results obtained by the participating teams covered ca. 47% of the ZOPA but their distribution was noticeably skewed towards its higher end.

Similar to the Benedict Basso simulation, in the case of John Kicker II, the highest salary was also accompanied by the second highest SVI evaluation. This resulted in the best total outcome among the teams representing John Kicker. The lowest salary produced the second lowest SVI evaluation and the second highest total outcome among The Rock's management.

The main challenge that we observed for the negotiating teams was finding the balance between the effectiveness of their value claiming strategies and relationship management. The results clearly showed that the substantive and relational outcomes do not have to negatively correlate with each other. The best performing John Kicker team was another strong example that even in distributive negotiation obtaining a good substantive outcome does not have to take place at the cost of damaging the relationship.

John Kicker II is a negotiation roleplay simulation suitable for introducing the topic of distributive negotiation and value claiming skills. It can also be used for analyzing the efficiency of first offer strategies and their potential impact on the relationships between negotiating parties.

Power Media

Author: **Peter Kesting**

Number of parties:	Preparation time:	Negotiation time:	Complexity level:
2	**15-30** minutes	**30-45** minutes	**inter-mediate**

Pedagogical focus

reservation point, BATNA, information exchange, value claiming strategies and tactics, combining them with trust creation and sustaining good working relationships, strategies of the first offer, anchoring, objective criteria, fairness, distributive negotiation

Short description

Power Media is a roleplay simulation concerning a two-party distributive negotiation for the pricing terms of an online advertising contract between a prominent national newspaper and a European based marketing agency. Specifically, an Icelandic newspaper, Reykjavik Evening News (REN), is interested in increasing its online advertising revenue by reducing its dependence on deeply discounted rates from Google AdSense. It has been approached by Power Media, a marketing agency that acts as an advertising reseller. Although Power Media has the ability to secure prime customers for REN and pay it significantly more than Google AdSense, the rates it offers are still significantly below its standard rates. If a deal can be reached, both parties stand to benefit enormously.

Confidential Instructions
for **Reykjavik Evening News**

You are working for the sales department of Reykjavik Evening News (REN). Founded in 1955, it is one of the oldest and most traditional newspapers in Iceland. However, despite its age, this newspaper has created the leading online news portal in Iceland, including a strong section in English. As with most newspapers, advertising is the leading source of income for REN. This is particularly important to its online news portal since the content is provided to viewers completely for free.

Although you are also working on a subscription-based premium online version of the paper, this may be a longer-term challenge due to a combination of people preferring their online news for free and the difficulty of finding the type of online content or services that people are willing to pay for. Therefore, you are currently more focused on a short-term goal of generating as much revenue as possible from online advertisements. Indeed, there is much pressure on you because the revenue from REN's traditional newspaper business is declining. Therefore, your performance will play an important role in the financial well-being the company.

On the REN website, there is a complex portfolio of different advertising categories and banner types that customers can purchase. In category two, which includes a secondary position on the front page and prime positions on secondary pages, the list price for banners is 40€ per 1,000 impressions.[8] However, in reality, very few customers pay this price. Instead, prices are routinely negotiated with advertisers and generous discounts are given. Because of the subjective nature of this, your current portfolio of

---

[8] Different than a click, an impression is a view. When an ad loads and displays in front of a user, that is one impression.

72

customers falls within a range of paying between 16€ and 32€ per 1,000 impressions. The highest prices are paid by inexperienced local customers. Lower prices are offered to market insiders who negotiate more aggressively. Despite this, REN's strong market position as one of the prime online advertising platforms in Iceland helps you to keep prices high. The customers with whom you negotiate directly and develop targeted advertising packages represent 60% of REN's category two advertising inventory (see *Table 3*).

Name	Share of advertisements	Price per 1,000 impressions (€)
Pharmaceuticals & Personal Care	4%	32
Whale Watchers	2%	32
Travel & Tourism	8%	26
Apparel & Accessories	10%	25
Automotive	6%	22
Food	20%	16
Financial Services	10%	16

Table 3. Reykjavik Evening News' portfolio of category two advertisements

The remaining 40% of category two advertisement space is filled with advertisements automatically generated by Google AdSense. In contrast to your direct customers, these automatically generated advertisements come from a wide range of advertisers enrolled through Google AdWords program. Google simply pays a very low price of 0.60€ per 1,000 impressions. Despite this being such a low price compared to your direct customers, it requires no customer search and acquisition effort on your part since Google automates the entire process and the space is always filled.

Some time ago, you were approached by Power Media, one of the leading media agencies in Germany. Their key focus is to market the share of the online advertising space that has not been managed directly by website operators. In your case, this means the 40% part of your category two advertising inventory that is filled with Google AdSense. You were excited to discover that Power Media has customers in whom you are very interested. As a result, in preparation for your upcoming meeting, you have the following considerations.

Any price above the 0.60€ that you receive from your current Google AdSense revenue (40% of your category two revenue) will increase your profit and is therefore desirable. On the other hand, since Power Media is going to use your advertising space for the type of direct customers for which you obtain a price range currently between 16€ and 32€, you would be very uncomfortable with prices far below this range.

You are aware that Power Media has a mix of customers. These include bargain hunters that do not want to get deeply involved in the advertising specifics and others who are focused just on specific websites for which they are willing to pay premium prices. Very important to you is your understanding that TLU, a large German travel agency, is engaging Power Media to acquire advertising space from you. Unfortunately, you do not know how determined TLU is to place their advertisements on your websites nor do you know how much TLU is paying to Power Media. Power Media obviously wants to keep this their secret.

Early communication with Power Media has established that this potential agreement will cover only the residual 40% of category two advertising space which you do not market directly. However, if you find new customers or lose old ones, the volume will be adapted accordingly so that your deal with Power Media will never restrict your direct sales of advertising space. Although you have been in contact with Power Media for some time and agreed on the general terms and technical details of the deal, you have not discussed the prices yet. Therefore, your primary goal is to reach an agreement on a price for REN. However, you are also interested in establishing a good relationship with Power Media since you think that a solid long-term relationship may prove beneficial for you as it can help you escape the low price Google AdSense dependency.

You are now meeting the representatives of Power Media. In brief:

- Try to negotiate the **best possible price.**
- At the same time, try to establish a **good relationship** for a future collaboration with Power Media.
- The share of the category two advertising space and any other aspects of the deal are **not negotiation issues.** The ranking will exclusively be based on the price and the relationship.
- A no-deal will be evaluated as anything below 0.60€ per 1,000 impressions.

Confidential instructions
for **Power Media**

You are working for Power Media, a young and upcoming marketing agency that is becoming a leading player in the German online advertising market. Like other marketing agencies, Power Media is a business-to-business matchmaker, linking companies (your customers) with an advertising need with portals and other website operators that provide advertising space (publishers).

The large publishers normally market their advertising space directly. Their prices are generally high, often about 40€ per 1,000 impressions. However, in reality, very few customers pay this price. Instead, prices are routinely negotiated with advertisers and generous discounts are often given. The highest prices are paid by inexperienced local customers. Lower prices are offered to market insiders, who negotiate more aggressively, sometimes up to a 60% discount, occasionally even more.

In recent years, for many publishers, revenue from online advertisement has become increasingly important. Indeed, for the traditional newspaper industry, this has become a particularly important issue since revenue from paper-based advertising is declining due to decreasing newsprint readership. Therefore, the advertising revenue from their online news has become an important source of income.

However, a challenge for operators of even the most popular websites is that they cannot sell all of their available advertising space even at their negotiated discounted prices. To deal with the remaining space they typically have three options: (i) they can use the unsold space to promote themselves, which generates no direct revenue (ii) they can leave the space blank, which also generates no revenue, or (iii) they can open the space for use by automatically generated advertisements from service providers like Google AdSense. However, with these type of organizations, the prices are very low at around 0.60€ per 1,000 impressions. This is painfully below what they can obtain from their direct customers.

Power Media has built a successful business model that focuses exactly on helping advertisers address this problem. It does this by buying any remaining underutilized advertising space and then through the power of its broad customer reach, resells it to advertisers at a premium price. In effect, it is an advertising retailer. Although Power Media's average 2€ per 1,000 impression price it pays to advertisers is extremely low compared even to the price they typically get from their most discounted customers, it is still higher than what they get from Google AdSense. Despite this, advertisers often seem uncomfortable with your value proposition. Although your offer is better than any other alternative they have and it certainly increases their revenue immediately, they perceive it as ridiculously low compared to what they can obtain directly from regular advertisers. As such, they often demonstrate resistance in lowering their prices that much. Moreover, they fear the potentially highly destabilizing effect such low prices could have on their ability to charge premium prices in direct sales.

You are about to re-approach the sales department of an Icelandic newspaper called Reykjavik Evening News (REN). Founded in 1955, REN is one of the oldest and most traditional newspapers in Iceland. In recent years, it has created the leading online news portal in Iceland, including a strong section in English for international visitors. You have been in email contact with REN for some time, and recently you have reached an agreement with them on the general terms of working together for their category two advertising space (secondary positions on the front-page and primary positions on secondary pages). Prices are the only issue that remains to be negotiated. Your understanding from REN is that they are only interested in discussing the category two advertising space that they are not able to market directly. Currently, this represents about 40% of category two. However, if REN finds new customers or loses established ones, the agreement will retain the required flexibility that the advertising volume will be adjusted so that the deal will never restrict the newspaper's direct sales of advertising space.

From your perspective, you know that you need the advertising space for your very important customer, TLU. They are the biggest travel agency in Germany. TLU has just decided to enter the Icelandic market. In doing so, they want to place advertising banners on prominent Icelandic websites. They are absolutely determined to place their advertisements in the Reykjavik Evening News and are willing to pay a high price for that, even if it means paying up to the list price of 40€.

This places you in a dilemma. On the one hand, you do not want to pay REN a price considerably higher than 2€, because this may set a precedent that impacts the prices that you can obtain from other suppliers. On the other hand, TLU is a very important customer. If you cannot close the deal with REN, you may lose them. Despite this, your absolute maximum price that you can pay is 10€ per 1,000 impressions. In addition, you want to establish good relations with REN because the Icelandic market is promising and the newspaper is an ideal partner for you. Therefore, despite the outcome, you are determined to end the negotiation amicably.

You are now meeting the sales representatives of Reykjavik Evening News. In brief:

- Try to negotiate the **lowest possible price**.
- At the same time, try to establish a **good relationship** for a future collaboration with Reykjavik Evening News.
- The share of the category two advertising space and any other aspect of the deal are **not negotiation issues**. The ranking will exclusively be based on the price and the relationship.
- A no-deal will be evaluated as anything above 40€ per 1,000 impressions

Debriefing

Power Media is a distributive negotiation roleplay simulation written for The Negotiation Challenge 2015. It was used during one of the qualification rounds for the final that took place in Munich.

The main issue in the negotiation between the representatives of Power Media and the sales team of Reykjavik Evening News (REN) is the price for 1,000 ad impressions for a marketing campaign that TLU, Power Media's most important customer is planning to run in Iceland. Both roles include various reference points that might be used to both calibrate their respective expectations and to develop their strategies. They are summarized in the following overview:

Figure 4. The structure of the Power Media roleplay simulation

REN's reservation point is 0.60€ per 1,000 impressions, the revenue they can reliably generate with Google AdSense. However, Power Media is not willing to offer them more than 10€ per 1,000 impressions. This results in a Zone of Possible Agreement (ZOPA) of 9.4€ per 1,000 impressions. Interestingly, nearly all reference points mentioned in the instructions are higher than the reservation point of Power Media.

As with other negotiations in this section, the complexity of this negotiation lies in the fact that a potential agreement is only the beginning of a working relationship between the parties. That is, focusing solely on obtaining the highest/lowest price at the expense of damaging a future working relationship would be a less than optimal outcome. Therefore, value claiming strategies and tactics applied in the negotiation must be weighed carefully and combined with relationship building measures.

Therefore, to evaluate the performance of the negotiators in this competition we combined the substantive outcome (price) that the parties agreed to with the relational outcome from the Subjective Value Inventory (SVI) score obtained from their negotiation partners. However, as each of these variables is expressed in different units, we needed to normalize them and convert them to z-scores. Both z-scores for the substantive and relational outcome were then added together. Although it could make sense to assign different weights to each partial z-scores, for this particular evaluation, we weighed them both equally since it best reflects both parties' objectives to maximize both salary and relationship outcomes. The final score approximates the relative performance of each team compared to the performance of all participating teams.

For the benefit of reference, the highest price obtained during The Negotiation Challenge 2015 was 12€ per 1,000 impressions, which is actually higher than Power Media's reservation point. However, we decided to accept this result as a legitimate agreement because, despite its potential negative consequence for future negotiations with other publishers, it is still lower than the list price and at the same time is clearly affordable for TLU, Power Media's client. The lowest price from TNC 2015 was 1.80€ per 1,000 impressions and the average 7.56€ per 1,000 impressions, which is a clear consequence of the reference points lying above the higher end of the ZOPA.

Also in this negotiation, the highest price negotiated was accompanied by the second highest SVI evaluation, which ultimately resulted in the best total outcome among the teams representing REN. Although the lowest price produced only an average SVI evaluation, it still gave the respective team the best total outcome among the Power Media teams.

The main challenge that we observed for the negotiating teams was finding the balance between the effectiveness of their value claiming strategies and relationship management. The results clearly showed that the substantive and relational outcomes do not have to negatively correlate with each other. The best performing REN team was another strong example that even in distributive negotiation obtaining a good substantive outcome does not have to take place at the cost of damaging the relationship.

Power Media is another roleplay simulation in this collection, which is well suitable for introducing the topic of distributive negotiation and the value claiming skills. It can also be used for analyzing the efficiency of first offer strategies and their potential impact on the relationships between negotiating parties.

3.2 Integrative Negotiation

The second type of negotiation that we model during The Negotiation Challenge is integrative negotiation. These type of negotiations are also called: non-zero-sum bargaining, collaborative or win-win negotiation. In integrative negotiations, the amount of benefits available to the parties is determined during the negotiation process by their negotiation skills. The parties have an opportunity to create value by potentially capitalizing on the differences between them (e.g., differences in interests, different predictions about the future, different risk aversions or time preferences) and by identifying and adding new issues. The objectives in integrative negotiations are more heterogeneous than those in distributive situations. Whereas some of the parties' objectives remain competitive and focused on claiming the biggest share of the available value, others become compatible and focused on engineering and exhausting the full potential available in the agreement.

For this type of negotiation, it is important to note the difference between the structure of the negotiation situation and the negotiation style demonstrated in it. To take full advantage of an integrative situation, the parties must recognize its potential and apply appropriate strategies. Pure value claiming strategies and tactics are likely to leave most of the negotiation situation's potential unexplored. Rather, the parties need to understand the issues, communicate their own interests and understand the interests of their negotiation partners to come up with value-generating options.

To contrast this difference further, distributive negotiations are based on inherently opposing interests. To reconcile them and find an agreement, one of the parties has to give in. In integrative negotiations, this is not necessary. If negotiated well, through identifying and pursuing value generating options, both parties have the possibility to get what is important to them and reach their objectives. They can achieve this because their interests and valuations of the negotiated issues are different. In the simplest settings, it means that by insisting on what they value the most and exchanging it for what they value relatively less the negotiators can create value.

This value creation process, however, comes with some risk. That is, a prerequisite for it is truthful revelation of what is important to us. This is very sensitive information, which our negotiation partner can either reciprocate to enable the exchange and unlock the potential of the situation or use it against us. Therefore, seasoned negotiators never negotiate to create trust. They build trust so that they can negotiate integratively.

Acknowledging such risk, there are various value-creating strategies that can be used. The simplest of them is the barter method, also known as logrolling. This method is built on two tenets. First, we need to make sure we know what is important to us. This can be easily operationalized in the form of a ranking or a rating of the negotiated issues. The ultimate form of assessing this importance is expressing the value of all issues in monetary terms. The second tenet is to identify and offer reasonable tradeoffs. If the value of a negotiated issue is different between the parties, value can be created by trading them off with each other.[9]

As should now be clear, the ability to distinguish an integrative negotiation situation from a purely distributive one and to deal with them appropriately is an important skill in the repertoire of The Great Negotiators. As mentioned in our introductory chapter, we call this ability negotiation intelligence and actively look for it during The Negotiation Challenge.

---

[9] The concept of value creation in negotiation is based on a similar principle as the theory of comparative advantage described by David Ricardo in his seminal work *On the Principles of Political Economy and Taxation* in 1817. In his famous example, Ricardo demonstrated that both England and Portugal could benefit from trading cloth for wine, if they can produce them at different relative marginal costs.

The roleplays in this chapter give negotiators an opportunity to test their ability to recognize this difference and to capitalize on such situations by combining their value creation and value claiming skills. To facilitate this, we have included only scoreable simulations, in which, based on the final outcome, it is possible to assess how well parties are able to engineer value both in terms of identifying and exploring the integrative potential of situations and claiming the biggest possible share for themselves. Therefore, while evaluating the negotiators' performance in the integrative scoreable rounds of The Negotiation Challenge, we focus on the substantive outcome and in justified cases, we combine it with the relational outcome.

Staple Rights

Author: **Peter Kesting**

Number of parties:	Preparation time:	Negotiation time:	Complexity level:
2	**15-30** minutes	**30-45** minutes	**inter-mediate**

Pedagogical focus

reservation point, BATNA, interest analysis, information exchange, strategies of the first offer, anchoring, logrolling, value creation and value claiming strategies, measuring negotiators efficiency, Pareto optimization, relationship building, trust creation, objective criteria, fairness, integrative negotiation

Short description

Staple Rights is two-party multi-issue, integrative negotiation roleplay simulation between the official trade delegation of the 15th century City of Leipzig and representatives of the Holy Roman Emperor, Maximilian I. Having enjoyed a long period of economic growth and prosperity, Leipzig is ready to take its place with the upper echelon of other Holy Roman Empire cities. To do this, it feels it must obtain the economic boosting staple rights that other key cities possess and that only the Emperor can bestow. Having already obtained a positive response from the Emperor, the details must now be negotiated with his trade delegation. However, the emperor will have greater regional economic and political stability in mind and will want to limit the terms.

Confidential Instructions
for the **Leipzig Delegation**

The year 1497 is a time of fundamental change in the world. It was only about fifty years ago, 1450, that Johannes Gutenberg invented a new printing technique using movable type that revolutionized communication and education. Five years ago in 1492, Christopher Columbus reached the Americas, and just this year Vasco da Gama started his journey to India starting what will be a new era of internationalization which will vastly change European culture. It will not be long from now that Martin Luther plants the seeds of the Reformation by publicizing his 95 theses, which will unleash a cultural and religious earthquake across Europe. Indeed, this year is deep in the middle of the time and events that will give birth to the Enlightenment and a new era of European culture and commerce.

Within this changing world is the city of Leipzig. Indeed, because it lies at the intersection of two ancient trade routes, the "via regia" and the "via imperii", over the centuries it has developed into a prosperous center of trade. Indeed, its influence and prosperity had grown so important that in 1165 Margrave Otto von Meißen officially bestowed it with full city rights, a designation that drove the development of a strong education and cultural infrastructure including famous institutions such as the University of Leipzig, the second oldest university in Germany and key churches including the Thomaskirche, famously associated with Johann Sebastian Bach.

As a very proud member of Leipzig's official trade delegation, you are in an important position to see its development and increasing prosperity continue. In this regard, the city council has applied to Maximilian I, the Emperor of the Holy Roman Empire for a Staple Right. A Staple Right is a medieval right awarded to certain municipalities that require passing merchants to unload their goods and display them for sale for a certain period before they can pass a city. As such, it will expand economic and cultural opportunities for the city and certainly set its status on par with other key cities of the Empire. Although he reacted quite positively to the request, his approval and any details remain uncertain. Therefore, you and your delegation will now need to meet with the representatives he is sending to Leipzig.

For this negotiation, your instructions are clear: the city council wants to be awarded a permanent Staple Right. Considering that many comparable cities such as Cologne, Berlin and Magdeburg already have the right, any other outcome would be considered by your party unfair and difficult to justify. However, because the Staple Right does force traders and merchants to stop in Leipzig for a period before moving on to their intended destinations, this delay has the ability to hamper trade in the wider region outside of Leipzig. Because of this, the delegation of Maximilian I will take care to minimize the negative impact on this region of his empire. With this in mind, you have to negotiate three different issues:

Staple time

This is the amount of time a passing merchant must offer his products for sale in the city. You know that granting the right implies allowing for some staple time, but on the other hand, the staple time also determines how much the merchant's journey is delayed. Your order is to extend this time as much as possible. In no circumstances should you allow for less than two days since your citizens will need a fair chance to be aware of the merchant's presence. This especially applies to citizens living outside of the city walls that do not enter the city every day.

Revenue sharing

Traditionally, the tax revenues generated by sales due to the Staple Right are shared with the Empire. Your order is to negotiate the lowest possible share that must be given to Maximilian I. You definitely should not go above the 50% level, the highest share paid by any other city.

Radius

To prevent merchants from circumventing the staple right obligation by simply passing around the city, a staple right is usually defined by an area. This is often a radius around the city that captures all possible transportation routes. The larger the radius, the more traders that fall under the staple right. Your order is to negotiate the largest possible radius, but in no circumstance allow for less than 40 km, otherwise it would be too easy to choose alternative routes. You are aware that there are cases where the radius is smaller, but these cities are located on rivers, and these staple rights particularly address passing ships that cannot easily change their route.

The city council has insisted on getting an agreement. Negotiation failure would leave a great opportunity unrealized. This is not acceptable. At the same time, the city council still requires you to negotiate the best possible result. Experience tells you that this requires determining the relative importance of the different issues and relating them to each other. After long discussions, you have internally agreed that an additional day of staple time is worth the same as a 10% lower share of the tax revenue or 10 km additional radius (1 day = 10 scoring points; 1% = 1 scoring point; 1 km = 1 scoring point). This scoring relationship exclusively determines the value of the agreement that you reach.

Summarizing, your objectives are:
- Make sure that **you reach an agreement** with Maximilian I on granting Leipzig the Staple Rights and settle their exact conditions (staple time, revenue split, and radius).
- Try to negotiate **the best possible agreement** for the city of Leipzig and the **highest number of scoring points**.

Confidential Instructions
for the **Delegation of Maximilian I**

The year 1497 is a time of fundamental change in the world. It was only about fifty years ago, 1450, that Johannes Gutenberg invented a new printing technique using movable type that revolutionized communication and education. Five years ago in 1492, Christopher Columbus reached the Americas, and just this year Vasco da Gama started his journey to India starting what will be a new era of internationalization which will vastly change European culture. It will not be long from now that Martin Luther plants the seeds of the Reformation by publicizing his 95 theses, which will unleash a cultural and religious earthquake across Europe. Indeed, this year is deep in the middle of the time and events that will give birth to the Enlightenment and a new era of European culture and commerce.

Within this changing world is the city of Leipzig. Indeed, because it lies at the intersection of two ancient trade routes, the "via regia" and the "via imperii", over the centuries it has developed into a prosperous center of trade. Indeed, its influence and prosperity had grown so important that in 1165 Margrave Otto von Meißen officially bestowed it with full city rights, a designation that drove the development of a strong education and cultural infrastructure including famous institutions such as the University of Leipzig, the second oldest university in Germany and key churches including the Thomaskirche, famously associated with Johann Sebastian Bach.

As the city council of Leipzig naturally wants to see its development and increasing prosperity continue, the city council has applied to Maximilian I, the Emperor of the Holy Roman Empire for a Staple Right. A Staple Right is a medieval right awarded to certain municipalities that require passing merchants to unload their goods and display them for sale for a certain period before they can pass a city. As such, it will expand economic and cultural opportunities for the city and certainly set its status on par with other key cities of the Empire. In this regard, impressed with their recent economic and cultural growth, he has reacted quite positively to Leipzig's written inquiry to obtain these staple rights. In response, he has sent you and your delegation to Leipzig to meet with the city's representatives and negotiate the conditions of the right.

Basically, your instructions are clear. Maximilian wants to grant Leipzig permanent Staple Rights. Facing the fact that many comparable cities in the Empire such as Cologne, Berlin and Magdeburg already have the right, any other outcome would be perceived by Leipzig as unfair and create political and economic frustration. However, Maximilian must also be concerned that the greater regional trade will not be excessively hampered by this privilege. Therefore, you must skillfully negotiate three different issues:

Staple time

This is the amount of time the passing merchant must offer his products for sale in the city. You know that granting the right implies allowing for some staple time, but on the other hand, the staple time determines how much the staple right delays a merchant's journey. Your order is to keep the time rather short. Under no circumstances should you allow for more than seven days since this delay could seriously hamper inter-regional commerce.

Revenue sharing

Traditionally, the tax revenues generated by sales due to the Staple Right is shared with the Empire. That is your share of the pie, and a key incentive to grant the Staple Right. Your order is to negotiate the highest possible share. You definitely should not go below the 20% level, the lowest level paid by any other city.

Radius

To prevent merchants from circumventing the Staple Right obligation by simply passing around the city, a staple right is usually defined by an area, often a radius around the city that captures all possible transportation routes. The larger the radius, the more traders that fall under the staple right. Your order is to negotiate the smallest possible radius, but in no circumstance to allow for more than 115 km because this would create conflicts of interests with neighboring cities.

Maximilian has insisted on getting an agreement. A failure of the negotiation could seriously harm his relationship with this important city and this is not acceptable. At the same time, Maximilian still demands that you negotiate the best possible result. Experience tells you that this will require determining the relative importance of the different issues and relating them to each other. After long discussions, you have agreed that one day less staple time is worth the same as 5% higher share of the tax revenue or 40 km of additional radius (1 day = 20 scoring points; 1% = 4 scoring points; 1 km = 0.5 scoring points). This scoring relationship exclusively determines the value of the agreement that you need to reach.

Summarizing, your objectives are:
- Make sure that **you agree** with the city of Leipzig on granting them the Staple Rights and settle their exact conditions (staple time, revenue split, and radius).
- Try to negotiate **the best possible agreement** for Maximilian I and the **highest number of scoring points**.

Debriefing

Staple Rights is a multi-issue, integrative negotiation roleplay simulation written for The Negotiation Challenge 2010 in Leipzig. The participating teams were asked to represent either the government of the City of Leipzig or Maximilian I, the ruler of the Holy Roman Empire in a negotiation concerning the exact conditions of the Staple Rights the city would like to obtain.

According to the instructions, the preferences of the negotiating parties can be quantified and expressed by the following formulas:

$$Score_{Leipzig} = 10 * Staple\ Time - 1 * Revenue\ Share + 1 * Radius$$

" (…) an additional day of staple time is worth the same as 10% lower share of the tax revenue or 10 km additional radius (1 day = 10 scoring points; 1% = 1 scoring point; 1 km = 1 scoring point)"

$$Score_{Maximilian} = 120 - 20 * Staple\ Time - 4 * Revenue\ Share - 0.5 * Radius$$

" (…) one day less staple time is worth the same as 5% higher share of the tax revenue or 40 km of additional radius (1 day = 20 scoring points; 1% = 4 scoring points; 1 km = 0.5 scoring point)"

The confidential instructions and the respective formulas clearly reveal the differences in valuations of the various negotiated issues. This exposes opportunity for capitalizing on these differences and gives each party an opportunity to engineer value.

It might be interesting to note that adding the remarks converting the preferences explicitly into scoring points is not absolutely necessary; we decided to do so only to improve the clarity of the instructions. Although 120 in Maximilian's scoring function is not directly mentioned in his confidential instructions, it has been added to place the graphical representation of the both parties' preferences closer to each other.

Additionally, the parties are instructed on their reservation points with respect to each of the negotiated issues. They are summarized in the table below:

Issue	Minimum	Maximum
Staple Time [days]	2	7
Revenue Share for Maximilian [%]	20%	50%
Radius [kilometres]	40	115

Table 4. Reservation points of the parties and the respective zone of possible agreement (ZOPAs)

Combining the scoring functions with the corresponding reservation points allows us to graph a Pareto efficiency frontier, which looks as follows:

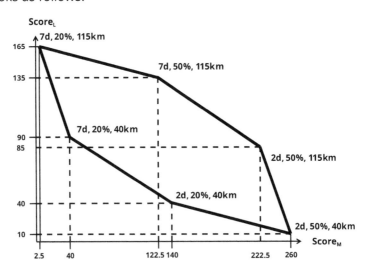

Figure 5. The structure of the Staple Rights roleplay including a sketch of the Pareto efficiency frontier

94

Quantified preferences allow us to draw inferences on the negotiators' performance based on the substantive outcome obtained in their negotiations. Based on the substantive outcome, we can assess the parties' success in value creation and claiming. Although it would be possible to evaluate value creation and claiming separately, for The Negotiation Challenge we decided to consider and compare only the final outcome. Also in integrative negotiations, the ultimate goal of each party is to maximize their own benefits, which emerge as a combination of their value creating and claiming skill.

For the benefit of reference, the best substantive result obtained by the teams representing the City of Leipzig during The Negotiation Challenge 2010 was 130 points and it was produced with an agreement including seven days of staple time, 50% of the tax revenues going to Maximilian I, and a radius of 110 kilometers. The best substantive result among the teams representing Maximilian I was 260 scoring points corresponding to an agreement including two days, 50%, and 40 kilometers. The average results obtained within each role differed substantially and amounted to 73.42 for the City of Leipzig and 174.67 for Maximilian I.

The key challenges for the negotiating teams were to create enough trust between them to share very sensitive information concerning their preferences, identify value-adding options and then exhaust the entire value potential of the negotiation. However, this is particularly difficult in a highly competitive context, which might incline the negotiators to focus solely on value claiming rather than combining it with value creation. Should they fall into this trap, it will produce a suboptimal agreement and leave value on the table.

Staple Rights is an integrative scoreable negotiation roleplay simulation suitable for practicing value creation and value claiming skills. Differences in parties' preferences and valuations of the negotiated issues allow them to create value by focusing on what is important to them.

The Vikings

Author: **Ditte Mathiasen**

Number of parties:	Preparation time:	Negotiation time:	Complexity level:
2	**30** minutes	**45-60** minutes	**high**

Pedagogical focus

reservation point, BATNA, interest analysis, information exchange, strategies of the first offer, anchoring, logrolling, value creation and value claiming strategies, measuring negotiators efficiency, Pareto optimization, relationship building, trust creation, objective criteria, fairness, integrative negotiation

Short description

The Vikings is two-party multi-issue, mixed-motive negotiation roleplay simulation. It takes place between the leaders of two early Icelandic Viking tribes over the distribution of the treasure recently obtained from a raid abroad including: longships, knarrs, silver coins, grain, cows, weapons, and alcohol. However, agreeing on a mutually acceptable distribution of this treasure will be a challenge due to various complicating issues. These include a recent degradation of their relationship and a growing mistrust which could even result in hostility. Moreover, both parties made different contributions to the raid, which they feel played a great role in its success. It will not be easy, but navigating through these complex barrires will be critical to reaching an amicable agreement.

Confidential Instructions
for **the Arnarson Tribe from the Southern Territory**

The year 885 has been an exceptionally cold one in Iceland. Eleven years ago, you, Ingólfur Arnarson, and your tribe arrived from the southeast in seven longships. When land was in sight, you threw a carved pillar into the water and decided to settle where the pillar washed ashore. You ended up at a place where geothermal steam rose from the earth and decided to name your village Reykjavík, the cove of smoke.

Soon after arriving, however, territorial disputes led to conflict with a local tribe to the north of your settlement. Their chief, Gunnar Garðarson simply did not like your presence and during the first three years, there were several battles between your respective tribes. Luckily, because you had experienced and strong warriors you did well during these battles including conquering a large area which has been important for your farming needs.

Despite this early conflict, territory boundaries eventually stabilized with your land becoming known as the Southern Territory and Gunnar Garðarson's land, the Northern Territory. For the last eight years, the relations between the tribes have improved so much that occasional intermarriages occur and both communities work on projects together. Indeed, just this previous winter you and Gunnar sent a joint raiding expedition to a wealthy land to the southeast.

The expedition consisted of five ships with 100 warriors. Although you agreed to nothing in advance on how any loot brought back would be split, you did agree on how the raiding party was structured. Since the tribe from the northern territory has more warriors than you, they sent 65 men. However, you feel this was balanced since your warriors are clearly stronger. Moreover, you provided three out of five longships.

However, something has recently changed. Since the warriors left this winter, Gunnar and his tribe have become unreliable and hostile, which causes you increasing concern including a strong feeling that he does not trust you. As an example, during the recent wedding between Biǫrnólfr Vésteinnson's daughter (Biǫrnólfr Vésteinnson is one of Gunnar's advisors) and one of your men, a fight almost erupted due to a misunderstanding about the dowry. Specifically, Gunnar accused you of increasing the agreed upon dowry from 2,700 to 3,800 grams of silver. You were extremely offended by this accusation because 2,700 grams of silver had only been an initial suggestion and never agreed upon. On another occasion, they tried to cheat you from your part of the profit of a joint trade made with some travelers. This resulted in a fight between your stepbrother, Hjörleifr Hróðmarsson and Gunnar. As a result, you have had no contact with them since.

Unfortunately, this degradation of the relationship and trust between the tribes could not have happened at a worse time since the joint raiding expedition that was sent out last winter has just successfully returned with much treasure. Now, concerned whether you can trust them to divide the treasure fairly, you and your stepbrother Hjörleifr Hróðmarsson, and your son Þorsteinn Ingólfsson, are to meet with Gunnar Garðarson, his wife, Halldóra Svararsdottir, and their wise man, Biǫrnólfr Vésteinnson to negotiate how to divide everything. Indeed, you are somewhat concerned as to what Gunnar might do, after his offensive behavior at the recent wedding and because his best warriors will escort him to the negotiation. However, you will also have your warriors at the ready and take confidence in knowing that they are stronger and are certainly ready to fight if necessary. Prior to arriving at the meeting, you received a list showing the inventory of the treasure brought back from the raid:

Longships

In addition to the original **five** ships they used for the raid, the warriors returned with five extra **longships**. These longships are considered very valuable. A longship is a light wooden boat primarily used for warfare and explorations. With its long and narrow hull, it is designed for speed and agility. It is therefore particularly suited for landings and troop deployments in shallow water. The five longships are in very good condition and very big with 30 rowing benches each. This makes them twice as long as the five you already had. You believe the value of the longships to be **around 2,800 grams of silver** each.

Knarrs

Apart from the longships, they also brought back **two knarrs**. Knarrs are also wooden ships. However, they are not as fast as the longships due to a broader hull, a deeper draft and a limited number of oars. Nonetheless, you believe them to be more expensive and very useful since they can carry a large cargo, a necessity when crossing the Atlantic Ocean. Moreover, these ships are much safer in the treacherous open ocean. You estimate the value to be **around 4,500 grams of silver** per knarr.

Coins

Although you have never actually seen one, for the last few years, you have been hearing about the concept of coins used as a means of payment instead of paying by weight, for example in silver. The expedition has now brought back from their raid **22,000 coins made of silver**, each of which consists of 1.5 grams of silver. For your entire life, you have only known paying with silver according to its weight. Indeed, to make sure you have a precise understanding of the value of various treasure that is why you still value treasure by grams of silver. Despite this, you know that these new coins are becoming increasingly important and that some communities rely heavily on them. Indeed, your stepbrother, Hjörleifr Hróðmarsson, knows a place where they value coins so much that they will pay you a **bonus of 3,000 grams of silver** for 20,000 pure silver coins you trade with them. You consider this a bit silly, but if they are willing to pay 3,000 grams of silver on top of the price of 1.5 grams of silver per coin, then you will certainly try to get 20,000 coins.

Grain

Grain is important for its use both as food and seed. If you travel to the east, each sack of grain is worth about **800 grams of silver**. Although the warriors brought back **ten sacks of grain**, you need just two sacks to provide you with enough food to get through next winter and enough seed for next spring's planting. If you get more than two sacks of grain, you will just sell the surplus on your next trading expedition to the east. If getting two sacks turns out too expensive, you are confident that you can arrange them from other sources.

Cows

The warriors returned with **eight cows**. Cows are highly valuable to you as they provide your tribe both milk and meat. You would like to have four cows out of the eight, but if it turns out too expensive now, you can always buy the difference in the cattle market. In general, a cow is sold for **1,200 grams of silver**.

Weapons

The warriors brought back an impressive number of **weapons, 400** in total. This includes helmets, shields, swords, spears and chainmail armor (a type consisting of small metal rings linked together). The price for a weapon is **100 grams of silver** regardless of its uniqueness. For many reasons, it is customary not to haggle over the price of every single weapon.

Alcohol

As Vikings, you consider alcohol very important. However, this type of **alcohol** is a lot stronger than the beer you normally drink. The warriors said that this kind of alcohol is called whisky. You have never tasted it before and consider it a special product. The warriors drank five casks on their way home, but there are still twenty casks left. These can either be used for special occasions or sold for **around 800 grams** of silver per cask.

The table below lists the items the Vikings brought back from the raid including their value per unit in silver and a possible bonus.

Item	Grams of silver per unit	Bonus
5 longships	2,800 grams of silver per ship	
2 knarrs	4,500 grams of silver per ship	
22,000 silver coins	1.5 grams of silver per coin	3,000 grams of silver if you sell 20,000 coins or more
10 sacks of grain	800 grams of silver per sack	
8 cows	1,200 grams silver per cow	
400 weapons	100 grams of silver per weapon	
20 casks of alcohol	800 grams of silver per cask	

Table 5. Inventory of the raided treasure together with their values for Arnarson

Even though you have a history of settling disputes violently, you cannot use violence or weapons to divide the treasure between the two tribes. Instead, you have to negotiate your way to a good deal.

Although, you may have a preference for some of the items specifically, at the end of the day only one thing matters: **value in total grams of silver**. Therefore, do not forget that each item has a value equaling a certain amount of silver. You want to **maximize that value** by dividing the treasure with the Northern Tribe in a way that leaves you with the **greatest value in terms of silver**. Also, do not forget that:

- You can only negotiate the items included in the loot. You are not allowed to invent options or introduce other items not mentioned above.
- A valid deal must involve an agreement on all seven items categories. If you can only agree on some of the items, there is no valid deal.
- In this negotiation, **the amount of silver you end up with is all that matters**. Any deal that gives you a positive amount of silver is acceptable. A no-deal means no silver.

THE LOOT
Arnarson's Tribe Valuation Table

Longships		Knarrs		Coins*		Grain*	
5	14,000	2	9,000	22,000	36,000	10	8,000
4	11,200	1	4,500	20,000	33,000	8	6,400
3	8,400			15,000	22,500	6	4,800
2	5,600			10,000	15,000	4	3,200
1	2,800			5,000	7,500	2	1,600
				1	1.5	1	800

Cows*		Weapons*		Alcohol*	
8	9,600	400	40,000	20	16,000
6	7,200	300	30,000	15	12,000
4	4,800	200	20,000	10	8,000
2	2,400	100	10,000	5	4,000
1	1,200	1	100	1	800

Table 6. Arnarson's Tribe Valuation Table

* Sample calculations for selected amounts of goods. You do not have to stick to the amounts listed in the table and can agree on other divisions from the allowed range e.g. 11,000 coins (16,500 grams of silver), 5 sacks of grain (4,000 grams of silver), 5 cows (6,000 grams of silver), 201 weapons (20,100 grams of silver), and 9 casks of alcohol (7,200 grams of silver).

Please do not let your negotiation partner(s)
see your Valuation Table!

Confidential Instructions
for **the Garðarson Tribe from the Northern Territory**

The year 885 has been an exceptionally cold one in Iceland. You have been living here in the northwestern part for almost 20 years. You, Gunnar Garðarson, arrived here with your father, Garðar Svavarsson, who discovered the island and originally named it *Garðarshólmi*. Later, you heard that a man called Flóki renamed it, *Ísland* (Iceland), which you found ironic due to the lack of ice. Although your father left, you decided to stay here with your family and build a community.

Eleven years ago, a man called Ingólfur Arnarson and his tribe arrived on the southern part of the island and settled in a place, which they named Reykjavík, meaning the cove of smoke. This place is two days travel south from your village.

Although there were several conflicts between your two respective tribes over the first three years following their arrival, things eventually settled down to a peaceful coexistence including a formal agreement on the territory boundaries with yours being known as the Northern Territory and his, the Southern Territory. Indeed, over the last eight years, relations have actually improved so much that occasional intermarriages occur and both communities work on projects together. In fact, just this previous winter you and their chief, Ingólfur Arnarson sent a joint raiding expedition to a wealthy land to the southeast.

The expedition consisted of five ships with 100 warriors. Although you agreed to nothing in advance on how any treasure brought back would be split, other than each keeping his own ships and men, you did agree on how the raiding party was structured. Since your tribe has more warriors than the Southern Tribe you provided 65 men. In return, they provided three out of five longships.

However, something has recently changed. Since the warriors left this winter, you have become increasingly concerned about Ingólfur and his tribe since they seem increasingly hostile. As an example, during the recent wedding between Biǫrnólfr Vésteinnson's daughter (Biǫrnólfr Vésteinnson is one of your advisors) and one of Ingólfur's men, a fight almost erupted due to a misunderstanding about the dowry. Specifically, on the very day of the wedding, they increased the dowry demand from 2,700 to 3,800 grams of silver. Had your best warriors not been away on a raid, the situation would have easily escalated to a fight. On another occasion, they tried to cheat you from your part of the profit of a joint trade made with some travelers. This resulted in a fight between you and Ingólfur's stepbrother, Hjörleifr Hróðmarsson. As a result, you have since had no contact with them.

Unfortunately, this degradation of the relationship and trust between the tribes could not have happened at a worse time since the joint raiding expedition that was sent out last winter has just successfully returned with much treasure. Now, concerned whether you can trust them to divide the treasure fairly, you, your wife, Halldóra Svararsdottir, and the wise man, Biǫrnólfr Vésteinnson, are to meet Ingólfur Arnarson, his step-brother Hjörleifr Hróðmarsson, and his son Þorsteinn Ingólfsson to negotiate how to divide everything. Indeed, as you are somewhat concerned about the southern tribe's hostile nature, you have arranged to have your best warriors wait outside the room in the event that they try something violent. Prior to arriving at the meeting, you received a list showing the following inventory of the treasure brought back from the raid:

Longships

In addition to the five ships they used in the raid, the warriors returned with **five** extra **longships**. These longships are considered very valuable. A longship is a light wooden boat primarily used for warfare and explorations. With its long and narrow hull, it is designed for speed and agility. It is therefore particularly suited for landings and troop deployments in shallow water. The five longships are in very good condition and very big with 30 rowing benches each. This makes them twice as long as the five you already had. You believe the value of the longships to be **around 3,200 grams of silver** each.

Knarr

Apart from the longships, they also brought back **two knarrs**. Knarrs are also wooden ships. However, they are not as fast as the longships due to a broader hull, a deeper draft and a limited number of oars. Nonetheless, you believe them to be more expensive and very useful since they can carry a large cargo, a necessity when crossing the Atlantic Ocean. Moreover, these ships are much safer in the treacherous open ocean. You estimate the value to be **around 3,000 grams of silver** per knarr.

Coins

Although you have never actually seen one, for the last few years, you have been hearing about the concept of coins used as a means of payment instead of paying by weight, for example in silver. The expedition has now brought back from their raid **22,000 coins made of silver,** each of which consists of 1.5 grams of silver. For your entire life, you have only known paying with silver according to its weight. Indeed, to make sure you have a precise understanding of the value of various treasure that is why you still value treasure by grams of silver.

Grain

Grain is important for its use both as food and seed. However, it is not the most valuable item for you. If you travel to the east, each sack of grain is worth **500 grams of silver**. Although the warriors brought back ten sacks of grain, you need just two sacks to provide you with enough food to get through next winter and enough seed for next spring's planting. If you get more than two sacks of grain, you will just sell the surplus on your next trading expedition to the east. If getting two sacks turns out too expensive, you are confident that you can arrange them from other sources.

Cows

The warriors returned with **eight cows**. Cows are highly valuable to you as they provide your tribe both milk and meat. You also know a place where you can sell a cow for **1,500 grams of silver**! You would like to have at least four out of the eight cows for your tribe but the more, the better.

Weapons

The warriors brought back an impressive number of **weapons**, **400** in total. This includes helmets, shields, swords, spears and chainmail armor (a type consisting of small metal rings linked together). The price for a weapon is **100 grams of silver** regardless of its uniqueness. For many reasons, it is customary not to haggle over the price of every single weapon. Despite this, you know of someone who is very eager to get their hands on a large cache of weapons. In fact, because of this, they will pay you a **bonus of**

3,000 grams of silver if you have more than 240 or more weapons to sell. This excites you!

Alcohol

As Vikings, you consider **alcohol** very important. However, this type of alcohol is a lot stronger than the beer you normally drink. The warriors said that this kind of alcohol is called whiskey. You have never tasted it before and consider it a special product. The warriors drank five casks on their way home, but there are still **twenty casks** left. These can either be used for special occasions or sold for **around 800 grams of silver** per cask.

The table below lists the items the Vikings brought back from the raid including their value per unit in silver and a possible bonus.

Item	Grams of silver per unit	Bonus
5 longships	3,200 grams of silver per ship	
2 knarrs	3,000 grams of silver per ship	
22,000 silver coins	1.5 grams of silver per coin	
10 sacks of grain	500 grams of silver per sack	
8 cows	1,500 grams silver per cow	
400 weapons	100 grams of silver per weapon	3,000 grams of silver if you sell 240 weapons or more.
20 casks of alcohol	800 grams of silver per cask	

Table 7. Inventory of the raided treasure together with their values for Garðarson

Even though you have a history of settling disputes violently, you cannot use violence or weapons to divide the treasure between the two tribes. Instead, you have to negotiate your way to a good deal.

Although, you may have a preference for some of the items specifically, at the end of the day only one thing matters: **value in total grams of silver**. Therefore, do not forget that each item has a value equaling a certain amount of silver. You want to maximize that value by dividing the treasure with the Southern Tribe in a way that leaves you with the **greatest value in terms of silver**. Also, do not forget that:

- You can only negotiate the items included in the loot. You are not allowed to invent options or introduce other items not mentioned above.
- A valid deal must involve an agreement on all seven items categories. If you can only agree on some of the items, there is no valid deal.
- In this negotiation, **the amount of silver you end up with is all that matters**. Any deal that gives you a positive amount of silver is acceptable. A no-deal means no silver.

THE LOOT
Garðarson's Tribe Valuation Table

Longships		Knarrs		Coins*		Grain*	
5	16,000	2	6,000	22,000	33,000	10	5,000
4	12,800	1	3,000	20,000	30,000	8	4,000
3	9,600			15,000	22,500	6	3,000
2	6,400			10,000	15,000	4	2,000
1	3,200			5,000	7,500	2	1,000
				1	1.5	1	500

Cows*		Weapons*		Alcohol*	
8	12,000	400	43,000	20	16,000
6	9,000	300	33,000	15	12,000
4	6,000	200	20,000	10	8,000
2	3,000	100	10,000	5	4,000
1	1,500	1	100	1	800

Table 8. Garðarson's Tribe Valuation Table

* Sample calculations for selected amounts of goods. You do not have to stick to the amounts listed in the table and can agree on other divisions from the allowed range e.g. 11,000 coins (16,500 grams of silver), 5 sacks of grain (2,500 grams of silver), 5 cows (7,500 grams of silver), 201 weapons (20,100 grams of silver), and 9 casks of alcohol (7,200 grams of silver).

Please do not let your negotiation partner(s)
see your Valuation Table!

Debriefing

The Vikings is a multi-issue, mixed-motive negotiation roleplay written for The Negotiation Challenge 2014 in Reykjavik, Iceland. It was negotiated at the Viking Village (Fjörukráin) in Hafnarfjörður close to Reykjavik. Prior to the negotiation, the participants enjoyed a short staged battle between actors dressed and equipped as traditional Vikings.

The negotiation described in the roleplay takes place between Ingólfur Arnarson from the Southern Territory and Gunnar Garðarson from the north. The main objective of the parties is to claim the most valuable share of the treasure brought back from their joint raid to a wealthy land to the southeast.

The confidential instructions reveal the following inventory of the treasure obtained in the raid together with their values for the respective parties:

Items	Amount	Value of 1 unit to Arnarson	Value of 1 unit to Garðarson
Longships	5	2,800	3,200
Knarrs	2	4,500	3,000
Coins	22,000	1.5	1.5
Sacks of grain	10	800	500
Cows	8	1,200	1,500
Weapons	400	100	100
Casks of alcohol	20	800	800

Table 9. Inventory of the raided treasure together with their values for Arnarson and Garðarson.

Longships			Knarrs			Coins*			Grain*		
5	14,000	0	2	9,000	0	22,000	36,000	0	10	8,000	0
4	11,200	3,200	1	4,500	3,000	20,000	33,000	7,500	8	6,400	1,000
3	8,400	6,400	0	0	6,000	15,000	22,500	15,000	6	4,800	2,000
2	5,600	9,600				10,000	15,000	22,500	4	3,200	3,000
1	2,800	12,800				5,000	7,500	30,000	2	1,600	4,000
0	0	16,000				0	0	33,000	0	0	5,000

Cows*			Weapons*			Alcohol*		
8	9,600	0	400	40,000	0	20	16,000	0
6	7,200	3,000	300	30,000	10,000	15	12,000	4,000
4	4,800	6,000	200	20,000	20,000	10	8,000	8,000
2	2,400	9,000	100	10,000	33,000	5	4,000	12,000
0	0	12,000	0	0	43,000	0	0	16,000

Table 10. Values of various divisions of the negotiated issues to the negotiating parties

Additionally, Arnarson can get a bonus in the amount of 3,000 grams of silver for obtaining at least 20,000 coins. A similar bonus of 3,000 grams of silver awaits Garðarson for getting 240 weapons. Table 10 illustrates the values of various possible negotiated divisions of the items to Arnarson and Garðarson. The first column for every item illustrates the amount of that item allocated to Arnarson. The middle column shows the value of the distribution to Arnarson and the right column to Garðarson.

Based on the information in both tables, it is evident that the complexity of this simulation is generated not only from the number of issues but also by the different types of issues. Longships, knars, grain, and cows are clearly integrative issues. The parties value them differently and therefore; it is possible to create value by allocating them to the parties that value them more. In contrast, alcohol is a purely distributive issue. The sum of values for each possible distribution of alcohol among the parties does not change and amounts to 16,000 grams of silver. Moreover, although the value of each coin appears the same at first sight, this is deceptive. The bonus that Arnarson can obtain for claiming 20,000 of them increase the value of each unit up to that point. The same is the case for Garðarson and the weapons. Any outlay beyond 20,000 coins for Arnarson and 240 weapons for Garðarson is distributive again.

To exhaust the entire potential of this negotiation, each party needs to identify and insist on getting what they value most. This means giving Garðarson all longships, cows, and at least 240 weapons. In turn, Arnarson should receive all knarrs, grain, and at least 20,000 coins. Dividing alcohol does not change the total value of the deal. A Pareto efficient outcome adds up to **140,000 grams of silver.**

Due to the complexity of the roleplay, Pareto efficient outcomes happen in less than 10% of the negotiating dyads. Such outcomes require establishing a trustful relationship and truthful information sharing between the parties. None of the teams participating in The Negotiation Challenge 2013 managed to negotiate a Pareto efficient agreement, though a few in each role ended up with more than 70,000 grams of silver, which is an even split of 140,000 grams.

Quantified preferences allow us to draw inferences on the negotiators' performance based on the substantive outcomes obtained in their negotiations. Based on them we can assess the parties' success in value creation and claiming. Although it would be possible to evaluate value creation and claiming separately, for The Negotiation Challenge we decided to consider and compare only the final outcome.

The key challenges for the negotiating teams were to create enough trust between them to share very sensitive information concerning their preferences, identify value-adding options from this and then exhaust the entire value potential of the negotiation. However, this is particularly difficult in a highly competitive context, which might incline the negotiators to focus solely on value claiming rather than combining it with value creation. Should they fall into this trap, it will produce a suboptimal agreement and leave value on the table.

The Vikings is an integrative negotiation roleplay simulation suitable for practicing value creation and value claiming skills. Differences in parties' preferences and valuations of the negotiated issues allows them to create value by focusing on what they value most.

Oasis Shipping

Author: **Peter Kesting**

Number of parties:	Preparation time:	Negotiation time:	Complexity level:
2	**30** minutes	**45** minutes	**intermediate**

Pedagogical focus

reservation point, BATNA, interest analysis, information exchange, strategies of the first offer, anchoring, logrolling, value creation and value claiming strategies, measuring negotiators efficiency, Pareto optimization, relationship building, trust creation, objective criteria, fairness, integrative negotiation

Short description

Oasis Shipping is a multi-issue, integrative negotiation roleplay simulation set between a Greek shipping company, Oasis Shipping, searching for a creative way to finance its explosive growth and a Danish finance company, Sørensen Invest A/S. Enjoying years of stellar management, Oasis Shipping needs five new ships to meet customer demand. Unfortunately, its current liquidity position limits its options to acquire them. Thus, the purpose of the meeting with Sørensen Invest is to identify and agree on a suitable solution. If successful, both parties have the potential to profit handsomely.

Confidential Instructions
for **Oasis Shipping Limited**

You are the managing director of Oasis Shipping Limited, a very successful medium-sized Greek shipping company based in Athens, Greece. Established in 1905, Oasis Shipping Limited remained for a long time only a small regional shipping company maintaining modest growth and reasonable profit. This changed however when your predecessor, Aristotle Oasis, the great-great-grandchild of the founder, took over. He was one of the first people in the company to realize the great potential of the Black Sea market as the newly elected USSR President and General Secretary, Mikhail Gorbachev was starting to liberalize Soviet trade policy. Opening the company's trade to this new market led to its first phase of explosive growth. Upon taking over from him, you led the company into its next phase of growth by recognizing that your Mediterranean location close to the Suez Canal provides you with competitive logistical advantages in the rising East African trade markets. Partly because of this, you have been able to acquire a healthy share of the growing trade between Africa and China.

Although the recent financial crises and the resulting slowdown in global trade and shipping placed significant pressure on company cash reserves and lines of credit, your strong infrastructure and efficient operations have allowed you not only to "weather the storm" but you have actually been able to expand your customer base as your competitors claimed insolvency. However, this unexpected growth has created another problem. In order to fulfill these new contracts, you need five more ships. You estimate them to cost around $300 million collectively. Now, as your cash position is currently too weak to purchase them outright and acquiring this much credit would be challenging, you have recognized that a creative financing solution must be found. Therefore, after talks with various finance providers, you have finally decided to engage Sørensen Invest A/S, a well-established Danish finance firm specializing in the shipping industry. Specifically, the idea that you have proposed to them is a "sale and leaseback" contract for ten existing ships in your fleet. This deal would entail that you sell these ships to Sørensen, who would then lease them back to you for a specified period. What happens with the ships after the leasing period is over is up to the new owner.

In preparation for your upcoming meeting with them, you, your Chief Financial Officer (CFO) and a separate external advisor have determined that the following issues will drive the negotiation. You have all agreed that the financial implications of the sale and leaseback contract will be fully determined by three parameters:

The sales price. This is the price for which you sell your ships to Sørensen. Here, the key requirement is that you get the $300 million to buy the five new ships that you need. Without at least this amount the deal is pointless. However, it would be quite nice to obtain more than the $300 million in this deal. Shipping is a risky business. Boosting your balance sheet with some extra cash liquidity will relieve much stress. Therefore, you really want the sale price to be about $350 million but the more, the better.

The leasing rate. This is the rate that you will pay annually to lease the ships back. Although you expect a gross profit of about 60% per year on these five ships, it is still a risky business. Thus, you want as low a rate as possible. However, you feel that 20% per year is fair since this rate will also need to cover the risk in the deal for the financer and also the depreciation of the ships. You know, of course, that any financial investor can refinance these assets under better terms anyway – that is a key source of their profit.

The duration of the lease contract. As you need some financial stability in this deal for many reasons, you want a contract duration of at least five years. A longer contract duration basically yields more profits for you. However, some of your key shipping contracts will expire in 10 years, so you would not like to go beyond this period.

Moreover, your CFO and his team have spent many hours calculating the financial implications of the contract. They found that given a sales price of $350 million, a leasing rate of 20% p.a. and a contract duration of 5 years, your base profit from the new ships will be $200 million. Also, every increase (reduction) of the sales price by $1 million increases (reduces) your profit by $2 million, every increase (reduction) of the leasing rate by 1% reduces (increases) your profit by $10 million, every increase (reduction) of the contract duration by 1 year increases (reduces) your profit by $50 million.

As you have already discussed the background and the substance of the deal with Sørensen, you are now meeting with their delegation consisting of the managing director and two project managers to reach agreement on the details outlined above. Your goal is to negotiate the highest possible profit for Oasis Shipping Limited.

Here is a brief summary of your most important instructions and objectives:
- Your net profit of the deal will be $200 million, given a sales price of $350 million, the leasing rate is 20%, and the contract duration is five years.
- Do not close any deal with a sales price below $300 million.
- Do not close any deal over ten years.
- Every increase (reduction) of the sales price by $1 million increases (reduces) your profit by $2 million.
- Every increase (reduction) of the leasing rate by 1% reduces (increases) your profit by $10 million.

- Every increase (reduction) of the contract duration by one year increases (reduces) your profit by $50 million.
- Your profit therefore be represented by the equation:

$$Profit_{Oasis} = 200 + 2 * [Sales\ Price - 350] - 10 * [Leasing\ Rate - 20] + 50 * [Contract\ Duration - 5]$$

- The ranking of this negotiation round is exclusively based on your profit.
- Your profit only consists of the elements above.
- Deals that violate any of your restrictions above are not valid.

The tables below show your profit for different combinations of leasing rates and contract durations for the three scenarios: a sales price of $300 million (*Table 11*); a sales price of $350 million (*Table 12*), and a sales price of $400 million (*Table 13*). Please note that the negotiations are NOT restricted to the combinations in the table – you can also negotiate ALL other combinations of sales prices, leasing rates and contract durations that do not violate the restrictions above.

	3 years	4 years	5 years	6 years	8 years	10 years
12%	80	130	180	230	330	430
16%	40	90	140	190	290	390
20%	0	50	100	150	250	350
24%	(40)	10	60	110	210	310
28%	(80)	(30)	20	70	170	270
32%	(120)	(70)	(20)	30	130	230
40%	(200)	(150)	(100)	(50)	50	150

Table 11. Profit of Oasis Limited for different combinations of leasing rates and contract duration at the sales price of $300 million

	3 years	4 years	5 years	6 years	8 years	10 years
12%	180	230	280	330	430	530
16%	140	190	240	290	390	490
20%	100	150	200	250	350	450
24%	60	110	160	210	310	410
28%	20	70	120	170	270	370
32%	(20)	30	80	130	230	330
40%	(100)	(50)	0	50	150	250

Table 12. Profit of Oasis Limited for different combinations of leasing rates and contract duration at the sales price of $350 million

	3 years	4 years	5 years	6 years	8 years	10 years
12%	280	330	380	430	530	630
16%	240	290	340	390	490	590
20%	200	250	300	350	450	550
24%	160	210	260	310	410	510
28%	120	170	220	270	370	470
32%	80	130	180	230	330	430
40%	0	50	100	150	250	350

Table 13. Profit of Oasis Limited for different combinations of leasing rates and contract duration at the sales price of $400 million

Confidential Instructions
for **Sørensen Invest A/S**

You are the owner of Sørensen Invest A/S, a Danish finance firm that is very experienced in the shipping industry. Your latest project is a "sale and leaseback" proposal with *Oasis Shipping Limited*, a very successful medium-sized Athens based Greek shipping company. Established in 1905, *Oasis Shipping Limited* was for a long time only a small regional shipping company with modest growth and profit. However, this changed when Aristotle Oasis, the great-great-grandchild of the founder took over. He was one of the first people in the company to realize the great potential of the Black Sea market as the newly elected USSR President and General Secretary, Mikhail Gorbachev started to liberalize Soviet trade policy. Opening the company's trade to this new market led to its first phase of explosive growth.

Upon taking over from Mr. Oasis, the new managing director continued this explosive growth by leveraging their Mediterranean location close to the Suez Canal to provide them with competitive logistical advantages in the rising East African trade markets and a healthy share of the growing trade between Africa and China.

Moreover, due to their strong infrastructure and efficient operations, they took advantage of the recent financial crises by expanding their customer base due to multiple insolvencies among their competitors.

However, to fulfill the contracts from these new customers, they need five more ships. In this regard, they have approached you about a creative financing option. Specifically, they are interested in a sale and leaseback contract for ten existing ships in their fleet. This deal would encompass Oasis Shipping Limited selling these ships to you, whereupon you would lease the ships back to them for a specified time horizon. What happens with the ships after the leasing period would be completely up to you as the new owner.

Sale and leaseback contracts are your core business. Therefore, together with your team, in preparation for your upcoming meeting with them, you have determined that the following issues will drive your negotiation and that the financial implications of the sale and leaseback contract will be fully determined by three parameters:

The sales price. This is the price that you pay for the ships. To take advantage of their new business opportunities, Oasis Shipping Limited needs $300 million. In return, you become the owner of ten of their ships. Although these ships are a little old, they are worth this price.

The leasing rate. Because you can refinance your capital needs at a much lower interest rate than most investors (you have an AAA credit rating), this rate is the main driver of your profit. However, with these leasing rates you have to also cover the risks involved in the deal and also the depreciation of the ships (the ships you buy will have a life expectancy between 15 and 20 years). Therefore, you aspire to a leasing rate of around 28-32% per year, the higher, the better.

The duration of the lease contract. Although the current economic health of the shipping market is good, you are slightly uncertain about the future. That is, although you are certain that you can sell the ships for a good price after five years, after 8-10 years your risk increases significantly. What price can you get for a ship with a life expectancy of 5-10 years? Therefore, to mitigate this risk, you want to keep the duration of the leasing contract as short as possible. Specifically, you aspire for a contract duration of 5 years, and you will not accept a contract duration of more than eight years.

Moreover, your CFO and his team have spent many hours calculating the financial implications of the contract. They found that your basic profit from the new ships will be $200 million, given a sales price is $300 million, a leasing rate of 28% p.a. and a contract duration of 5 years. Also, every increase (reduction) of the sales price by $1 million reduces (increases) your profit by $1 million, every increase (reduction) of the leasing rate by 1% increases (reduces) your profit by $20 million, every increase (reduction) of the contract duration by 1 year reduces (increases) your profit by $20 million.

So far, you have already discussed the background and the substance of the deal with them and after signing a letter of intent have conducted a thorough due diligence (a detailed investigation of the physical condition of the ships and all other relevant issues for the deal). You are now meeting with their delegation consisting of the managing director, the CFO and an external advisor to reach agreement on the above details. Your goal is to negotiate the highest possible profit for you.

Here is a brief summary of your most important instructions and objectives:

- Your net profit of the deal will be $200 million, given a sales price is $300 million, the leasing rate is 28% and the contract duration is five years.
- Do not close any deal over eight years.
- Every increase (reduction) of the sales price by $1 million reduces (increases) your profit by $1 million.
- Every increase (reduction) of the leasing rate by 1% increases (reduces) your profit by $20 million
- Every increase (reduction) of the contract duration by one year reduces (increases) your profit by $20 million.
- Your profit therefore be represented by the equation:

$$Profit_{Oasis} = 200 - 1 * [Sales\ Price - 300] + 20 * [Leasing\ Rate - 28] - 20 * [Contract\ Duration - 5]$$

- The ranking of this negotiation round is exclusively based on your profit.

- Your profit only consists of the elements above.
- Deals that violate any of your restrictions above are not valid.

The tables below show your profit for different combinations of leasing rates and contract durations for the three scenarios: a sales price of $300 million (*Table 14*); a sales price of $350 million (*Table 15*), and a sales price of $400 million *(Table 16)*. Please note that the negotiations are NOT restricted to the combinations in the table – you can also negotiate ALL other combinations of sales prices, leasing rates and contract durations that do not violate the restrictions above.

	3 years	4 years	5 years	6 years	8 years
12%	(80)	(100)	(120)	(140)	(180)
16%	0	(20)	(40)	(60)	(100)
20%	80	60	40	20	(20)
24%	160	140	120	100	60
28%	240	220	200	180	140
32%	320	300	280	260	220
40%	480	460	440	420	380

Table 14. Profit of Sørensen Invest for different combinations of leasing rates and contract duration at the sales price of $300 million

	3 years	4 years	5 years	6 years	8 years
12%	(130)	(150)	(170)	(190)	(230)
16%	(50)	(70)	(90)	(110)	(150)
20%	30	10	(10)	(30)	(70)
24%	110	90	70	50	10
28%	190	170	150	130	90
32%	270	250	230	210	170
40%	430	410	390	370	330

Table 15. Profit of Sørensen Invest for different combinations of leasing rates and contract duration at the sales price of $350 million

	3 years	4 years	5 years	6 years	8 years
12%	(180)	(200)	(220)	(240)	(280)
16%	(100)	(120)	(140)	(160)	(200)
20%	(20)	(40)	(60)	(80)	(120)
24%	60	40	20	0	(40)
28%	140	120	100	80	40
32%	220	200	180	160	120
40%	380	360	340	320	280

Table 16. Profit of Sørensen Invest for different combinations of leasing rates and contract duration at the sales price of $400 million

Debriefing

Oasis Shipping is a multi-issue, integrative negotiation roleplay written for The Negotiation Challenge 2012 in Athens, Greece. The participating teams were asked to represent Oasis Shipping Limited or Sørensen Invest A/S in a negotiation concerning the detailed conditions of a sale and leaseback contract between them.

According to the confidential instructions, the preferences of the negotiating parties can be quantified and expressed by the following formulas. Each formula describes the profit that each of the parties can obtain given the exact agreement they strike across the three variables: sales price, leasing rate and contract duration:

$$Profit_{Oasis} = 200 + 2 * [Sales\ Price - 350] - 10 * [Leasing\ Rate - 20] + 50 * [Contract\ Duration - 5]$$

> "(...) every increase (reduction) of the sales price by $1 million increases (reduces) your profit by $2 million, every increase (reduction) of the leasing rate by 1% reduces (increases) your profit by $10 million, every increase (reduction) of the contract duration by 1 year increases (reduces) your profit by $50 million (...)"

$$Profit_{Oasis} = 200 - 1 * [Sales\ Price - 300] + 20 * [Leasing\ Rate - 28] - 20 * [Contract\ Duration - 5]$$

> "(...) every increase (reduction) of the sales price by $1 million reduces (increases) your profit by $1 million, every increase (reduction) of the leasing rate by 1% increases (reduces) your profit by $20 million, every increase (reduction) of the contract duration by 1 year reduces (increases) your profit by $20 million (...)"

These instructions and respective formulas clearly reveal the differences in valuations each party places on the various issues being negotiated. These differences expose opportunity for capitalizing on disparities and gives each party an opportunity to engineer value.

As in the Staple Rights roleplay, one will notice that the profit formulas include more details than what is described narratively in the parties' preferences. As with Staple Rights, this information is added solely as an aid to place the graphical representation of both parties' preferences close to each other.

Additionally, the parties are instructed on their reservation points with respect to some of the negotiated issues. They are summarized in the table below:

Issue	Minimum	Maximum
Sales price [$]	300m	unspecified
Leasing rate [%]	unspecified	unspecified
Contract duration [years]	3 years	8 years

Table 17. The parties' reservations points and the respective zone of possible agreement (ZOPAs)

Combining these reservation points with the corresponding scoring functions allows us to graph a Pareto efficiency frontier, which looks as follows:

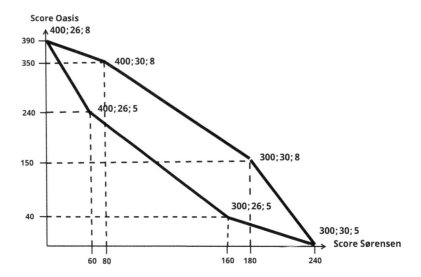

Figure 6. The structure of the Oasis Shipping negotiation roleplay including a sketch of the Pareto efficiency frontier

Quantified preferences allow us to draw inferences on the negotiators' performance based on the substantive outcome obtained in their negotiations. Based on the substantive outcome, we can assess the parties' success in value creation and claiming. Although it would be possible to evaluate value creation and claiming separately, for The Negotiation Challenge we decided to consider and compare only the final outcome.

For the benefit of reference, the best substantive result obtained by the teams that represented Oasis Shipping during The Negotiation Challenge 2013 was a total profit of $480 million and it was produced by an agreement with a sales price of $390 million, a leasing rate of 35%, and a contract duration of 8 years. The best substantive result among the teams representing Sørensen Invest A/S was a total profit of $440 million corresponding to an agreement with a sales price of $380 million, a leasing rate of 44%, and a contract duration of 5 years. The average results obtained within each role differed substantially and amounted to $180 million for Oasis Shipping and $264 million for the Sørensen Invest negotiators.

The key challenges for both negotiating teams in Oasis Shipping are to create enough trust between them to share very sensitive information concerning their preferences, identify value-adding options from this and then increase the efficiency of the outcome. Another key challenge is not to stop this process too early. Overcoming these challenges will be particularly difficult in a highly competitive context, which might incline the negotiators to focus solely on value claiming rather than combining it with value creation. Should they do so, it will produce a suboptimal agreement and leave value on the table.

It is interesting to note that the structure of this roleplay allows **unlimited value creation**, at least theoretically. Contract duration is the only issue that has clearly stated reservation points. For the remaining issues: price and leasing rate, the negotiators have much more flexibility. Offsetting a price increase with a higher leasing rate creates value for both parties at the same time. This process has no upper limit and theoretically could continue infinitely. Of course, at some point, the combinations of sales prices and leasing rates become absurd and defy common business sense. Nevertheless, having tested this roleplay during The Negotiation Challenge as well as in many courses with our graduate students, we have learned that this unlimited potential for value creation is **unnoticed**.

There are many possible explanations for this phenomenon. Despite the seeming clarity of preferences given in the confidential instructions of the roleplay, just as in real-world negotiations, for various reasons negotiators can remain unfocused on what they precisely want or on how important one issue is compared with another. This can be further complicated by the reticence of each party to exchange very sensitive information on the relative importance of the involved issues in order to recognize and unlock the potential of a negotiation. Finally, many negotiators myopically perceive negotiation only as a competitive value claiming process and do not utilize the prerequisites and the mechanics of value creation. A combination of any of these reasons might cause the parties to settle for agreements that leave even unlimited potential untapped.

Oasis Shipping is an integrative scoreable negotiation roleplay simulation suitable for practicing value creation and value claiming skills. Differences in parties' preferences and valuations of the negotiated issues allows them to create value by focusing on what they value most. Moreover, this roleplay can also be used to illustrate an extreme example of negotiators' inability to recognize and exhaust the full potential of a negotiation.

Cocoa Negotiation

Authors: **Dwaipayan Bhowmik,**
Kamal Ganeriwala and Ina Yotova
under the supervision
of **Remigiusz Smolinski**

Number of parties:	Preparation time:	Negotiation time:	Complexity level:
2	**30-45** minutes	**45-60** minutes	**high**

Pedagogical focus

reservation point, BATNA, interest analysis, information exchange, strategies of the first offer, anchoring, logrolling, value creation and value claiming strategies, measuring negotiators efficiency, Pareto optimization, relationship building, trust creation, objective criteria, fairness, integrative negotiation

Short description

Cocoa Negotiation is a multi-issue, mixed-motive negotiation role-play simulation between the founders of a German chocolate manufacturing company, Natura Chocolate GmbH and the CEO and of a cocoa beans supply company CBS (Cocoa Beans Supply) Limited. Looking to enter the European market for the first time to sell its high-quality fair-trade derived cocoa beans, CBS Limited is interested in striking a deal with Natura Chocolate, who happens to be searching for a new supplier but only one that can supply the highest quality beans that come from sustainable fair-trade farms. However, Natura is a start-up, which means they must be highly discerning on all financial issues. They are now meeting to negotiate the terms and conditions of a cocoa beans supply contract.

Confidential Information
for **CBS Limited**

Growing mainly in world's equatorial regions, cocoa beans are the key source component for the billion-dollar chocolate industry. Although the third largest producer of cocoa beans in the world, the country of Ghana is also known for the premium quality of its cocoa. In fact, Ghanaians call it *"pa pa paa"* which means the best of the best.

Unfortunately, despite the high quality of this commodity, general economic underdevelopment in Ghana has allowed farming practices such as child labor that many characterize as unethical. To combat this, the industry recently introduced a Sustainability and Equity Certification (S&E Certification) Program. The key goals of this program are to promote sustainable agricultural practices, improve farm yield management and address social and living conditions among farm workers. An encouraging sign of its impact, according to a recent report, is the comparatively higher yields, better quality and higher profitability of S&E certified cocoa farms when compared to conventional farms.

Your team represents **Cocoa Beans Supply Limited** (CBS). As a cocoa bean supplier to chocolate manufacturing companies in the United States, you work closely with a key cocoa farmer union in Ghana that is a source for high-quality S&E certified cocoa beans. Unfortunately, after a recent economic downturn in the USA, CBS's business has been struggling. As a result, after considering several alternative strategies to deal with this downturn in customer demand, the company has decided to enter the European market where chocolate demand remains high especially for high-quality cocoa beans. However, to establish your presence in the European market, you need to sign up your first customer as soon as possible. Unfortunately, this has turned out to be more challenging than expected.

However, after recently meeting one of the representatives of a German start-up company called Natura Chocolate GmbH at a trade show, you discovered they are in the process of searching for a reliable supplier of premium quality cocoa beans. Since they produce premium organic chocolate products (chocolate bars, chocolate candy, etc.) by using only high-quality ingredients, this could be a perfect opportunity.

As a result, you have organized a meeting with Natura to discuss acquiring them as a new customer. During this meeting, issues that will be important for you to discuss with them will be:

- Price
- Quantity
- Quality (based on percentage of defective cocoa bean and yield of cocoa butter)
- Incoterms (International Commercial Terms)
- Certification
- Flavor

Each of these issues has a different priority as is indicated by the weight assigned to it. The most important issue for you as a supplier is the price for your premium quality product. This is followed by the minimum order quantity per year and the percentage of defective cocoa beans. Yield, flavor, Incoterms, and certification all have an equal weight. The weights of the different issues are outlined in the following table:

Issues	Priority/Weight CBS Limited
Price	0.3
Quantity	0.15
Defective cocoa beans	0.15
Yield of cocoa butter	0.1
Incoterms	0.1
Certification	0.1
Flavor	0.1

Table 18. Negotiation issues and their priorities for CBS Limited

You have asked your analysts to prepare a short briefing for the upcoming meeting with Natura Chocolate and here is what they came up with:

- **Price:** This is the most important issue for CBS. The higher the price, the better. The current average market price for cocoa beans is 2.14 € per kilogram. The prices for premium certified beans can sometimes exceed 4 € per kilogram. To reach the desired level of profitability in the European market, CBS must sell at a price of **at least 2.1 € per kilogram** (weight: 0.3).

- **Quantity:** This is the fixed minimum amount of cocoa beans that CBS will sell to Natura Chocolate. On this issue, you are concerned about the risk of working with a startup company. Yes, they may grow and drive your European operations, but they could also fail and go bankrupt. Therefore, you would like to keep the fixed quantity as high as possible in order to minimize your shipment, custom and warehouse costs. Thus, you require a minimum commitment of at least 3,000 tons of cocoa beans per year (weight: 0.15).

- **Percentage of defective cocoa beans** in a random sample is one of the standard measures of quality widely recognized in the industry. Depending on the beans' origin, an average value is between 6% and 8%. You are aware that some of your competitors claim they can deliver their products with only 2% defective beans. The farmers in your union can meet such high standards, but you also know that this level of quality comes at a premium price (weight: 0.15).

- **Percentage of yield:** The yield is one of the most important indicators of cocoa beans' quality. It describes the amount of cocoa butter in the nibs. Nibs are just the fragmented pieces of cocoa beans that result from the roasting and husk separation process. Higher levels of cocoa butter mean that lower levels will need to be added later in the manufacturing process. Nib yields are determined in the laboratory[10] (weight: 0.1).

- **Incoterms:** International Commercial Terms are a series of pre-defined commercial terms, which are used in international commercial transactions or procurement processes, with the intention to clearly inform about the tasks, costs, and risks associated with the delivery and transport of goods.[11] Maritime transport will take place between the harbors of Accra (Ghana) and Hamburg (Germany). Cocoa beans will be transported in containers by the rules for sea transport. There are four Incoterms rules relevant in this case:

  - FAS Accra – Free alongside Ship – the seller delivers when the goods are placed alongside the buyer's vessel at the named port of shipment. This means that the buyer has to bear all costs and risks of loss of or damage to the goods from that moment.

---

[10] Source: http://www.icco.org/
[11] Source: http://en.wikipedia.org/wiki/Incoterms

- FOB Accra – Free on Board – the seller pays for transportation of goods to the port of shipment and the loading cost. The buyer pays the cost of marine freight transportation, insurance, unloading and transportation cost from the arrival port to destination. The passing of risk occurs when the goods are in buyer's account.

- CFR Hamburg – Cost and Freight – Seller must pay the costs and freight to bring the goods to the port of destination. However, risk is transferred to the buyer once the goods are loaded on the vessel. Insurance for the goods is NOT included.

- CIF Hamburg – Cost, Insurance and Freight – Exactly the same as CFR except that the seller must, in addition, procure and pay for the insurance.[12]

These rules clearly define which costs need to be covered by which party and who bears the financial risk of loss of or damage to the freight. For CBS, FAS Accra is certainly the best option, as the buyer has to bear all costs and risks of loss or damage (weight: 0.1).

- **Certification:** Although price is clearly the most important issue for CBS, as a loyal representative of the farmers' union you have to protect their interests and make sure they are properly rewarded for their hard work. Therefore, you prefer to operate with partners who respect the norms of Fairtrade[13] and honor the Sustainability and Equity

---

[12]   Source: http://en.wikipedia.org/wiki/Incoterms
[13]   **Fairtrade** is a trading partnership, based on dialogue, transparency, and respect, that seeks greater equity in international trade. It contributes to sustainable development by offering better trading conditions to, and securing the rights of, disadvantaged producers and workers – especially in the South"(FINE, 1998).

Certificates. These certificates are awarded each year based on a yearly assessment of operations by an independent certification organization. Criteria for the assessment are the sustainable use of resources, fair-trade, fair labor conditions and no child labor. Despite a series of disturbing reports in the press concerning child labor in your farmers' union, ethical conduct has always been more important to you than profits. Therefore, a high level of the S&E Certification would strengthen your reputation and be very helpful in entering the European market (weight: 0.1).

- **Flavor** quality of the cocoa beans is also important for chocolate manufacturers. Experienced tasters determine the flavor quality, and can give it a rating of high, medium or low. Ghanaian cocoa beans are especially famous for their flavor, and your farmers have consistently met the highest standards in this area (weight: 0.1).

Your objective for the upcoming negotiation is to:
- make sure you **reach an agreement with Natura Chocolate** – this is a great opportunity to enter the European market and improve your financial situation;
- agree on the set of options that **maximizes your score**;
- agree on **all seven issues** indicated in the table below. Only such agreements are valid. Leaving any of the issues unsettled means no agreement at all and 0 points for both parties.
- Please make sure the final agreement includes **only the options explicitly mentioned in the payoff table** below.

Your **total score** for the negotiation is the sum of the product of points corresponding to the agreed options and their weights (see a sample calculation below).

Payoff Tables of CBS Limited

Price per kilogram (weight 0.3)	Points CBS Limited
< = 2.00 €	0
2.25 €	0.125
2.50 €	0.25
2.75 €	0.375
3.00 €	0.5
3.25 €	0.625
3.50 €	0.75
3.75 €	0.875
> = 4.00 €	1

Defective cocoa beans in % (weight 0.15)	Points CBS Limited
> = 10	1
9	0.875
8	0.75
7	0.625
6	0.5
5	0.375
4	0.25
3	0.125
< = 2	0

Incoterms (weight 0.1)	Points CBS Limited
FAS Accra	1
FOB Accra	0.67
CFR Hamburg	0.33
CIF Hamburg	0

Certification (weight 0.1)	Points CBS Limited
platinum level	1
gold level	0.75
silver level	0.5
bronze level	0.25
no certification	0

Quantity in tons (weight 0.15)	Points CBS Limited
< = 3,000	0
3,500	0.28
4,000	0.46
4,500	0.58
5,000	0.69
5,500	0.77
6,000	0.84
6,500	0.89
7,000	0.94
7,500	0.98
> = 8000	1

Yield cocoa of cocoa butter in % (weight 0.1)	Points CBS Limited
< = 50	1
51	0.9
52	0.8
53	0.7
54	0.6
55	0.5
56	0.4
57	0.3
58	0.2
59	0.1
> = 60	0

Flavor (weight 0.1)	Points CBS Limited
low	0
medium	0.5
high	1

Table 19. Payoff Tables of CBS Limited

Sample Calculations:

Final Score = Points(**Price**) $*$ 0.3 + Points(**Quantity**) $*$ 0.15 + Points(**Defective**) $*$ 0.15 + Points(**Yield of cocoa butter**) $*$ 0.1 + Points(**Incoterms**) $*$ 0.1 + Points(**Certification**) $*$ 0.1 + Points(**Flavor**) $*$ 0.1

Example:

Issues	Weights	Agreement	Payoff	Score
Price	0.3	3.00€	0.5	0.15
Quantity	0.15	5,000 tons	0.69	0.1035
Defective cocoa beans	0.15	5%	0.375	0.05625
Yield of cocoa butter	0.1	53%	0.7	0.07
Incoterms	0.1	CFR Hamburg	0.33	0.033
Certification	0.1	Gold level	0.75	0.075
Flavor	0.1	Medium	0.5	0.05
			Total Score:	**0.5378**

Table 20. Sample calculations of the final score for CBS Limited

Confidential Information
for **Natura Chocolate GmbH**

Growing mainly in world's equatorial regions, cocoa beans are the key source component for the billion-dollar chocolate industry. Although the third largest producer of cocoa beans in the world, the country of Ghana is also known for the premium quality of its cocoa. In fact, Ghanaians call it *"pa pa paa"* which means the best of the best.

Unfortunately, despite the high quality of this commodity, general economic underdevelopment in Ghana has allowed farming practices such as child labor that many characterize as unethical. To combat this, the industry recently introduced a Sustainability and Equity Certification (S&E Certification) Program. The key goals of this program are to promote sustainable agricultural practices, improve farm yield management and address social and living conditions among farm workers. An encouraging sign of its impact, according to a recent report, is the comparatively higher yields, better quality and higher profitability of S&E certified cocoa farms when compared to conventional farms.

Your team represents **Natura Chocolate GmbH**, a German start-up company that produces high-quality organic chocolate products (chocolate bars, chocolate candy, etc.) with a focus on using only premium high-quality ingredients. The mission of your company is to provide your customers with a unique, high-quality organic chocolate confectionary, which is also produced in a sustainable, environmentally friendly, and socially responsible way. It is also important to you that the acquisition of your source supplies follows the spirit of Fairtrade. This means that you are ready to pay a higher price for cocoa beans.

Currently, Natura Chocolate is in the process of searching for a new supplier of premium quality cocoa beans. Indeed, the success of the company depends on a long-term relationship with a reliable supplier. After a recent introduction to them and some preliminary research, you have discovered that Cocoa Beans Supply Limited (CBS) might be a suitable choice. CBS is a cocoa bean supplier that works closely with a cocoa farmer union in Ghana to supply chocolate manufacturing companies in the United States with premium quality cocoa beans.

You are about to meet key members of their company to assess the potential of a supplier relationship. Important in this discussion will be your ability to assess how premium the quality of their beans are which depends on three key factors: the percentage of defective cocoa beans, the percentage of yield of cocoa butter from the cocoa nib and the flavor quality of the cocoa beans.

The success of your negotiation will be determined by your **final score**, which is a function of the following negotiation issues:

- Quality (based on percentage of defective cocoa bean and yield of cocoa butter)
- Quantity
- Price
- Incoterms (International Commercial Terms)
- Certification
- Flavor

Each issue has a different priority indicated by the weight assigned to it. The most important issue for you as a manufacturer is the yield of cocoa butter followed by the minimum order quantity per year and the percentage of defective cocoa beans. Price, flavor, Incoterms, and Certification have an equal weight. The weights of the different issues are outlined in the following table:

Issues	Priority/Weight Natura Chocolate GmbH
Yield of cocoa butter	0.3
Quantity	0.15
Defective cocoa beans	0.15
Price	0.1
Incoterms	0.1
Certification	0.1
Flavor	0.1

Table 21. Negotiation issues and their priorities for Natura Chocolate GmbH

You have prepared a short briefing for the upcoming negotiation with CBS and here is its short summary:

- **Percentage of yield:** The yield is one of the most important indicators of cocoa beans' quality. It describes the amount of cocoa butter in the nibs. Nibs are just the fragmented pieces of cocoa beans that result from the roasting and husk separation process. Higher levels of cocoa butter mean that lower levels will need to be added later in the manufacturing process. Nib yields are determined in the laboratory[14] (weight: 0.3).

- **Quantity:** This is the fixed minimum amount of cocoa beans that Natura Chocolate will buy from CBS. Natura Chocolate would like to keep the fixed quantity as low as possible to maintain flexibility and keep warehouse costs low. Ideally, you want an agreement with a very low fixed commitment- less than 4,000 tons of cocoa per year. However, you certainly do not want to commit to anything more than 8,000 tons of cocoa beans per year (weight: 0.15).

---

[14] Source: http://www.icco.org/

- **Percentage of defective cocoa beans** in a random sample is one of the standard measures of quality widely recognized in the industry. Depending on the beans' origin, an average value is between 6% and 8%. However, some of CBS's competitors claim they can deliver their products with only 2% defective beans, and this is what you are planning to request from CBS as well (weight: 0.15).

- **Price**: The current average market price for cocoa beans is 2.14 € per kilogram. Although quality has its price, the less you can pay for it, the better. The prices for premium certified beans can sometimes exceed 4 € per kilogram, and that is the maximum you are willing to pay (weight: 0.1).

- **Incoterms**: International Commercial Terms are a series of pre-defined commercial terms, which are used in international commercial transactions or procurement processes. They clearly define the responsibilities, costs, and risks associated with the delivery and transport of goods between contracting parties.[15] Maritime transport will take place between the harbors of Accra (Ghana) and Hamburg (Germany). Cocoa beans will be transported in containers by the rules for sea transport. There are four Incoterms rules relevant in this case:

  - FAS Accra – Free alongside Ship – the seller delivers when the goods are placed alongside the buyer's vessel at the named port of shipment. This means that the buyer has to bear all costs and risks of loss of or damage to the goods from that moment.

---

[15] Source: http://en.wikipedia.org/wiki/Incoterms

- FOB Accra – Free on Board – the seller pays for transportation of goods to the port of shipment and the loading cost. The buyer pays the cost of marine freight transportation, insurance, unloading and transportation cost from the arrival port to destination. The passing of risk occurs when the goods are in buyer's account.

- CFR Hamburg – Cost and Freight – Seller must pay the costs and freight to bring the goods to the port of destination. However, the risk is transferred to the buyer once the goods are loaded on the vessel. Insurance for the goods is NOT included.

- CIF Hamburg – Cost, Insurance and Freight – Exactly the same as CFR except that the seller must, in addition, procure and pay for the insurance.[16]

These rules clearly define which costs need to be covered by which party and who bears the financial risk of loss of or damage to the freight. For Natura Chocolate, CIF Hamburg is certainly the best option, as all costs including insurance, are paid by the seller (weight: 0.1).

• **Certification**: Although CBS enjoys a very good reputation in the industry, it does have some history of acquiring beans harvested under unethical labor practices including the use of child labor. As it is a matter of great importance for you as Natura Chocolate GmbH that your chocolate products are based on fair labor conditions and sustainable farming practices, it is extremely important that CBS holds a Sustainability and Equity Certification with a high level.

---

[16] Source: http://en.wikipedia.org/wiki/Incoterms

These Certificates are awarded each year based on a yearly assessment of operations by an independent certification organization. Criteria for the assessment are the sustainable use of resources, fair-trade, fair labor conditions and no child labor. As social responsibility is important to you and your customers, it is unacceptable to work with companies that do not share this value. Therefore, the higher the Certification level, the better (weight: 0.1).

- **Flavor quality** of the cocoa beans is also important for chocolate manufacturers. Experienced tasters determine the flavor quality, and can give it a rating of high, medium or low. You expect CBS to meet the highest standards in this area (weight: 0.1).

Your objective for upcoming the negotiation is to:
- make sure you **reach an agreement with CBS** – they seem to be a suitable supplier for your premium chocolate business.
- agree on the set of options that **maximize your score**.
- agree on **all seven issues** indicated in the table below. Only such agreements are valid. Leaving any of the issues unsettled means no agreement at all and 0 points for both parties.
- Please make sure the final agreement includes **only the options explicitly mentioned in the payoff table** below.

Your total score for the negotiation is the sum of the product of points corresponding to the agreed options and their weights (see a sample calculation below).

Payoff Tables of Natura Chocolate GmbH

Price per kilogram (weight 0.1)	Points Points Natura Chocolate GmbH
< = 2.00 €	1
2.25 €	0.875
2.50 €	0.75
2.75 €	0.625
3.00 €	0.5
3.25 €	0.375
3.50 €	0.25
3.75 €	0.125
> = 4.00 €	0

Defective cocoa beans in % (weight 0.15)	Points Points Natura Chocolate GmbH
> = 10	0
9	0.125
8	0.25
7	0.375
6	0.5
5	0.625
4	0.75
3	0.875
< = 2	1

Incoterms (weight 0.1)	Points Points Natura Chocolate GmbH
FAS Accra	0
FOB Accra	0.33
CFR Hamburg	0.67
CIF Hamburg	1

Certification (weight 0.1)	Points Points Natura Chocolate GmbH
platinum level	1
gold level	0.75
silver level	0.5
bronze level	0.25
no certification	0

Quantity in tons (weight 0.15)	Points Natura Chocolate GmbH		Yield cocoa of cocoa butter in % (weight 0.3)	Points Natura Chocolate GmbH
< = 3,000	1		< = 50	0
3,500	0.98		51	0.1
4,000	0.94		52	0.2
4,500	0.89		53	0.3
5,000	0.84		54	0.4
5,500	0.77		55	0.5
6,000	0.69		56	0.6
6,500	0.58		57	0.7
7,000	0.46		58	0.8
7,500	0.28		59	0.9
> = 8,000	0		> = 60	1

Flavor (weight 0.1)	Points Natura Chocolate GmbH
low	0
medium	0.5
high	1

Table 22. Payoff Tables of Natura Chocolate

Sample Calculations:

Final Score = Points(**Yield of cocoa butter**) * 0.3 + Points(**Quantity**) * 0.15 + Points(**Defective**) * 0.15 + Points(**Price**) * 0.1 + Points(**Incoterms**) * 0.1 + Points(**Certification**) * 0.1 + Points(**Flavor**) * 0.1

Example:

Issues	Weights	Agreement	Payoff	Score
Yield of cocoa butter	0.3	53%	0.3	0.09
Quantity	0.15	5,000 tons	0.84	0.126
Defective cocoa beans	0.15	5%	0.625	0.09375
Price	0.1	3.00€	0.5	0.05
Incoterms	0.1	CFR Hamburg	0.67	0.067
Certification	0.1	Gold level	0.75	0.075
Flavor	0.1	Medium	0.5	0.05
			Total Score:	0.5518

Table 23. Sample calculations of the final score for Natura Chocolate GmbH

Debriefing

Cocoa Negotiation is a multi-issue, mixed-motive negotiation role-play written for The Negotiation Challenge 2015 in Munich. It was negotiated during one of the online qualification rounds prior to the main event in Munich.

The negotiation described in the roleplay takes place between the founders of a chocolate manufacturing company Natura Chocolate GmbH and the CEO of CBS (Cocoa Beans Supply) Limited, cocoa beans supply company. The parties are to negotiate the terms and conditions of a cocoa beans supply contract. The main objectives of the parties are to protect their substantive interests in a mutually beneficial manner and create a positive foundation for future collaboration.

The confidential instructions reveal the following issues on which agreement must be reached. For each party, this includes the relative importance of each issue expressed as the weight it plays on their scoring function:

Issue	Importance of issues for CBS	Importance of issues for Natura Chocolate
Price	0.30	0.10
Yield of cocoa butter	0.10	0.30
Quantity	0.15	0.15
Defective cocoa beans	0.15	0.15
Incoterms	0.10	0.10
Certification	0.10	0.10
Flavor	0.10	0.10

Table 24. Negotiated issues together with their importance to CBS and Natura Chocolate

Table 25 below illustrates the values of various options of the negotiated items to CBS and Natura Chocolate as stated in their confidential instructions.

At first sight, it seems that price and yield are distributive. However, when we consider the differences in their importance for the negotiating parties as shown in *Table 24*, we recognize that value creation potential exists by trading off price against yield.

The next interesting insight concerns the quantity to which the parties agree. Many negotiation roleplays use linear preferences to illustrate value creation. This means that the maximum value generating options are corner solutions, lying at the ends of the ZOPAs. However, since the parties' preferences concerning quantity are non-linear, the maximum value generating option is not a corner solution but occurs at 5,500 tons.

Price per kilogram	Points CBS Limited	Points Natura Chocolate GmbH
< = 2.00 €	0.3	1
2.25 €	0.125	0.875
2.50 €	0.25	0.75
2.75 €	0.375	0.625
3.00 €	0.5	0.5
3.25 €	0.625	0.375
3.50 €	0.75	0.25
3.75 €	0.875	0.125
> = 4.00 €	1	0

Quantity in tons	Points CBS Limited	Points Natura Chocolate GmbH
< = 3,000	0	1
3,500	0.28	0.98
4,000	0.46	0.94
4,500	0.58	0.89
5,000	0.69	0.84
5,500	0.77	0.77
6,000	0.84	0.69
6,500	0.89	0.58
7,000	0.94	0.46
7,500	0.98	0.28
> = 8,000	1	0

Defective cocoa beans in %	Points CBS Limited	Points Natura Chocolate GmbH
> = 10	1	0
9	0.875	0.125
8	0.75	0.25
7	0.625	0.375
6	0.5	0.5
5	0.375	0.625
4	0.25	0.75
3	0.125	0.875
< = 2	0	1

Flavor	Points CBS Limited	Points Natura Chocolate GmbH
low	0	0
medium	0.5	0.5
high	1	1

Yield cocoa of cocoa butter in %	Points CBS Limited	Points Natura Chocolate GmbH
< = 50	1	0
51	0.9	0.1
52	0.8	0.2
53	0.7	0.3
54	0.6	0.4
55	0.5	0.5
56	0.4	0.6
57	0.3	0.7
58	0.2	0.8
59	0.1	0.9
> = 60	0	1

Incoterms	Points CBS Limited	Points Natura Chocolate GmbH
FAS Accra	1	0
FOB Accra	0.67	0.33
CFR Hamburg	0.33	0.67
CIF Hamburg	0	1

Certification	Points CBS Limited	Points Natura Chocolate GmbH
platinum level	1	1
gold level	0.75	0.75
silver level	0.5	0.5
bronze level	0.25	0.25
no certyfication	0	0

Table 25. Negotiated issues, options and their values to the negotiating parties

This is followed by the percentage of defective beans and inco-terms. Both remain distributive. In contrast, the last two issues, certification and flavor, are compatible issues. That is, it is in the best interests of both parties to agree to a platinum level of certification and the highest standard of flavor. However, before getting to this agreement, it should not be forgotten that compat-ible issues are often used to strategically exert additional conces-sions on other negotiated issues.

To exhaust the entire potential of this negotiation, each party will need to recognize and give the other what they value most. This means agreeing to a price of at least 4.00€ per kilogram, 60% yield or more, 5,500 tons, platinum level certification, and high standards of flavor. An agreement on the percentage of de-fective beans and incoterms does not change the total value of the agreement; it only determines its distribution. A Pareto effi-cient outcome adds up to **1.481 points**.

Due to the complexity of the roleplay, Pareto efficient outcomes happen in less than 10% of the negotiating dyads. Such outcomes require establishing a trustful relationship and transparent infor-mation sharing between the parties. None of the teams partici-pating in The Negotiation Challenge 2015 managed to negotiate a Pareto efficient agreement.

Quantifying negotiating preferences and combining them with the substantive outcome allows us to gain important insights into the negotiators' performance and better assess the parties' suc-cess in the total outcome of value creation and claiming. Although it would be possible to evaluate them separately, we considered and compared only the final outcome.

Cocoa Negotiation is a roleplay simulation suitable for prac-ticing the recognition and application of an appropriate combi-nation of value creation and value claiming skills. Differences in parties' preferences and valuations of the negotiated issues al-lows them to create value by focusing on what they value most. The key challenges for the negotiating teams were to create enough trust between them to share very sensitive information concerning their preferences, identify value-adding options from this and then exhaust the entire value potential of the negotiation. However, this is particularly difficult in a highly competitive context, which might incline the negotiators to focus solely on value claiming rather than combining it with value creation and as a result, produce a suboptimal agreement and leave value on the table.

3.3 Complex Multi-Issue Negotiations

We are convinced that the search for negotiation intelligence in a negotiation competition should not be limited only to scoreable negotiation scenarios. One reason for this is that it is not consistent with the reality of the majority of real-life negotiations, in which parties' interests are typically not expressed by scoring or utility functions. Even if it was theoretically possible, given the time constraints for preparation during the competition, negotiators would often find it too difficult or even practically impossible to quantify them.

Another strong reason is that a scoring mechanism inherently limits a negotiator's creativity. In scoreable negotiation roleplays, the parties are explicitly asked to stay within the confines of the variables used in the scoring functions. Integrating new issues is possible only if their value can be identified and added to the remaining part of the score. In contrast, negotiations over non-scoreable issues enable open-ended, unconstrained creativity that might be applied in the search for value-generating options.

However, since negotiated outcomes cannot be the only basis for comparing performance in non-scoreable rounds of The Negotiation Challenge, they can pose serious operational challenges for evaluating performance. First, superior outcomes in these types of negotiations will include creative, out-of-the-box, value-generating solutions. Because these type of open-ended solutions cannot be effectively predefined and captured as a comparable scoring function, they cannot be objectively compared with each other. Instead, the only way to compare the negotiators' performance is to involve negotiation experts as judges and equip them with a list of criteria by which to structure their observations and the judging process. This allows us to assess various aspects of the negotiators' skills throughout the process, rather than only focusing on its outcomes. For similar reasons, evaluations for this type of negotiation are indicative in character. That is, scoring is a function of the relative ranking of the teams representing each role, which the judges collectively calibrate and agree on immediately following the round. This judging process and the criteria used are described in chapter 2.2.

Moreover, a second challenge is that involving judges in the evaluation process exposes results to natural biases inherent in a judge's cultural background, experience, education, etc. As such, judges can subjectively interpret our judging criteria differently, meaning that a risk exists that similar negotiation performances may be assessed differently by different judges. To address this subjectivity risk, we spend a considerable amount of time prior to the negotiation explaining the evaluation criteria to the judges and suggest the observable behaviors that they should be focusing on during the negotiation process that demonstrate these criteria.

The evaluation conducted by the judges during the negotiation has an indicative character. All we need for the purpose of the competition is a relative ranking of the teams representing each role. Therefore, directly after the negotiation round, the judges meet to calibrate their evaluations and come up with the final ranking of the participating teams.

In summary, including these modifications into the evaluation process allows for more flexibility in the design of the negotiation roleplay simulations, which we use to increase the complexity of the negotiation rounds. Although the negotiation process itself is similar to those based on the simulations introduced previously, the main difference is a more extensive and challenging phase of interest exploration and in identifying value generating options best reflecting these interests. For the teams, the challenge lies in extracting, analyzing and prioritizing their interests and in executing a strategy developed from this knowledge.

The roleplay simulations included in this chapter display a high level of complexity and mastering them will require from the negotiators the highest level of their negotiation skills.

Greekonia

Authors: **Alexander Pflaum and Andre Vörtler**
under the supervision of **Remigiusz Smolinski**

Number of parties:	Preparation time:	Negotiation time:	Complexity level:
2	**30** minutes	**45-60** minutes	**intermediate**

Pedagogical focus

reservation point, BATNA, interest analysis, information exchange, strategies of the first offer, anchoring, combining scoreable and non-scoreable issues, value creation and value claiming strategies, relationship building, trust creation, objective criteria, fairness, integrative negotiation

Short description

Greekonia is a two-party, multi-issue negotiation roleplay simulation between the government of Greekonia and financial representatives of the United Union, the supra-national political, economic and monetary union to which it is a member. Greekonia, after years of mismanagement, is faced with an imminent national debt default and now must make some tough choices. Unless it takes significant austerity measures, it will default on its sovereign debt and its creditors will cease to provide it continuing liquidity. This will plunge the country into economic chaos. However, these very austerity measures may set off a social revolution and topple the government. On the other side, because Greekonia uses the Uro, the United Union's common currency, the Union is also faced with a dilemma. Because their banking systems are so tightly interwoven, a potential bankruptcy of Greekonia could not only end the Uro but could also cause a global economic crisis. Therefore, if it cannot convince Greekonia to take the appropriate and sustainable measures that will ensure sustainable economic stability, Greekonia will be forced to leave the United Union.

General Instructions

Greekonia is a charming country in southern Europe, which recently has been undergoing severe financial difficulties. Experts believe that this situation was caused by a combination of an inefficient tax system, a bloated administration and the fact that the country was seriously affected by the global recession in 2008 and 2009. Currently, Greekonia is not only heavily indebted (140% of the GDP) but is also unable to refinance its debt because interest rates for Greekonian bonds have skyrocketed. The labor market situation is also tense. The unemployment rate has doubled within the last two years, reaching a historic high of 20% in November 2011. Moreover, Greekonia's next interest and redemption payments to international investors are due in the upcoming weeks. However, with no external financial support given, the market issues the country is facing these obligations may prove difficult to meet. The first austerity measures, such as tax system reform and spending cuts, which Greekonian government has undertaken recently, have not had enough time to reverse the fears of insolvency.

This situation worries the 27-member United Union (UU) to which Greekonia is a member state because, as it shares a common currency called the Uro with 17 of these member states, its financial situation has also negatively affected the Uro. Indeed, because the economies of the UU countries and their banking systems are so tightly interwoven a potential bankruptcy of Greekonia could not only be the end of the Uro but could also cause a global economic crisis. Therefore, the UU has a strong need for Greekonia to regain its financial liquidity and economic stability.

As a result, the UU's finance ministers are now under great pressure to help resolve this issue. However, although the ministers are willing to provide Greekonia with the financial support needed to stave off bankruptcy, they are not willing to support

Greekonia if its government does not show a satisfactory level of self-initiative including introducing necessary structural reforms. Thus, a UU financial bailout of Greekonia is contingent upon the implementation of certain reforms.

The Greekonian government is under great pressure. While focusing on the financial rescue of their country, it also needs to calm their citizens who fear potential adverse measures such as job and benefit cuts as well as tax increases. Despite the government's efforts, a vast majority of Greekonians are very unhappy with the current situation. Supported by the Greekonian Labor Union, angry citizens have organized regular public protests and nationwide labor strikes. Implementing even more reforms can be politically explosive, as its citizens fear job losses, painful benefit cuts and tax increases.

Clearly, this situation poses a serious threat to the Greekonian government and needs to be resolved quickly in a way that is carefully balanced. Greekonia must try to sustain their member status in the United Union and advocate for keeping Uro as their currency. Exclusion from the Union and the return to the "Greekonian Pound" would mean an economic catastrophe both for the Greekonian government as well as for the Union.

Therefore, the main objective of the upcoming negotiation between the Greekonian government and the UU is to agree on the magnitude of the necessary reforms to be implemented in order to restore Greekonian liquidity. However, this will not be easy since the debt is large, currently 200 billion Uro, and the debtors are multiple. The largest creditor is the Germonian Bank, holding 25% of the Greekonian bonds. The remaining 75% is held by other UU's member state banks and private investors, who in the upcoming negotiation will be represented by the UU.

Specifically, the parties are expected to discuss the level of any potential debt relief (so-called debt haircuts), the timing of the necessary reforms, and changes in the Greekonian tax system focusing mainly on corporate income tax (CIT) and value-added tax (VAT). Currently, the CIT rate in Greekonia is 20% and the VAT rate is 10%. Both will most likely need to be raised, but the exact amount of any new tax rates would need to be negotiated.

The press expects a long and heated debate during which the negotiating parties will insist on the most favorable terms for their constituencies. However, the main objective of both negotiation parties is to reach an agreement and settle the conditions of the Greekonian bailout.

Confidential Instructions
for the **Greekonian Government**

Greekonia faces very serious economic issues! Your country is approaching financial insolvency and political instability. All the major labor unions are routinely striking, and thousands of outraged citizens publically protest against the government's "failings." However, as a condition for a necessary financial bailout, the United Union (UU) is demanding radical economic reforms including draconian spending cuts and increased taxes. You know that the UU is right. Even the experts agree that under the current tax policy, Greekonia will be insolvent within six months. Even more distressing, you know that if it is not possible to restore balance in the Greekonian economy, the UU might even consider excluding Greekonia from the United Currency Union (UCU). Therefore, although you are well aware that many are following their own interests, you are grateful to the UU for their willingness to support your country in these difficult times and even more so to your creditors for their readiness to restructure the Greekonian debt.

However, since you would like to get re-elected for another term in office, you also need to improve your image with Greekonian voters, especially with the labor unions that are upset with Greekonia's austerity measures. Before this can be addressed though, your number one immediate priority is to make sure Greekonia regains its financial liquidity. To achieve this goal, three measures need to be undertaken:

1. **Greekonian debt must be restructured.** The experts agree that given the current Greekonian fiscal situation, the government would have to borrow even more money to avoid defaulting on the payments due within the next year.

However, the financial markets perceive Greekonian bonds as significantly riskier than they used to be and as a result require an increased risk premium (i.e., higher interest rates). Therefore, there is a strong risk that increased borrowing will just increase the probability of an eventual Greekonian default soon.

2. **Tax revenues must be increased.** Even if the Greekonian debt is restructured, the government will still need to pay something back to lenders. Given the current state of Greekonian public finance and the persistent fiscal deficit, tax increases seem inevitable. These changes are most likely to affect value added tax (VAT) and the corporate income tax (CIT).

3. **Necessary reforms must be legislated.** In addition to increasing the tax revenue, Greekonia needs to cut its budgetary expenditures, streamline its tax system, reform its pension system, liberalize the market, and privatize the national electricity transmission grid. These reforms must be passed within the upcoming three years, but a detailed schedule has not been discussed yet.

Moreover, the following information has been provided to you by your finance minister:
- The restructuring of Greekonian debt is absolutely necessary and is the most important issue in the upcoming negotiation. According to finance ministry estimations, to help restore Greekonian liquidity in the upcoming years, **a minimum 40% debt reduction** is necessary. Smaller debt reductions are unacceptable since even if coupled with the most draconian tax increases and spending cuts they will not save Greekonia from bankruptcy. To send a strong positive signal to the highly critical and angry public, you must try to

convince the United Union to reduce Greekonian debt as much as possible, ideally to 60-80% of its current level (i.e., restructured balances would be approximately 20-40% of current balances outstanding).

- You must increase the value-added tax (VAT) by at least three percentage points in order to improve your country's liquidity and reduce the fiscal deficit. Although this change has already been announced, it will likely be considered as insufficient by the UU. Although they will likely demand a higher VAT rate, every additional percentage point could trigger a level of social resistance proportional in its severity to the magnitude of the VAT rise. The average level of VAT in the UU currently lies at nearly 20%. Member states probably expect Greekonian VAT to approach that level as well. However, you anticipate that **a VAT rate higher than 18%** would cause violent social unrest and riots and potentially topple the government. Therefore, this is unacceptable.

- Your last election campaign was financed mainly by Greekonian entrepreneurs and their companies. The more taxes they have to pay, the less inclined they will be to support you politically. Therefore, they will be quite upset about any CIT raises and will find it especially hard to accept a CIT higher than 25%. If a higher CIT rate is required from the UU, your wealthiest supporters might shift their future contributions to your political opponents. This would be the end of your political career. Therefore, you need **to keep the CIT as low as possible and make sure it does not exceed 25%.**

- To avoid borrowing money in the future, Greekonia needs to reduce its budgetary deficit and generate a surplus as soon as possible. Although the necessity of the reforms is indisputable, their timing must be chosen carefully not to fuel further escalation of social tensions. Three years are probably sufficient to prepare, consult and pass the necessary measures. You are planning to **distribute them along the full span of this period**, starting with those that are the least controversial and/or affect the least citizens (reducing governmental expenses, privatization, market liberalization) and delaying the most controversial ones (changing the pension system, improving tax collection, cutting salaries and jobs in the public administration).

Lastly, your economic and political advisors have provided you with the following information concerning your preferences for the upcoming meeting:

- The most important issue for the Greekonian government is maximizing the debt haircut, followed by minimizing the CIT and VAT increases, and a reasonable timing and sequence of the necessary reforms.
- Increasing the debt haircut by one percentage point is twice as important as a reduction of CIT by a percentage point.
- Changes in CIT are three times more important than changes in VAT, as an additional percentage point of CIT affects only your political future, whereas raising VAT leads to social resistance, riots, and other social unrest in your country.
- An appropriate timing and sequence of the necessary reforms could de-escalate some of the social tensions, but saving Greekonia from defaulting is much more important, and therefore, if absolutely necessary, you are ready to reconsider your preferences.

Your objective in the upcoming negotiation is to **reach an agreement** with the representatives of the United Union on all of the issues above and obtain the **best possible outcome** for the Greekonian government given the above-listed constraints.

Good luck!

Confidential Instructions
for the **United Union**

As the representative of the United Union (UU), you are highly concerned about the integrity of the UU and the future of your common currency, the Uro. Since a bankruptcy of Greekonia would likely lead to a complete collapse of the Uro, you have two options. First, you can focus on stabilizing the currency by helping the Greekonian government regain their country's financial liquidity and thus improve its credibility in the financial markets. Second, you can force Greekonia to leave the United Currency Union (UCU).

Unfortunately, excluding Greekonia from the UCU would be a very expensive endeavor for the UU and could also potentially result in political and social instability in the Union. Therefore, assuming that the Greekonian negotiators are both fully willing and committed to making the appropriate sacrifices, you prefer the former option, which is to help push forward Greekonian financial reforms. Therefore, your number one priority is to help Greekonians restore financial liquidity. To achieve this, three measures need to be undertaken:

1. **Greekonian debt must be restructured**. The experts agree that given the current Greekonian fiscal situation, the government would have to borrow even more money to avoid defaulting on the payments due within the next year. However, the financial markets perceive Greekonian bonds as significantly riskier than they used to be and as a result require an increased risk premium (i.e., higher interest rates). Therefore, there is a strong risk that increased borrowing may inadvertently lead to a Greekonian default in the long term.

2. **Tax revenues must be increased.** Even if the Greekonian debt is restructured, the government will still need to pay something back to lenders. Given the current state of Greekonian public finance and the persistent fiscal deficit, tax increases seem inevitable. These changes are most likely to affect value added tax (VAT) and the corporate income tax (CIT).

3. **Necessary reforms must be legislated.** In addition to increasing the tax revenue, Greekonia needs to cut its budgetary expenditures, streamline its tax system, reform its pension system, liberalize the market, and privatize the national electricity transmission grid. These reforms must be passed within the upcoming three years, but a detailed schedule has not been discussed yet.

Moreover, the following information has been provided to you by your analysts:

- To avoid borrowing money in the future, Greekonia needs to reduce its budgetary deficit and generate a surplus as soon as possible. The necessity of the reforms is undisputable, and despite the social tensions, they need to be passed as soon as possible. Three years are certainly more than sufficient to prepare, consult and pass the necessary measures. You are planning to maximally condense them, starting with those that have the highest revenue or cost-saving potential (changing the pension system, improving tax collection, cutting salaries and jobs in the public administration). The greekonian government should pass them during the first year and follow up with the remaining reforms in the second year.
- According to your estimations, a debt haircut of more than 50% could require the UU to grant additional financial guarantees to the banks. Moreover, although generally

supportive, because the banks have already insured most of their loans to the Greekonian government they are unwilling to write off more than half of their value. Indeed, you have agreed with them not to set a complicating precedent for future UU countries in trouble and in turn will attempt to convince the Greekonian government to pay back as much of their debt as possible. You are **not authorized to accept a higher debt haircut than 50%** and hope that the agreed level of debt haircut will be significantly lower (30-40% is deemed reasonable by the banks).

- VAT is the highest source of tax revenue for Greekonia. Thus it **must be raised as much as possible.** The Greekonian government seems to understand this necessity as it has recently announced its intention to raise VAT from its current 10% rate to a 13% rate. The UU is pleased with this announcement and perceives it as the absolutely necessary minimum. However, it strongly encourages further VAT increases. Although increasing the VAT rate too radically (above the 18% mark) might trigger an even stronger wave of protests and strikes, the experts believe that even the smallest VAT raises will most likely lead to a linear increase in tax revenues. The average level of VAT in the UU lies at nearly 20%, and the member states expect Greekonian VAT to approach that level as well.

- Since the CIT (which is currently at 20%) is far below the average of the rest of the UU (25%), you are concerned that if the country is saved, the comparatively lower rate will create an unfair competitive situation by attracting companies away from other UU states. Therefore, you agreed with all UU member states **not to accept a CIT rate lower than 23%**, which is the UU average. Generally, the higher the CIT rate, the more tax revenue can be expected. However, this effect is not linear, since high taxes might also incentivize Greekonian companies to relocate their businesses to other

UU countries. Although you would like the Greekonian government to raise CIT as much as possible, a CIT rate above
30% would be among the highest in the UU and is unlikely
to be accepted by the Greekonian government.

Fortunately, your economic experts provided you with the following information concerning your preferences with respect to
the negotiated issues:
- The most important issue for the UU is definitely the legislat-
  ing of the necessary reforms as soon as possible, followed by
  minimizing the debt haircut and raising VAT and CIT.
- An appropriate timing and sequence of the necessary reforms will send an important signal that the financial support for Greekonia can only be provided, once structural
  changes have been passed.
- Decreasing the debt haircut by one percentage point increases your score twice as much as an additional percentage point in VAT rate.
- Raising VAT is three times more important than raising CIT
  as an additional percentage point of VAT generates three
  times as much tax revenues than an additional percentage
  point of CIT.

Your objective in the upcoming negotiation is to **reach an agreement** with the Greekonian government on all issues mentioned
above and obtain the **best possible outcome for the UU** given
the constraints listed above.

Good luck!

Debriefing

Greekonia is a multi-issue, non-scoreable negotiation roleplay simulation written for The Negotiation Challenge 2012 in Paris. It was used during the final, in which the best two teams from the previous four negotiation rounds: HHL Graduate School of Management and ESSEC Business School, represented the Greekonian government and the United Union in a negotiation concerning the exact measures that need to be taken to save Greekonia from defaulting on its debt.

The structure of this simulation is similar to the one described in Staple Rights. The main difference lies in integrating a non-scoreable issue (timing and sequence of reforms) with scoreable issues (debt haircut, VAT and CIT rates). According to the instructions, the preferences of the negotiating parties can be only partially quantified and expressed by the following formulas:

$$Score_{Greekonian\ Government} = 6 * Debt\ Haircut - 3 * CIT - 1 * VAT + a_{GG} * Reforms$$

> "(...) increasing the debt haircut by one percentage point is twice as important as a reduction of CIT by a percentage point. Changes in CIT are three times more important than changes in VAT.

$$Score_{United\ Union} = 6 * Debt\ Haircut + 1 * CIT + 3 * VAT + a_{UU} * Reforms$$

> "(...) decreasing the debt haircut by one percentage point increases your score twice as much as an additional percentage point in VAT rate. Raising VAT is three times more important than raising CIT."

The confidential instructions and these respective formulas reveal the differences in how each party values the negotiated issues. With the exception of the debt haircut, the weights of the other variables are different for each party. This exposes opportunity for capitalizing on disparities and gives each party an opportunity to engineer value.

Although we cannot quantify exactly the importance of the timing and sequence of the necessary reforms to the negotiating parties (a_{GG} and a_{UU} are not specified in the formulas) and the value of different options within this issue, we know that it is the most important issue for the United Union and the least important issue for the Greekonian government.

Additionally, the parties are instructed on their reservation points with respect to each of the negotiated issues. They are summarized in the table below:

Issue	Minimum	Maximum
Debt haircut [%]	40%	50%
VAT [%] (currently 10%)	13%	18%
CIT [%] (currently 20%)	23%	25%

Table 26. Reservations points of the parties and the respective zone of possible agreement (ZOPAs) for the scoreable issues.

The fourth issue concerning the timing and the sequence of the necessary reforms does not include the parties' clear reservation points but instead mentions their aspiration points. Specifically, the Greekonian government is planning to distribute reforms along the full span of this period, starting with those that are the least controversial and/or affect the least number of citizens. They want to delay the most controversial reforms until social tensions around the financial crisis significantly reside. In contrast, the United Union expects the Greekonian government to condense their reforms, starting with those that have the highest revenue or cost-saving potential. They want the Greekonian government to implement them during the first year, followed by the remaining reforms in the second year.

As is now evident, because one of the variables in the scoring function cannot be quantified, we cannot combine them to graph a Pareto efficiency frontier. For the same reason, we cannot assess the negotiators' performance only based on a substantive outcome obtained in their negotiations. Therefore, as described in the introduction to this chapter, expert judges are needed to evaluate the parties' success in value creation and claiming.

Lastly, supporting video material also exists for this simulation that can be used in addition to the general and confidential instructions. Directed by Stoyan Yankov, a talented young filmmaker, we have produced three short videos that, in the form of a TNC News report, summarize the content of the simulation and present the consequences of its two potential outcomes.

Moderated by Larry McQueen (Nyasha Ngara), it discusses the situation in Greekonia as seen by the representatives of the key stakeholders and experts:

- Herbert Schmidt, Germonia Finance Minister, who emphasizes the necessity for the Greekonian government to take immediate political action and introduce necessary fiscal reforms, especially tax increases. He signals United Union's willingness to support Greekonia with moderate debt haircuts.
- Jo Bergmann, the CEO of the Germonian Bank, Greekonia's biggest lender. He points out that granting Greekonia a high debt haircut might encourage other countries to increase their deficits as well. He insists that Greekonia change their financial policy as a prerequisite for receiving financial support.
- Dimitrios Papadopoulos, the President of Greekonia, who underlines the gravity of the situation and an urgent need for restructuring its debt. He admits that some tax increases might be indispensable.

- Patroula Papayiannidou, the Chief of Greekonian Labor Union, who describes the social tension around the debt crisis and warns not to increase taxes at the moment. She suggests that increasing taxes might escalate social unrest.
- Vaidas Armonas, a finance scholar, who summarizes and analyzes the negotiation issues, focusing on the debt haircut and increasing VAT and CIT.

The two remaining videos briefly discuss the consequences of an agreement between the parties and the consequences of no-agreement.

Greekonia is a negotiation roleplay simulation suitable for practicing value creation and value claiming skills based on a combination of quantified and not quantified issues. Differences in parties' preferences and valuations of the negotiated issues allow them to create value by focusing on what they value most. The main challenges for the negotiating teams are to combine a non-quantified issue (timing and sequence of reforms) with quantified distributive and integrative issues and also create enough trust between them to share very sensitive information concerning their preferences, identify value-adding options from this and then exhaust the entire value potential of the negotiation. However, this is particularly difficult in a highly competitive context, which might incline the negotiators to focus solely on value claiming rather than combining it with value creation. Should they fall into this trap, it will produce a suboptimal agreement and leave value on the table.

The Battle of the Nations

Author: **James Downs and Jared Cardon**
under the supervision
of **Remigiusz Smolinski**

Number of parties:	Preparation time:	Negotiation time:	Complexity level:
2	**45** minutes	**45-60** minutes	**high**

Pedagogical focus

preparation, defining negotiation issues, information exchange, understanding mutual interests, reservation point, BATNA, generating value creating options, value claiming, principle-based negotiation, relationship building, trust creation, objective criteria, fairness, integrative negotiation

Short description

The Battle of Nations is a two-party multi-issue negotiation role-play simulation set during the 1813 German War of Liberation. Facing an imminent attack, Napoleon must reinforce the defenses of the city of Leipzig strongly enough to repel the enemy. He can only do so if his ally, Prince Jozef Poniatowski of the Duchy of Warsaw will agree to provide sufficient military support. However, the Prince, fearing a post-battle invasion of his homeland, must save enough of his resources to protect it and his own political and economic goals.

General Instructions

It is October 1813. Napoleon's *Grande Armée* has recovered from the disaster of the Russian invasion and is now in Saxony. The Prussians and Austrians have joined with the Russian army to attack Napoleon as he attempts to build another army. After a brief armistice, the Emperor won a decisive victory at Dresden in August against a numerically superior force and inflicted heavy casualties on the Allies. However, a defeat of one of his generals in Berlin has forced the Emperor to move his troops to Leipzig. Napoleon intends to fortify the city and fight a battle of his choosing.

Arrayed against Napoleon is an allied army of 350,000 Russians, Prussians, Austrians and Swedes, commanded by Austrian Field Marshal Karl von Schwarzenberg. With the Emperor are 220,000 troops including 140,000 troops under his personal command. These include French, Italians, Saxons, various members of the Confederation of the Rhine, and 80,000 Polish troops led by Prince Jozef Poniatowski of the Duchy of Warsaw.

In preparation for this upcoming battle, Napoleon plans to meet with Prince Poniatowski at Penig, a small village outside Leipzig, to discuss his strategy. This meeting is critical because if France loses the upcoming battle at Leipzig, it will force Napoleon's full retreat back to within the borders of France. It also means that he will lose control over the Confederation of the Rhine, territory for which his armies have paid with the loss of thousands of lives. Moreover, not only would he lose a significant tax base to fund his military campaigns, but it will also embolden all remaining countries under his control to revolt against him. Therefore, winning the Battle of Leipzig[17] is the key to maintaining his political and military control of Europe!

---

[17] On October 22, 1813, shortly after the smoke and dust have settled over Leipzig, Armin von Arnim in his article for a Berlin newspaper *Preußischer Correspondent* used the term *Völkerschlacht* (The Battle of the Nations) for the first time to describe The Battle of Leipzig.

Confidential Field Documents
for **Prince Jozef Poniatowski, Commander of the Polish Army, Duchy of Warsaw**

As Prince Jozef Poniatowski of the Duchy of Warsaw, you are one of the most powerful individuals in Europe. The Duchy of Warsaw is just one piece of what was the proud and powerful Kingdom of Poland, which was invaded and partitioned by Russia, Austria and Prussia less than 20 years ago. You are the nephew of the former King of Poland, and you are currently the head of the Polish armies for the Duchy of Warsaw. Since 1811, you have been a close ally and friend to Napoleon, and you have felt the mutual trust and respect grow between you both during the long Russian campaign. Now you and your 80,000 strong army have just arrived in Leipzig following a great victory at the Battle of Dresden against the allied forces of Prussia, Russia and Austria. It is now important that a defensive works be built around the city of Leipzig in order to successfully defend against the upcoming attack from the regrouped and angry coalition of allied armies. You know that Field Marshall Schwarzenberg's forces are fast approaching from Dresden and it is possible that they will attack before construction is finished. This would be a disaster. You have a meeting with Napoleon to discuss the key issues around this situation. However, you have just discovered through another commander that Napoleon may ask you to initially defend the city exclusively with your troops until his men can finish the defensive works.

This concerns you greatly due to the strength and size of Field Marshall Schwarzenberg's forces, a total of 350,000 cavalry, infantry and artillery. Standing alone against them could result in your losing a significant portion (if not all) of your army. This would be unacceptable. You know that your homeland will soon fall under threat from an emboldened Russian army. Should you lose the majority of your troops defending Leipzig you will have no way to defend your home country. The resulting invasion would end the proud history of your country and ruin any chance of restoring the Kingdom of Poland, including the possibilty of you becoming its king. Therefore, you will need many of your troops to defend the Duchy from a potential Russian invasion.

On the other hand, you realize that if Napoleon wins the upcoming battle your fortunes would be vast. With the defeat of the Russian, Prussian, and Austrian coalition, Prussia would be an easy target for an invading army. As a landlocked country, this could give the Duchy access to the Prussian Baltic seaport cities of Königsberg, Danzig, Rostock and Stettin. If you could obtain one or more of these key port cities, it would give the Duchy access to sea trade for the first time. The vast wealth that the trade and taxes from these cities would provide could fund the re-establishment of the Kingdom of Poland. As the nephew of the former King of Poland, the prestige that this would bring to you would ensure that you become King!

After considering your options, you have determined that should Napoleon ask you to defend Leipzig exclusively, you can do so only if he agrees to offer you total control of one or more of these Prussian cities. However, to be able to defend yourself against Russia, you will need a minimum of 20,000 troops. The more men you have after the battle in excess of 20,000, the less likely Russia will even attack Warsaw. Based on their vast experience and the size of the attacking allied army, your staff has developed the following table that predicts what kind of losses you can expect defending the city.

Troops Promised to Napoleon		30,000	40,000	50,000	60,000	70,000	80,000
Surviving Troops After	**1 day**	75,500	74,000	72,500	71,000	69,500	68,000
	2 days	67,850	63,800	59,750	55,700	51,650	47,600
	3 days	57,140	49,520	41,900	34,280	26,660	19,040
	4 days	50,000	40,000	30,000	20,000	10,000	0

Table 27. Estimated losses of the Polish army while defending Leipzig

From creating the Duchy of Warsaw's Polish army, you know that to pay for approx. 12,000 to 15,000 soldiers, you would require the tax revenues of one whole city.

From reliable and well-informed sources from Napoleon's closest circles, you have recently learned that he is thinking about offering you one of the highest and most prestigious titles in the Empire, the title of Imperial Marshal.[18] Although there are many great generals fighting in Napoleon's armies across the world, he has only nominated 20 Imperial Marshals so far. All of them are Napoleon's close friends and all of them are French. Admitting a foreigner into their noble ranks would certainly leave some of them unamused and lead to a new wave of rumors and speculations. As privileged and grateful as you feel to find out about Napoleon's plans, your heart beats only for Poland, and you are not interested in anything less than following the footsteps of your uncle and becoming the next King of Poland. Hopefully, Napoleon's offer is not meant to distract your attention from your

---

[18] Imperial Marshal or Marshal of the Empire (Maréchal d'Empire) was a civil dignity granted during the First French Empire. A Marshal was a grand officer of the Empire, with a prominent position at the Court and entitled to the presidency of an electoral college. Although this title was initially meant for "the most distinguished generals", Napoleon has consistently interpreted it in his own way, making at least a few controversial choices. Source: https://en.wikipedia.org/wiki/Marshal_of_the_Empire.

most important objective in comparison with which becoming an Imperial Marshal is nearly worthless.

For many years, you and your men have fought countless battles for your biggest dream, a dream shared with millions of his countrymen, a dream to reestablish the Kingdom of Poland. The Prussian Baltic seaport cities would significantly improve the country's economic stability, and getting them together with Napoleon's anointment would make you the most serious candidate for the Polish throne.

As a committed bachelor, you were not amused to find out from your sources that Napoleon is planning to arrange your marriage with his sister Pauline, the princess of Guastalla. Pauline is a 33 years old woman of great beauty and charm, adored and admired by countless noblemen and high officers across Europe but not you. She is just not your type. Although you have only met her just a couple of times, she seems to have developed a reputation of a notoriously promiscuous seductress, which is not necessarily the best prerequisite for a future queen. Despite her beauty and charm, Pauline has not had much luck with her husbands so far. The first one died on a military expedition to Haiti and recently, the second drew his last breath in her arms. You refuse to be next!

You believe that this is the perfect time to insist on Napoleon to reestablish the Kingdom of Poland. The enemies are joining forces and advancing quickly and to keep your dream alive you must win the upcoming battle. It is evident that Napoleon's success in The Battle of the Nations and the future of his Empire depends largely on the degree of your support. This dependency is a great opportunity to advance your strategic and operational objectives. Remember, however, that Napoleon as the Emperor and Commander chose to discuss these matters with you instead of simply enforcing his will. Weigh your arguments carefully, use your assets wisely, and make Poland proud!

Troops under your command: 80,000
60,000 Infantry and Irregular foot soldiers
10,000 Cavalry
5,000 Light Cannon
5,000 Grenadiers

Napoleon's Troops: 140,000 strong
80,000 Infantry and Irregular foot soldiers
20,000 Cavalry
20,000 Dragoons (mounted infantry, mounted for travel but dismount and fight on foot)
10,000 Imperial Guard and Marines (Napoleon's personal guard and reserve troops)
5,000 Artillery and Gun pieces
5,000 Grenadiers

As a last note, you MUST reach an agreement with Napoleon. Should he lose to the allied army, he would potentially lose his Empire, and consequently, you could lose your homeland and any chance of restoring the Kingdom of Poland.

Good luck!

Confidential Field Documents
for **Emperor Napoleon Bonaparte**

As Napoleon, you know that to win the upcoming battle it is critical that you construct defensive works around the city. You also know that the allied armies are quickly approaching and it is likely that they will attack before you are finished with construction. This would be a disaster. Therefore, to finish as quickly as possible you need to commit all of your troops to the construction work. Yet, to ensure that the city is protected against any early attacks by the approaching allied army before construction is complete, you need the help of your long-time Polish ally, Prince Poniatowski. He and his Polish army of 80,000 have just returned with you from your key victory at the Battle of Dresden.

Specifically, you need to convince Prince Poniatowski to commit as many troops as possible and for as long as possible to the outer perimeter defense of Leipzig so that you can prepare a successful defense. At a minimum, you need two days to prepare even the most basic of defenses. Anything less than two days will result in losing the battle and is therefore unacceptable to you. If the Prince can delay Field Marshall Schwarzenberg for four days, you are confident that you can complete extensive defense preparations that would withstand even the most determined enemy. In addition to the number of delay days, you also need Prince Poniatowski to deploy at least 40,000 troops to delay Schwarzenberg and his army but the more, the better. Any less and you know that the Warsaw troops will never be able to hold off the advancing allied armies. You are sure that with 80,000 troops he could easily hold off the allied armies until your defensive preparations were complete.

You know that Prince Poniatowski will need to be convinced to agree to this and that he will also be reluctant. By delaying Field

Marshall Schwarzenberg with his troops alone, he will risk the lives of thousands of his men. However, you also know that he would be very interested in obtaining the Prussian Baltic seaport cities of Königsberg, Danzig, Rostock and Stettin. If he could obtain one or more of these key port cities, it would give Warsaw access to sea trade for the first time! (The Duchy of Warsaw is a landlocked country). Moreover, the Duchy of Warsaw is just one piece of what was the proud and powerful Kingdom of Poland. Since Prince Poniatowski is the nephew of the former King of Poland, the prestige that this would bring him could help him restore the Kingdom of Poland with himself as the King! As an incentive for him to commit the maximum amount of troops for as long as possible, you are potentially willing to cede control of the cities of Königsberg, Danzig, Rostock and Stettin after they fall during your planned invasion of Prussia next year. However, you realize that because they are key seaport trade cities, each of these four cities will represent about 10% of your Prussian territorial tax base. Therefore, as giving all four away would represent 40% of this significant tax base, you could be jeopardizing your ability to fund future campaigns. From your extensive experience, you know that one city's tax revenue would pay for 10,000-15,000 troops.

Another idea that could potentially offset some of the tax revenue would be to grant Prince Poniatowski one of the highest and most prestigious titles in the Empire and make him your Imperial Marshal.[19] Although many great generals are fighting in your armies across the world, you have only nominated 20 Imperial Marshals so far. All of them are your close friends and all of them are French. Admitting a foreigner into their noble ranks would

---

[19] Imperial Marshal or Marshal of the Empire (Maréchal d'Empire) was a civil dignity granted during the First French Empire. A Marshal was a grand officer of the Empire, with a prominent position at the Court and entitled to the presidency of an electoral college. Although this title was initially meant for "the most distinguished generals", Napoleon has consistently interpreted it in his own way, making at least a few controversial choices. Source: https://en.wikipedia.org/wiki/Marshal_of_the_Empire.

certainly leave some of them unamused and lead to a new wave of rumors and speculations. You are determined, however, to face the potential resistance and live with the consequences. Prince Poniatowski deserves it more than anyone else!

From your countless conversations with Prince Poniatowski, you know, however, that his biggest dream, which he shares with millions of his countrymen, is the reestablishment of the Kingdom of Poland. The Prussian Baltic seaport cities would significantly improve his country's economic stability, and getting them, together with your anointment, would make Prince Poniatowski the most serious candidate for the Polish throne and a perfect match for your favorite sister Pauline, the princess of Guastalla.

Pauline is a 33 years old woman of great beauty and charm, adored and admired by countless noblemen and high officers across Europe. You never believed the rumors that made a notoriously promiscuous seductress out of your sweet little sister. She has always been warm, loving and loyal to you and your siblings. Despite her beauty and charm, Pauline has not had much luck with her husbands so far. The first one died on a military expedition to Haiti, and recently, the second drew his last breath in her arms. Pauline deserves to be a queen and her marriage with Prince Poniatowski would solidify your ties with the future Kingdom of Poland.

Although you have come to know your Polish soldiers and generals as honorable and brave men, you are uncertain whether fulfilling their dream and establishing the Kingdom of Poland at this point would not weaken their fighting morale. Would they still fight so fiercely at your side, once they obtained what they were fighting for? Would loyalty and gratefulness prevail?

You believe that the reestablishing of the Kingdom of Poland is a strategically wise decision and you are inclined to make the necessary arrangements but the timing could not be possibly worse. The enemies are joining forces and advancing quickly to put an end to your reign and your Empire. Therefore, your main priority now is to make the necessary preparations for the upcoming battle.

Troops under your command: 140,000 strong
80,000 Infantry and Irregular foot soldiers
20,000 Cavalry
20,000 Dragoons (mounted infantry, mounted for travel but dismount and fight on foot)
10,000 Imperial Guard and Marines (Napoleon's personal guard and reserve troops)
5,000 Artillery and Gun pieces
5,000 Grenadiers

Prince Poniatowski's Troops: 80,000
60,000 Infantry and Irregular foot soldiers
10,000 Cavalry
5,000 Light Cannon
5,000 Grenadiers

Your staff has developed the following information summarizing the time required to complete the construction of the defense fortifications together with their consequences.

Construction days	1	2	3	4
% of Leipzig protected	25%	50%	75%	100%
Effect on Napoleon's troops	1 allied troop will be worth 3 French You will lose	1 allied troop will be worth 2 French You might lose	Parity, with 75% of the city defended the two forces will be equal You might win	French troops able to defeat twice their number in allied troops You're confident you will win

Table 28. Construction of Leipzig City Defense and its consequences

As Napoleon, you **MUST** produce an agreement during this meeting. Due to the Prince's success as a commander and the sacrifice that the Polish troops have made in your previous campaigns, you do not feel that you can simply order him to deploy all his men. You have developed a great respect and admiration for him over the years of fighting together. You are also fearful that he might defect with his troops to the allied side as many of your former commanders have like Field Marshall Schwarzenberg. Therefore, you must do your best to convince and persuade the Prince. Otherwise, if no agreement is made, you are well aware that you will lose the battle and probably even your Empire!

Good luck!

Debriefing

The Battle of Nations is a two-party multi-issue negotiation roleplay simulation written for The Negotiation Challenge 2016 in Vienna. It was negotiated during the last qualification round at the Diplomatic Academy of Vienna. Experienced negotiation academics and professionals judged the performance of the participating teams. It is suitable for practicing value creation and value claiming skills based on a combination of quantified and not quantified issues.

The negotiation described in the simulation takes place between a team representing Napoleon Bonaparte and his advisors and Prince Jozef Poniatowski and his advisors in preparation for the defense of the city of Leipzig during the Napoleonic Wars. The task of the negotiating teams is to resolve how best to share their respective resources in a way that maximizes both their chance to effectively win the battle and that also best achieves their respective post battle political and economic goals. Specifically, defensive works must be built around the city to defend it against the upcoming attack from the angry coalition of allied armies. However, the attack may come before the finish. To complete it on time, Napoleon must commit all of his troops to construct the defenses and thus needs Poniatowski to delay the attack by defending at the outskirts of the city with his army alone. However, because of the enemy's size, Poniatowski may lose a significant amount of his army. This would be unacceptable to him because he would not be able to defend his homeland from an upcoming Russian attack, which would result in the destruction of his homeland, ruin the chances of restoring the Kingdom of Poland and him becoming king.

The confidential instructions reveal the following major issues that need to be agreed on in the negotiation:

1. **Troops committed to the defense**
   Napoleon must convince Poniatowski to hold off the attacking army with his army alone while he prepares defensive works. He needs him to commit a minimum of 40,000 of his troops. Anything less will result in sure defeat. Anything above 40,000 will increase the chance of success.

   Poniatowski has 80,000 troops. If he commits them to help Napoleon, he will surely lose some. However, he cannot afford to lose more than 60,000 troops since he must retain at least 20,000 to defend his homeland from an anticipated Russian invasion. However, the more that he can retain the better the chances are that Russia will not attack at all.

2. **Days committed to the defense**
   Napoleon needs Poniatowski to commit to holding off the attack for a minimum of two days in order to prepare even the most basic of defenses and give them at least a chance of victory. Anything less is unacceptable since it will result in sure defeat. Anything more and their chances will increase. Four days will lead to sure victory

   For Poniatowski, the more days that he commits to, the more troops he will lose. The rate of loss is directly tied to how many troops he commits (see *Table 27*). However, it is unacceptable to end up with less than 20,000 troops no matter for how many days he commits.

3. **The Kingdom of Poland**
   Poniatowski believes that this is the perfect moment to insist on Napoleon to reestablish the Kingdom of Poland. He realizes that the level of his military commitment to the upcoming battle will have a decisive impact on Napoleon's success and the future of his Empire. He sees this dependency as a unique opportunity to advance his strategic and operational objectives and wants to discuss them with Napoleon now.

Napoleon believes that the reestablishing of the Kingdom of Poland is a strategically wise decision and is inclined to make the necessary arrangements, but the timing could not possibly be worse. With the enemy forces approaching, his main priority is to make the necessary preparations for the upcoming battle.

4. **Imperial Marshal**
To honor Poniatowski's military merits and to thank him for his support, Napoleon wants to grant him the highest and most prestigious titles in the Empire and make him one of his 20 Imperial Marshals.

Poniatowski understands and appreciates this great honor, but it is much more important to him to become the next King of Poland. He hopes that the title offered by Napoleon is not meant to distract his attention from reaching his main objective.

5. **Number of Baltic port cities ceded**
Following a successful defense and defeat of the attacking Allies, an invasion of a weakened Prussia would yield four key Baltic port cities. Attaining one or more of these cities from Napoleon would help Poniatowski fund (trade and tax wealth) the reestablishment of the Kingdom of Poland and become King. The more cities that he can attain, the better his chances.

For Napoleon, each of four cities ceded would reduce his Prussian territorial tax base by 10%. Giving away all four (40% tax base) would jeopardize his ability to fund future military campaigns.

6. **Pauline, the princess of Guastalla**
Napoleon believes that his favorite sister Pauline would be a perfect match for the future King of Poland. Although she

has not had much luck with her husbands so far, she deserves to be a queen and her marriage with Poniatowski would solidify his ties with the Kingdom of Poland.

Poniatowski was not amused to find out about Napoleon's plans. He is a committed bachelor and Pauline is just not his type. Besides, her reputation as a promiscuous seductress is not necessarily the best prerequisite for a future queen.

Poniatowski's main interests are to sufficiently support Napoleon to ensure the battle is won in order to unleash a subsequent chain of opportunities, which will reestablish the Kingdom of Poland and place him as King. However, he faces a tradeoff dilemma. He knows that the more that he supports Napoleon, the greater the chances are they will win the battle. Winning provides Poniatowski the greatest leverage in obtaining concessions from Napoleon on a number of Baltic port cities. However, if he overcommits to Napoleon, he will have too few troops remaining to defend against an anticipated post-battle invasion from Russia, ending all hopes of restoring the Kingdom. Thus, he believes maintaining the survival of at least 20,000 of his troops to defend his homeland is critical as insurance against a worst-case scenario of the battle being lost.

Moreover, the negotiation is complicated by the fact that two of the issues (troops and days), though separate negotiation criteria, are for him, synergistically interrelated since they affect the survival rate of his soldiers. This is shown in *Table 27* of his confidential instructions. Therefore, he must carefully balance negotiating for as many cities as possible while losing as few soldiers as possible.

Lastly, since reestablishing the Kingdom of Poland and becoming King is really the main issue he cares about, he will need to be diplomatically careful not to get distracted about the minor issues of the title of Imperial Marshal or a potential marriage to Napoleon's sister, Pauline.

Napoleons Main interests are to successfully win the battle by gaining from Poniatowski a combination of the most troops and days of commitment as possible. Indeed, he needs as many troops as possible for as long as possible to maximize his chance of success. Specifically, two days and 40,000 troops are his reservation points. Anything less and he would be sure to lose. If he can manage four days, he can ensure 100% chance of success. Realizing how passionately Poniatowski is to reestablish the Kingdom of Poland and become King and understanding that possessing a Baltic port city is the key to achieving that, he is willing to trade Poniatowski's commitment for such a city (or more). However, his dilemma is the future loss of revenue (10% of his Prussian tax base) for each. As such, he will only want to give away the smallest number necessary.

Instead of discussing the difficult issue of reestablishing the Kingdom of Poland directly before the decisive battle, Napoleon is willing to offer Poniatowski the prestigious title of Imperial Marshal and a potential marriage to his sister, Pauline, now and postpone the rest.

Lastly, as the Emperor and Commander, he could impose his will on Poniatowski. However, he prefers to involve the Prince in the decision-making, especially since there is always the risk that Poniatowski and his army could defect to the other side.

In general, based on the negotiators' ability to recognize each other's respective interests, as well as to employ necessary negotiation skills, this negotiation might result in one of the following outcomes:

1. **Creative, collaborative solution**
   The main underlying interest that both parties share is winning the battle. Napoleon needs Poniatowski's commitment of troops and days to ensure a successful defense of Leipzig and stabilize his hold on Central Europe. Poniatowski needs Napoleon's post-battle support with one or more Baltic port cities to reestablish the Kingdom of Poland and him as its King.

If the parties share their confidential information, they will realize that two days and 40,000 troops are the minimum level of defense that Napoleon can consider. This establishes a loss of 16,200 troops as the benchmark against which to compare better options. However, they may also realize that days are much more important than the troops committed by Poniatowski for the outcome of the battle. Moreover, it appears that if Poniatowski achieves obtaining just one city, it should be enough to achieve his goals of reestablishing the Kingdom of Poland and becoming King.

As a result, there exists a large solution space, which can either be creatively explored to its limits or unnecessarily narrowed by premature compromises. Which path is chosen will be determined by such key factors as quality relationship development between the negotiating parties and effectively navigating the dynamics of the negotiation process.

The following are just some examples of integrative options:

- Napoleon may promise the Prince a certain number of troops to help defend Warsaw after the battle.
- Napoleon and the Prince may trade a certain number of troops in order to ensure that the Prince has enough surviving troops to defend Warsaw.
- Napoleon may reassign some of his troops from building the city's defense to the Prince to increase the number of troops delaying the Allies.
- The Prince may offer to share a percentage of the tax revenue of any newly gained port cities with Napoleon.

2. **Competitive process and solution**
Despite largely compatible interests of the involved parties, alternative plans for Poniatowski's military resources can sometimes evolve into a conflict between the parties. This conflict can intensify if, at the beginning of

the negotiation, one of the parties decides to demand an unreasonably high/low share of the troops (anchoring). Such tactics increase the competitive pressure between the parties and shift their focus from value creation to value claiming.

Moreover, the negotiators representing Poniatowski need to find the balance between being supportive and helping Napoleon win The Battle of the Nations and using this unique opportunity to advance their own interests and reestablish the Kingdom of Poland. Winning the upcoming battle is crucial for the future of both parties and as such their joint interest. Although for Napoleon this is the most important issue, for Poniatowski, however, it is only a step in the pursuit of his dream of becoming the next King of Poland. Therefore, the negotiators representing him need to weigh their arguments carefully so that they do not come across as blackmailing or threatening.

Due to the parties' high degree of compatible interests, even a highly competitive negotiation typically ends up with an agreement. However, the more competitive the process, the more the agreement is focused on securing the necessary time and troops for the upcoming battle versus reflecting the future of the Duchy of Warsaw and Prince Poniatowski.

3. **No agreement**

   Given their common interests and the clear negative consequences that both parties would suffer should they fail to reach an agreement, finishing this negotiation without an agreement happens rather rarely. When it happens, however, it is typically a result of the negotiators' damaged relationship and their hurt egos.

   Should the parties not reach an agreement, the parties should be informed of the following:

Napoleon should be informed that he was severely defeated by Field Marshall Schwarzenberg. As a consequence, he was forced to retreat to France and subsequently lost his empire and was banished to the Island of Elba.

Poniatowski should be informed that due to the confidence gained from defeating Napoleon, Russian armies invaded the Duchy of Warsaw, subjected all of its inhabitants to severe conditions and incorporated it as a province of Russia. His homeland no longer exists.

Most of the teams negotiating this simulation in The Negotiation Challenge 2016 managed to reach an agreement that secured the necessary time and military resources to change history and win The Battle of The Nations. The quality of the agreements, however, differed strongly between the parties. Whereas some teams focused only on the upcoming battle, some managed to reestablish the Kingdom of Poland and help Poniatowski become King. Only one dyad finished the negotiations without an agreement.

Plato's Academy

Author: **Remigiusz Smolinski**

Number of parties:	Preparation time:	Negotiation time:	Complexity level:
2	**45** minutes	**60** minutes	**high**

Pedagogical focus

preparation, defining negotiation issues, information exchange, understanding mutual interests, reservation point, BATNA, generating value creating options, value claiming, principle-based negotiation, relationship building, trust creation, objective criteria, fairness, integrative negotiation

Short description

Plato's Academy is a multi-issue, non-scoreable negotiation simulation that is set in ancient Greece in the midst of an argument between Plato, the founder of the Academy, an ancient center of learning, and his top protégé and potential successor, Aristotle. They have found themselves in a passionate disagreement over what the future vision of the Academy should be. As their less emotional representatives, the negotiators need to resolve this dispute by coming to an agreement on multiple issues to both repair their deteriorating relationship and to establish a bright future for the Academy. However, the negotiators must navigate this carefully! Their mentors are very stubborn about the importance of their respective positions.

Confidential Instructions
for **Aristotle's Team**

As the sun sets over the hills of the Acropolis, Aristotle walks slowly through the sacred grove of the Academy with his head hanging low:

> *"He just doesn't get it. We could do so much more for Athens and the Academy. This stubborn old man didn't even consider what I proposed. He sees risk everywhere and is simply not willing to change anything regardless of how strong my arguments are."*

Since the meeting with Plato this afternoon, Aristotle has been very disappointed and depressed. He could not believe that his beloved mentor could be so myopic and blind to such a great opportunity.

The Academy

In 384 BC, after having traveled throughout Italy, Sicily, Egypt and Cyrene, Plato returned to Athens. By that time, at the age of 40, he was already an established scholar and a highly respected Athenian citizen. Not much later, Plato founded his Academy on an inherited property about one mile north of Athens containing a sacred grove of olive trees dedicated to the goddess of wisdom, Athena.

Since the very beginning, Plato's Academy lacked official structures. It was merely a series of informal but regular gatherings attracting the greatest minds of Athens at the time. Although the Academy did not charge any fees for membership, it maintained an elite character and remained closed to the general public. It never had a formal curriculum, and the distinction between teachers and students was rather vague. It was always important to Plato not to put any constraints on the process of educating new members. "*Wisdom likes no limits,*" he used to say. After joining the Academy, typically at the age of 16-20, junior members acquired knowledge and wisdom by solving verbally-posed problems through endless discourse with their mentors. Plato often encouraged scientific research by motivating members to look for the simplest explanation of observable phenomena.

Plato's Academy has had many famous members including Aristotle, his protégé and devoted follower, who has studied there for the last twenty years, 367 to 347 BC. After all of this, who could have thought that this devotion would turn into disappointment?

Meeting with Plato

Aristotle felt that he had raised multiple important issues during today's meeting with Plato. Namely, Aristotle believes that to strengthen its reputation in Athens and abroad, the Academy needs more structure. It needs to become a formal institution with a formal, well-structured curriculum adjusted to the needs of Athenian society instead of being just an unorganized neverending discourse between junior and senior members. At its beginning, the unofficial gatherings of wise Athenians and their endless debates were good, but now it is time to get organized and focusd on a practical education, which is based on observation, cooperative research and documentation of philosophical history instead of pursuing Plato's mysterious forms and ideals. Moreover, the Academy must provide its members with a holistic education focusing not only on intellectual growth but also on body-strengthening physical education. The main reason why Aristotle decided to propose these changes to Plato was to make the Academy even better and to set it on a path of sustainable growth by focusing on what Athenians really need.

However, after listening to Aristotle, Plato became very angry. With a raised voice he argued that the Academy would not have gained its great reputation had it not been organized the way it was. Indeed, it is the very reason why Athen's noble class sends their children to the Academy. *"How can we be sure that we won't waste decades of our hard work, by changing it? Never!"* concluded Plato.

Aristotle then went on to suggest that the Academy should broaden its admission policy so that more Athenians could bene-fit from its intellectual riches. Specifically, he argued for admitting younger members (12-16 years old), basing entry on merit rather than social status and giving students a structured and pragmatic education that they could use to benefit Athenian society.

Angrily interrupting Aristotle, Plato asked, *"Very noble of you, but who will pay the bills? You know that we can only afford to ad-mit a few members per year[20] from the patrician families that sup-port the Academy. You know that their parents would not welcome the idea of integrating members from other social classes. Keeping them happy was the key to the Academy's success. Losing their sup-port would cause big financial problems for the Academy."*

Aristotle did not get a chance to explain that his analysis indi-cates that an average yearly intake of around 60 students would generate a similar income and make them independent of the do-nors. Indeed, with the combined strong reputation of Plato and the Academy's and their broad network, the likelihood of success for his plan were very high. Most importantly, with an alternative, stable source of income, the Academy would have a better plat-form for sustainable growth.

---

[20] Typically, no more than five junior members joined the Academy per year. An average length of membership of a junior member at the Academy was ca. 5 ye-ars. After leaving the Academy, the alumni typically pursued political, academic or military careers ultimately becoming senators, generals, philosophers, mathema-ticians. Additionally, 10-20 senior members constituted the Academy's permanent faculty which was occasionally supported ca. 10 visiting scholars per year.

Instead, he waited for Plato to calm down, and continued with the general idea that each student would pay only according to what their family could afford. Those who could not pay at all would work at the Academy. However, on this idea, Plato again erupted with displeasure. He has been the only person running the Academy since its inception. He considered having students take over any role of his as nonsense.

However, after some thought, Plato did admit that stabilizing the revenue sources of the Academy would make it easier for him to plan and administer its budget. Although introducing formal tuition for studying at the Academy had been discussed on various occasions in the past, he firmly believed that given the elite character of the Academy and with so few members, the tuition would have to be set at such a high level that it could seriously impair the generosity of the donors. However, he was still so upset that he did not give Aristotle a chance to explain that to maintain the current budget the tuition fee would not have to be higher than 40 drachmas.

Lastly, Aristotle pointed out that the Academy urgently needed a library and volunteered to create it. He urged Plato to start gathering historical and philosophical works and make them available to all Academy members. It was the only issue that did not fuel Plato's anger. He acknowledged that it might be worth considering, but the subsequent discussion on the potential budget for this library ended in another disagreement. Aristotle insisted on 750-1,000 drachmas per year, which would be about 10% of the Academy's annual budget.[21] Plato offered 500 drachmas. It was not much, but it would be sufficient at the beginning assuming that more would follow later.

---

[21] One drachma in ancient Greece was an equivalent of a skilled worker's daily pay which in modern Europe amounts to ca. 100 Euro. The typical costs of goods in ancient Greece: loaf of bread 1 obol (6 obols = 1 drachma), lamb 8 drachmas, gallon of olive oil 5 drachmas, shoes 8 to 12 drachmas, slaves 200 to 300 drachmas, houses 400 to 1000 drachmas. Source: http://en.wikipedia.org/wiki/Greek_drachma.

Aristotle has been the best member that the Academy has ever seen. He is very ambitious, a great philosopher, and an excellent teacher who is highly regarded by all Academy members. Despite the outcomes of today's meeting, Aristotle has always highly respected Plato. However, this time he is so convinced about his ideas that if Plato does not show more flexibility concerning the necessary changes, he will leave the Academy and found a new institution. Although he realizes it would be extremely difficult to recruit students and attract funding without Plato's reputation and network, he cannot imagine staying at the Academy if no satisfactory agreement can be reached.

The Mandate

You are the smartest members of Plato's Academy and Aristotle has personally designated you to represent him at the upcoming meeting with Plato's team. Aristotle wants to see the Academy prosper and grow and has given you an unconstrained mandate to represent his interests. He is allowing you to make all decisions, commitments and obligations reflecting these interests. Try to find the best possible solution, restore peace and secure a bright future for the Academy, but remember that Aristotle is ready to leave the Academy and pursue his ideas on his own if he is not happy with the result of your negotiation.

Καλή τύχη!

Confidential Instructions
for the **Plato's Team**

As the sun sets over the hills of the Acropolis, Plato's raised and outraged voice runs through the walls of the Academy:

"This is ridiculous! It makes absolutely no sense! He wants to ruin me! He wants to destroy the Academy! I will never let him do it! NEVER!"

Since the meeting with Aristotle this afternoon, Plato has been furious. He cannot believe that his beloved student wants to destroy the Academy – the great work of his lifetime.

The Academy

In 384 BC, after having traveled throughout Italy, Sicily, Egypt and Cyrene, Plato returned to Athens. By that time, at the age of 40, he was already an established scholar and a highly respected Athenian citizen. Not much later, Plato founded his Academy on an inherited property about one mile north of Athens containing a sacred grove of olive trees dedicated to the goddess of wisdom, Athena.

Since the very beginning, Plato's Academy lacked official structures. It was merely a series of informal but regular gatherings attracting the greatest minds of Athens at the time. Although the Academy did not charge any fees for membership, it maintained an elite character and remained closed to the general public. It never had a formal curriculum and the distinction between teachers and students was rather vague. It was always important to Plato not to put any constraints on the process of educating new members. *"Wisdom likes no limits,"* he used to say. After joining the Academy, typically at the age of 16-20, junior members acquired knowledge and wisdom by solving verbally posed problems through endless discourse with their mentors. Plato often encouraged strictly scientific research by motivating members to look for the simplest explanation of observable phenomena.

Plato's Academy has had many famous members including Aristotle, his protégé and devoted follower who has studied there for the last twenty years, 367 to 347 BC. After this, who could have thought that this devotion would turn into disappointment?

Meeting with Aristotle

Plato considered the various points that Aristotle raised during today's meeting with him. Namely, Aristotle repeatedly asserted that the Academy needed to become more formal and insisted on introducing new organizational structures. Plato did not really understand how, but it was supposed to generate positive reputational effects for it in Athens and abroad. Aristotle also argued that the Academy needed to become a formal educational institution with a formal, well-structured curriculum adjusted to the needs of Athenian society instead of being just an unorganized never-ending discourse between junior and senior members. He expressed how the current format of endless debates at unofficial gatherings between wise Athenians, although good at the beginning, now needed improvement. Specifically, it was time to focus on a practical education, which is based on observation, cooperative research and the documentation of philosophical history instead of just pursuing Plato's ideals. Moreover, Aristotle suggested that the Academy provide its members with a holistic education focusing not only on intellectual growth but also on strengthening the body through physical education.

Upon hearing this, Plato could not believe his ears. Indeed, he felt disappointed and even angry. He felt that Aristotle, who was to become his successor and the next head of the Academy, apparently wanted to ruin everything that was so valuable to him. He felt these changes were not needed. Lectures and philosophical discourse were the best pedagogical methods that he knew. They have worked well at the Academy for years. He could never abandon idealism as an underlying philosophical doctrine. Physical education was especially nonsensical. Most of the senior members were in their 50s and 60s.

In addition, Aristotle demanded the broadening of the Academy's admission policy by admitting younger members whose entry would be based on merit rather than social status and giving them a structured and pragmatic education they could use to the benefit of Athenian society.

At this point, Plato angrily interrupted, *"Very noble of you, but who will pay the bills? You know that we can only afford to admit a few members per year[22] from the patrician families that support the Academy. You know that their parents would not welcome the idea of integrating members from other social classes. Keeping them happy has been the key to the Academy's success. Losing their support will cause big problems for the Academy."*

Despite the interruption, Aristotle continued with the general idea that each student would pay and would do so only according to what their family could afford. Those who could not pay at all would pay their tuition through working at the Academy. However, on this idea, Plato again erupted with displeasure. He has been the only person running the Academy since its inception. He considered having students take over any role of his as nonsense.

---

[22] Typically, no more than five junior members joined the Academy per year. An average length of a junior member's membership at the Academy was ca. 5 years. After leaving the Academy, the alumni typically pursued political, academic or military careers ultimately becoming senators, generals, philosophers, mathematicians. Additionally, 10-20 senior members constituted the Academy's permanent faculty, which was occasionally also supported by ca. 10 visiting scholars per year.

However, after some thought, Plato did admit that stabilizing the revenue sources of the Academy would make it easier for him to plan and administer its budget. Although introducing formal tuition for studying at the Academy had been discussed on various occasions in the past, he firmly believed that given the elite character of the Academy and with so few members, the tuition would have to be set at such a high level that it could seriously impair the generosity of the donors. Indeed, the more Plato thought about this, the less inclined he was to take the risk and change the status quo.

Lastly, Aristotle pointed out that the Academy urgently needed a library. He urged Plato to start gathering historical and philosophical works and make them available to all Academy members. In contrast, to his other ideas, on this point Plato knew that Aristotle was right. It would be a great development for his Academy. If Aristotle would agree to take on the task of acquiring and cataloging the works, he would do his best to secure the necessary funding from the patriarchs of Athens with whom he is so well connected. Realistically, with significant effort, he could probably secure an additional budget of around 500 drachmas per year for the library at the beginning. He thought Aristotle's demands of 750-1,000 drachmas per year were exaggerated and completely unrealistic as they would amount to about 10% of the Academy's yearly budget.[23]

Despite the outcomes of today's meeting, Plato has always highly respected Aristotle and appreciated his advice. In his opinion, Aristotle is the best member in the Academy's history. He is very ambitious, independent, a great philosopher and an

---

[23] One drachma in ancient Greece was an equivalent of a skilled worker's daily pay, which in modern Europe amounts to ca. 100 Euro. The typical costs of goods in ancient Greece: loaf of bread 1 obol (6 obols = 1 drachma), lamb 8 drachmas, gallon of olive oil 5 drachmas, shoes 8 to 12 drachmas, slaves 200 to 300 drachmas, houses 400 to 1000 drachmas. Source: http://en.wikipedia.org/wiki/Greek_drachma.

excellent teacher who is highly regarded by all Academy members. Because of this, he has started introducing Aristotle to Athenian high society in preparation for him to become the new head of the Academy. Now, however, he is having second thoughts: *"I'm not sure whether it was such a good idea... He is probably not ready yet... Maybe he is not even the right person...? Speusippus is perhaps not as smart as Aristotle and lacks his vision and leadership skills, but at least we seem to share the same views on the Academy's future... Maybe I should choose him instead...? If Aristotle could only understand that the way the Academy is currently organized is already financially sustainable and pedagogically sound... It would be so sad to see him leave..."*

The Mandate

You are smart and trusted members of the Academy and Plato has personally designated you to represent him at the upcoming meeting with Aristotle's supporters. Plato wants to see the Academy prosper and grow and explicitly gave you an unconstrained mandate to represent his interests and the interests of the Academy. He has allowed you to make all decisions, commitments and obligations reflecting these interests. Try to find the best possible solution, restore peace and secure bright future for the Academy, but remember that Plato needs to hear very convincing reasons before any changes can be successfully introduced at the Academy.

Καλή τύχη!

Debriefing

Plato's Academy is a multi-issue, non-scoreable integrative negotiation roleplay simulation written for The Negotiation Challenge 2013 in Athens. It was negotiated in the final between teams representing HHL Leipzig Graduate School of Management and Reykjavik University. This negotiation was filmed and can be found on YouTube at: https://www.youtube.com/watch?v=6vOv6RL6IUE. It is highly suitable for practicing principle-based negotiation as introduced by Roger Fisher, William Ury, and Bruce Patton in Getting to Yes: Negotiating Agreement Without Giving In in 1981.

The negotiation described in the roleplay takes place between representatives of Plato, the founder of the Academy and those representing Aristotle, his best student and potential successor. The main objective of the parties is to resolve a dispute between Plato and Aristotle over the future of the Academy. While focusing on protecting their substantive interests, the parties also need to restore the damaged relationship between the two men and create a positive foundation for future collaboration.

The confidential instructions reveal the following issues that need to be agreed on in the negotiation and each party's interests concerning them:

1. **Level of formalism**

   Plato's Academy lacks official structures. It is merely a series of informal but regular gatherings attracting the greatest minds of Athens at the time.

   Aristotle insists on a more formal and structured curriculum to strengthen the Academy's reputation and to set the foundations for future growth.

   Plato does not understand how introducing new structures could contribute to the Academy's success. It is important to him not to put any constraints on the process of educating its new members ("wisdom likes no limits").

2. **Teaching philosophy**
According to Aristotle, the Academy must provide its members with a holistic, pragmatic education focusing not only on intellectual growth but also strengthening the body by offering physical education.

For Plato, lectures and philosophical discourse are the best pedagogical methods that he knows, and they have worked well at the Academy for years. Plato would never abandon idealism as his underlying philosophical doctrine.

3. **Students' profile**
Aristotle argues for admitting students based on merit and not social status. He also wants to allow younger members (12-16 years old).

Plato is reluctant to change here. He is concerned that enlarging the student body might have a negative effect on the elite character of the Academy as well as on the budget.

4. **Financing**
The Academy is currently financed solely from the donations of wealthy Athenians. Aristotle argues that each student should pay a small fee based on what their family can afford. Those who could not pay for their education would earn their tuition by assisting in the administration of the Academy.

Plato agrees that stabilizing the revenue sources of the Academy would make it easier for him to plan and administer its budget. However, at the same time, he firmly believes that given the elite character of the Academy and with so few members, the tuition would have to be set at such a high level that it could seriously impair the generosity of the donors.

Aristotle does not get a chance to present his new financial concept, which would maintain the current budget while keeping the tuition at or below 40 drachmas (an equivalent of three pairs of shoes).

5. **Library**
   It is a compatible issue – both parties are interested in founding a library and operating it as a part of the Academy.

   Plato acknowledges the need and Aristotle volunteers to manage the project.

   Aristotle's estimate of the necessary budget of 750-1,000 drachmas is higher than Plato's which is 500 drachmas.

In general, based on the negotiators' ability to recognize each other's respective interests, as well as to employ necessary negotiation skills, the negotiation might result in one of the following outcomes:

1. **No agreement**
   Initially, it seems that both parties' interests are so different and their relationship so damaged that they will have a difficult time finding common ground. Trying to convince each other who is right and who is wrong only magnifies these differences and potentially escalates the conflict between them.

   Not overcoming these differences would result in the worst potential result and produce a lose-lose outcome for the parties. In such a case, Aristotle leaves the Academy and tries to set up his own educational institution. The Academy stays as it is and loses an opportunity to develop and grow. Moreover, Plato loses his best student and a potential successor.

   Although the roleplay is fictitious, some of the elements mentioned in it are based on historical events. Aristotle indeed left the Academy and in 335 BCE founded "The Lyceum," an educational institution reflecting his ideas, philosophical doctrine and pedagogical approach.

2. **Compromise – changes at the Academy**

   In the second possible outcome, Plato and Aristotle work out a compromise deal which reflects only some of their interests. That is, the way the Academy is organized will change but most likely not all changes suggested by Aristotle will be implemented. Various options are possible and depend largely on respective individual valuations and the negotiation dynamics.

3. **Creative, collaborative solution**

   Finally, Plato and Aristotle can also try to actively look for solutions that build upon the differences between their interests. They keep working together at the Academy and help it flourish and grow.

   A useful example that reflects this is the outcome agreed on during the final of The Negotiation Challenge 2013. Here a separate unit as envisioned by Aristotle is created at the Academy for younger students (12-16 years old), which he also leads. With an intake of around 60 students per year, this unit can be sustainably financed by a tuition fee of about 40 drachmas per student. The best graduates of this unit could continue working at the Academy, whereas the rest could start working in Athens.

   The education of older students would remain organized the way it currently is. Plato can then continue his life's work and the new enlarged Academy becomes his legacy. No compromise is necessary and both parties can pursue and realize their interests.

A key challenge in this roleplay, unlike all previous simulations in this book, is that the negotiation issues are not stated explicitly. Instead, they need to be identified by the negotiators during their initial interactions. Their ability to do so helps them identify the core of the conflict between Plato and Aristotle, which is the key to resolving the conflict in their subsequent discussion. Indeed, by not describing the negotiation issues explicitly in the roleplay, we try to emulate a very common scenario for many real-world negotiations in which issues first need to be identified despite a variety of sometimes overlapping chaotic dynamics including differing positions, contrasting perspectives of past events and divergent interests.

A second key challenge for the negotiators in this roleplay is the large solution space, which can either be creatively explored to its limits or unnecessarily narrowed by premature compromises. Which path is chosen will be determined by such key factors as quality relationship development between the negotiating parties and effectively navigating the dynamics of the negotiation process.

King Polo

Author: **Remigiusz Smolinski**

Number of parties:	Preparation time:	Negotiation time:	Complexity level:
2	**60** minutes	**60-90** minutes	**very high**

Pedagogical focus

preparation, defining negotiation issues, information exchange, understanding mutual interests, reservation point, BATNA, generating value creating options, value claiming, principle-based negotiation, relationship building, trust creation, objective criteria, fairness, integrative negotiation

Short description

King Polo is a two-party non-scoreable, integrative negotiation roleplay simulation between a global confection manufacturer and an independent Icelandic importer and wholesaler. After years of enjoying a quasi-monopolistic position in the distribution of King Polo, a chocolate covered wafer that has attained cult-like popularity over the years, its sales have dropped. Moreover, the announced recipe and package changes are causing severe anxiety to the impact it may have on its customers. The upcoming contract renewal meeting is a perfect time for both parties to address these issues and negotiate a better path forward.

General Instructions[24]

The first shipment of King Polo, a chocolate covered wafer from Poland, arrived in Iceland in 1955. Since then, it has become an integral part of Icelandic culture, just like elves and scratchy wool sweaters. Kids grow up accompanied by this chocolaty treat at school, on camping trips, or just visiting grandparents. Although Icelanders certainly love and cultivate all things indigenous to their own culture, over the years foreign culinary items such as hot dogs, Loca-Cola and King Polo have become so omnipresent and integrated that they are now considered almost as Icelandic as local foods like Hákarl (rotten shark). Indeed, as a testament to this embeddness, it is not difficult to find it being frequently referenced throughout Icelandic popular culture, literature and politics.

The history of King Polo in Iceland started with Poland's fondness for herrings. Securing sufficient stocks of this popular fish in the centrally planned economy of post war communist Poland required some creativity. Initially, the Polish government approached Iceland, a herring exporter, and offered a simple exchange: herrings for vodka. Icelandic negotiators were initially hesitant. However, after the Poles added King Polo to the offer, handshakes followed.

For almost three decades following this trade agreement, due to a loophole in Icelandic import laws, King Polo enjoyed a quasi-monopolistic position in Iceland as the only imported confectionery product on the market. Olaf Asbjørnsson, the owner and CEO of Olaf Asbjørnsson ehf., a mid-sized wholesaler specializing mainly in importing branded consumer goods to Iceland and the sole importer of King Polo, could not believe his eyes as he watched his rising sales. King Polo rapidly conquered Icelandic tastes and hearts, melted into their culture and the revenues continued to

---

[24] This role play is inspired by true events described in: http://podroze.gazeta.pl/podroze/1,114158,15452911.html. However, it also contains many fictitious elements added for educational purposes.

rise. Indeed, at the pinnacle of its popularity in the 1970s, Olaf Asbjørnsson was selling almost 6 million Polish wafers per year, topping 300 tons. This means that on average every Icelander was consuming about one kilogram of King Polo per year (significantly more than the citizens of other countries where it was sold, including Poland, Slovakia, Hungary, Latvia, Lithuania and Ukraine).

King Polo was a gold mine. For many decades, the sales kept rising and almost no marketing investments were necessary. This was an ideal situation for a wholesaler like Olaf Asbjørnsson, who during that time operated an efficient and highly profitable King Polo business in Iceland. With only around 40 employees and over 100 different products in portfolio, efficiency is a key success factor driving profitability in the company's business model.

The first major advertising campaign for King Polo was launched in 1995, 45 years after its introduction to the Icelandic market. Although it had a heavy impact on Olaf Asbjørnsson's profitability, it was necessary because of the customers' massive complaints connected with the introduction of new packaging and their perceived decline in King Polo's quality. The campaign managed to neutralize most of the negative financial implications of this change and was generally considered a success. Nevertheless, the Icelanders were so attached to the old wrapping that even after all these years they still miss their "old King Polo."

Today, it is estimated that Olaf Asbjørnsson sells about 140-160 tons of King Polo wafers (almost 3 million wafers per year or around 14 wafers per person). Also, its brand recognition in Iceland remains high, on a similar level as Loca-Cola's, and is associated with positive traditional values. Although, it remains a very profitable business, the golden era is long gone. Since opening up the Icelandic confection market to international competition in 1982, the demand for King Polo has been steadily declining. In 2014 demand was only half of what it was in the 1970's.

The history of King Polo itself is equally interesting. In 1955 King Polo was also introduced in Poland. It was manufactured by Elsa

SA, a Polish confectioner company founded in 1920 as a chocolate factory. Over time, it experimented with various types of confectionery products, but it was not until the 1950's that they achieved a breakthrough with King Polo. The wafers were received very well in Poland and very quickly became the most popular chocolate bar in the country.

In 1993, shortly after the fall of communism and liberalization of the market, Elsa SA was acquired by Jacobs AG, which in 2012, after being involved in several mergers, acquisitions and name changes became Mondelex International. Today Mondelex is a global player in the confectionery, food and beverage industry. It has annual revenue of approximately $36 billion and has 100,000 employees operating in more than 80 countries.

Over the years, the cooperation between Olaf Asbjørnsson and the string of companies that eventually became Mondelex has worked quite well. At the moment, however, both parties are not comfortable with the dynamics of the business in Iceland, and both are seeking measures to fix it.

The current distribution contract between the manufacturer of King Polo and its Icelandic wholesaler will expire at the end of the year. The representatives of Mondelex have recently signaled that they are planning to modify the packaging and adjust the recipe. The management of Olaf Asbjørnsson is not amused by these plans. They still remember the long crisis meetings and the heavy investment needed to neutralize the effects of the changes introduced in 1995. Nonetheless, both parties have agreed to explore whether a new distribution contract is an option they should pursue.

The upcoming meeting between the representatives of Mondelex International and Olaf Asbjørnsson is a great opportunity to discuss quality issues and agree on the provisions of a new agreement.

Confidential Instructions
for **Olaf Asbjørnsson efh**[25]

You are the representatives of Olaf Asbjørnsson efh, one of the main consumer brand importers and wholesale distributors in Iceland. Your company was founded in 1937 by Olaf Asbjørnsson, whose strategy was to use his country's size to help create a profitable business model. This model was built on obtaining exclusive import and distribution rights for Iceland from well-known premium brands around the world. For these multinationals, the Icelandic market was too small to establish their own local operations, so many of them accepted Olaf Asbjørnsson's offer to generate incremental sales without investing additional resources. Today, with 40 employees, Olaf Asbjørnsson is believed to generate nearly € 50 million in revenue with gross profit margins ranging from 20% to over 100%, depending on the product.

Because the current import and distribution contract between you and Mondelex (the manufacturer of King Polo) will expire at the end of the year, you will be meeting with them to discuss important issues related to its renewal. However, you also want to explore a joint venture idea that you have and use the opportunity to discuss issues related to the planned package and recipe changes they have announced. Your main objective in discussing all of these issues is to lay a solid foundation for the future growth of your King Polo business in Iceland based on a **participative and profitable** relationship with Mondelex. Specifically, the meeting should focus on the following issues:

---

[25] efh is the Icelandic form of plc (private limited company)

Upcoming Package and Recipe Changes

Mondelex is planning to make packaging and recipe changes to its King Polo product. Despite your appreciation for being informed early about this, you are still very concerned with these changes due to the disastrous consequences the last changes had on your business. Specifically, in 1995, due to EU regulations originally introduced in 1992 that chocolate bars must be individually sealed, Mondelex changed the open-wrap King Polo package design to a new sealed format and at the same time changed the packaging design from the traditional muted colors to a shiny gold design. Unfortunately, they informed you of the change on such short notice that you had no time to prepare sufficiently. As a result, although it seemed like only a minor change, it was received by customers with an avalanche of criticism and complaints.

Björn Guðmundursson, the general manager at Olaf Asbjørnsson, still remembers the day they announced the changes. "It got a lot of attention. People were trying to buy up old stock. It would be the Icelandic equivalent to when Loca-Cola changed their recipe and everything went berserk," he says bemusedly. "One guy even called me and said. 'What are we going to do next, change our national flag?' "We still hear some say things like, 'Why in the hell did you change King Polo?'" Guðmundursson says. "Like it was up to us!" he adds.

In response, although it completely consumed King Polo's annual gross profit,[26] Olaf Asbjørnsson reacted with a nearly €1 million advertising campaign, which stabilized sales at 140-160 tons per year where it has since remained. Moreover, since then, your customers have repeatedly voiced their dissatisfaction with King Polo's declining quality. Disturbed by these complaints,

---

[26] Generally, gross profit is the difference between net sales and cost of goods sold. In the case of Olaf Asbjørnsson, it does not include the marketing and distribution cost which amount to 10-20% of the revenues.

your management has inquired with King Polo's brand manager whether the recipe for the product has been changed. He insisted that nothing has changed. Apparently, the only objective basis for this perception of declining quality was the new packaging.

You are very concerned that another package design change combined with a new recipe might significantly damage your King Polo business. Were these changes to take place, you would need an intense marketing campaign to counter the negative impact, which would be financially painful. Indeed, a simulation prepared by your marketing experts suggests that to counter the negative effects of a change and keep King Polo revenues at their current level, you would need to invest about €500,000 in a marketing campaign starting immediately and running continuously until year end. They also project that the relationship between the budget for the marketing effort and King Polo revenues will be linear. That is, decreasing the marketing budget for this campaign by €100,000 will reduce King Polo revenues by 10%. Taking no marketing actions at all will cut your King Polo revenues by half. Increasing the budget beyond €500,000 is not expected to generate any additional positive revenue effects.

Moreover, because your cash is tied up in other more promising and urgent projects, you do not have enough money even to run this marketing campaign nor can you consider debt as an option. If absolutely necessary, you could reallocate around €200.000 from other projects, but you would prefer to avoid it.

Therefore, unless you can convince Mondelex to help prevent your revenue loss by financially contributing to your marketing campaign, your strongest preference is to convince them either to **stay with the current package or even better restore the old package** and certainly **not change the traditional King Polo recipe.** Should they insist on implementing the changes, you will need to explain to them the potential consequences and demand that they finance the necessary marketing countermeasures.

New Contract

The current distribution contract between Olaf Asbjørnsson and Mondelex is very simple. Olaf Asbjørnsson can purchase King Polo at a discounted wholesale net price of €5,000 per ton and can exclusively import and distribute it in Iceland. Since King Polo is so popular in Iceland, it sells at an average net wholesale price that exceeds €10,000 per ton, averaging nearly €12,000 and sometimes reaching even €14,000. Wholesale price selection in Iceland is at the sole discretion of Olaf Asbjørnsson. However, all marketing and distribution cost, which range from 10% to 20% of revenues, must be covered by Olaf Asbjørnsson. All marketing efforts implemented by Olaf Asbjørnsson are subject to prior approval from Mondelex.

However, in order to stimulate King Polo sales growth in Iceland, the structure of the new contract needs to be changed. You need to convince Mondelex that a closer more collaborative relationship is needed. This would involve Mondelex's direct involvement in your operations and in sharing your marketing and distribution expenses.

More specifically, the most important issue you want to address in the upcoming negotiation is the **fee structure**. You are still very interested in purchasing King Polo at a discounted net price of around €5,000. However, you would like Mondelex to indirectly subsidize your marketing and distribution costs as much as possible by paying you a **distribution fee.** A distribution fee is a common practice in the beverage industry, but the amounts vary heavily based on the relative strength of the transacting parties. In your case, the management of Olaf Asbjørnsson wants to use this distribution fee entirely to pay for King Polo marketing campaigns to stimulate its growth. As both parties want growth, it feels that this measure is more than fair and long overdue. Additionally, you would also like to receive a sales-based **variable bonus**. In summary, the greater the anticipated payments that you can negotiate from Mondelex (e.g., distribution fee, performance bonus, etc.), the more resources you will have to drive the growth of your King Polo business in Iceland.

However, successfully negotiating for these changes alone may not necessarily be enough to turn around King Polo sales in Iceland. Though it has become a part of Icelandic culture and for many decades has been a great business, the opening up of the Icelandic confectionary market to foreign products, combined with very limited marketing activities carried out by Olaf Asbjørnsson, have led to a gradual decline of the King Polo business. Though regaining the market position from the 1970s is unfortunately not possible anymore.

Your experts agree that growth is certainly possible. They recommend several options that, if also incorporated into the new contract, could drive growth. Thus, in the spirit of a more participative and profitable relationship with Mondelex, these should be objectives negotiated in this meeting with them:

- **Localizing the package** – Tradition plays an essential role in Iceland. It seems to be much more important than in other King Polo country. Customers would appreciate if tradition could be reflected in the package design. As such, it would be ideal if King Polo's new packaging could reflect the old traditional design. If this is not possible, then at least staying with the current package design would be next best. Changing it again to something completely different is an option you must avoid. Therefore, because you certainly understand that customers in other King Polo countries have different expectations and needs, you would like to explore the possibility to have customized packaging. Perhaps it would even make sense to build a local packaging facility in Iceland. Indeed, a local packaging facility would be your strongest preference, especially since you know that customized packaging would increase revenue by 10%. However, since this option would cost around €3 million, it would only be possible if Mondelex mostly financed it.

- **Partnership with Loca-Cola** – Loca-Cola's soft drinks are often sold together with hotdogs or other simple meals and King Polo. These combinations are very common in Iceland, and after a recent and very promising meeting with Loca-Cola's local representatives, you are planning to intensify this relationship by launching a series of joint marketing activities. According to your estimates, these joint activities could increase your King Polo revenue by at least 20% for the duration of this partnership. However, you have heard rumors that executives of Loca-Cola and Mondelex have a sour relationship with each other. As such, you anticipate this to be a rather difficult conversation with King Polo's brand management. Nevertheless, you are convinced that this partnership is a great growth opportunity for King Polo and would not hesitate to invest the required €200,000 per year in joint projects if you only currently had this money. You could postpone the start of this partnership until next year and finance it from operating cash flow. However, you are afraid that in the meantime Loca-Cola would contract with Nesty to run a similar campaign with their SitCat candy bar, which is King Polo's main competitor in Iceland. Therefore, though you want to get approval from Mondelex for this partnership with Loca-Cola, you also want to convince them to finance it completely for at least the first year and then contribute 25% of the investment for subsequent years. If they cannot do this, you will need to reprioritize other ongoing projects which you would prefer to avoid.

- **Regular marketing campaigns** – the secret behind the steadily rising popularity of SitCat is its regular marketing campaigns. Ever since it was introduced in the Icelandic market in the 1980s, it has gradually increased in market share to the point that it has almost caught up with King Polo. Your experts suggest that if other King Polo promotional efforts could be supported by regular advertising campaigns, sales and market share would improve and be maintained. Specifically, the relationship between the annual advertising budget and its effect on sales is expected to be positive and linear between €300,000 and €500,000. That is, below €300,000 there would be no effect. €300,000 would increase sales by 30% whereas €500,000 would drive growth up to 50%. Above €500,000, diminishing returns would rapidly apply and no additional improvement above 50% would be realized. Ideally, you would like Mondelex to completely offset your financing of these campaigns with the distribution fee. This would neutralize the impact these costs would play on your profit. You would like to start these regular campaigns next year since you may be very busy this year addressing any upcoming product changes announced by Mondelex.

Joint Venture

In addition to these issues, you can also imagine extending your business relationship with Mondelex by forming a joint venture with them for King Polo. This would combine your knowledge of the local market with their quality products, commercial knowledge and financial support. Importantly, this would also simplify the potential introduction of other Mondelex products in Iceland. You estimate that the initial financing for such a company should be €5 million. Mondelex should contribute 80% of the capital and Olaf Asbjørnsson the remaining 20%. This level of financing would help King Polo's realize its full potential in Iceland since it would provide the needed investment to enable sales enhancing projects such as the installation of a €3 million local product packaging facility and important marketing campaigns. Although you have some flexibility on the exact split of financing, you expect that the vast majority of it to come from Mondelex.

This joint venture would be staffed with salespeople and a general manager from Olaf Asbjørnsson and a senior marketing executive from Mondelex. Profits could be either reinvested into the core business or distributed equally between the partners. Should these or similar conditions not be acceptable to Mondelex then you are fine to continue your relationship with them as a commercial (non-equity) partnership.

The main objective of the upcoming contract negotiations is to create a basis for the sustainable and profitable growth of your King Polo business in Iceland. You have the authority to decide on and commit to any solution you consider beneficial for your company. Negotiate wisely.

Gangi þér vel!

Confidential Instructions
for **Mondelex International**

You are the representatives of Mondelex International, a global powerhouse in the confectionery, food and beverage industry managing well-known snack brands, including cookies, chocolates and candy. With over 100,000 employees in more than 80 countries, Mondelex generates $4 billion USD in net income on an annual revenue of approximately $36 billion USD.

The current distribution contract between you and Olaf Asbjørnsson efh., the exclusive importer and distributor of King Polo chocolate wafers in Iceland, will expire at the end of the year. In the upcoming negotiation for its renewal, your main objective is to lay a solid foundation for the growth of your King Polo business in Iceland that is based on a fair and profitable relationship with Olaf Asbjørnsson. You anticipate that the following topics will be discussed during the meeting:

Upcoming Package and Recipe Changes

Mondelex is planning to make packaging and recipe changes to its King Polo product. After a series of thorough market studies for your important Polish market, you have realized that the two main reasons driving why competitors are gaining market share are that King Polo has a thinner chocolate cover than competitors have and that many customers now consider the packaging too flashy and pretentious. Designing a new package to address this has been rather straightforward, and you quickly came up with a modern and friendly alternative while still including some of the main style elements of the old one. However, developing a new recipe has been a time consuming and resource intensive process, especially since the cost of producing the new King Polo cannot be greater than the current version. You are convinced that the solution you have identified will have a very positive impact on your business. Focus group market testing reveals that customers like it and you are hoping for an increase of gross profitability of up to 10 percentage points to nearly 60% without raising the prices.

You intend to support the launch of the new packaging and recipe with a strong marketing campaign. You have reserved €3 million for this purpose, which, though you were initially planning to spend it only in Poland, you are considering using it to support any international partners that may also need it. However, any support that you do provide in this regard should follow a ratio similar to the split of revenues generated by them and under no circumstances should the amount used to support them exceed €200,000.

You are very excited to see the success that this product change will generate since the last one went so well. That change took place in 1995 due to EU regulations originally introduced in 1992 that chocolate bars must be individually sealed. To meet this standard, Mondelex changed the traditional open-wrap King Polo package design to a new sealed format and at the same time changed the design from the traditional muted colors to a shiny gold design. This change was very well received in almost every country that King Polo was sold. Indeed, market studies following the launch of the new design revealed that customers perceived King Polo as a modern, classy, premium snack. This was exactly the intention of the brand management team who considered the change a great success.

The only exception was Iceland. There, the change was received with an avalanche of customer criticism and complaints, which resulted in disastrous consequences for the product's revenue for your Icelandic distributor, Olaf Asbjørnsson. It could be that Mondelex, unfortunately, contributed to this since, in the turmoil of the package redesign, they were not informed well in advance of the change. Indeed, they were quite unhappy. However, to address this, they launched a major marketing campaign, which supposedly cost a fortune to calm the criticism. This campaign successfully stabilized sales at a level of 140-160 tons per year where it has since remained. Moreover, since then, Icelandic customers have repeatedly voiced their dissatisfaction with King Polo's declining quality. Disturbed by these complaints, the management of Olaf Asbjørnsson asked you whether the wafers' recipe had been changed. You assured your partners that they were still selling exactly the same product as in 1955. Apparently, the only objective basis for the perception of declining quality was the new packaging.

So, with this in the background, you are very concerned that another package design change combined with a new recipe might have a negative impact on the King Polo business in Iceland. To help mitigate this risk, this time you have informed Olaf Asbjørnsson well in advance of the planned changes. Moreover, you are determined to support them in an efficient rollout of the new King Polo in Iceland, including with any financial support they need as long as that support is reasonable and necessary.

New Contract

The current distribution contract between Olaf Asbjørnsson and Mondelex is very simple. Olaf Asbjørnsson can purchase King Polo at a discounted wholesale net price of €5,000 per ton and can exclusively import and distribute it in Iceland. Since King Polo is so popular in Iceland, it is estimated to have an average wholesale net domestic price of €12.000 or higher. Wholesale price selection in Iceland is at the sole discretion of Olaf Asbjørnsson. However, all marketing and distribution cost must be covered by Olaf Asbjørnsson. All marketing efforts implemented by Olaf Asbjørnsson are subject to prior approval from Mondelex.

However, to better stimulate sales growth of King Polo in Iceland and bring greater equity in the relationship with your distributor, the structure of the new contract needs to be changed. You need to convince Olaf Asbjørnsson that a closer more collaborative relationship is needed. More specifically, the most important issue that you want to address in the upcoming negotiation is the **fee structure**. For many years, you have tolerated the fact that Olaf Asbjørnsson has probably been earning a greater profit with King Polo in Iceland than you – its manufacturer. It is time to change this inequality. To do so, you are planning to base the new contract on a gross profit sharing model. Although your cost of your goods sold amounts to around 50% of sales, you estimate that currently, your gross profit is not even a half of Olaf Asbjørnsson's.[27] It is very important to you that Olaf Asbjørnsson's gross profit does not significantly exceed yours. To equalize this, you estimate that you would need to claim around a 30% share of Olaf Asbjørnsson's gross profit. If they agree to this profit sharing model, you would, in turn, be prepared to cover a part of their marketing and distribution cost. Additionally, if possible, you would also like to receive a fixed licensing fee for sharing your sales and marketing expertise. Mondelex management feels that this combination of deals is more than fair, long overdue and certainly demonstrates its financial commitment to help drive King Polo's growth in Iceland.

In this regard, you really hope that these negotiations go well. That King Polo has become so ingrained in Icelandic culture drives a sense of pride in Mondelex. For many decades, the revenue from exporting King Polo to Iceland has been a very nice addition to that of your core market of Poland. Indeed, this success has been almost effortless for you. Olaf Asbjørnsson was a very solid and reliable trading partner with exemplary payment behavior. All you had to do was manufacture King Polo, ship it to Iceland

---

[27] Generally, gross profit is the difference between net sales and cost of goods sold. In the case of Olaf Asbjørnsson, it does not include the marketing and distribution cost which amount to 10-20% of the revenues.

and issue the invoices. This is probably the reason why the current contract between you has never been changed. However, the opening up of the Icelandic confectionary market to foreign products, combined with very limited marketing activities carried out by Olaf Asbjørnsson, have led to a gradual decline of the King Polo business. Moreover, despite King Polo's great brand awareness in Iceland, the share of Icelandic sales in the whole King Polo's business have never exceeded 5%, lately oscillating mostly around 2%-3%. Since performance there is not reaching its full potential, some action must be taken.

Your experts agree that, although regaining the market position from the 1970s is unfortunately not possible, solid growth is. So, in addition to addressing the issues above, they recommend several other growth-oriented issues that should be discussed in this meeting that are in the spirit of a more participative and profitable relationship with Olaf Asbjørnsson:

- **Localizing the package** – Olaf Asbjørnsson keeps reminding you that tradition plays a very important role in Iceland. Indeed, it does seem to be much more important than in other King Polo markets. Your partners have suggested that their customers would appreciate if these values were reflected in the package design. They claimed that it would be ideal if you could use King Polo's old wrapping again or at least make sure that the new design looks similar to the old one. Unfortunately, you currently do not have the ability to use localized package designs in the manufacturing process. However, you fully understand that customers in different King Polo national markets might have different preferences. As such, maybe it would make sense to build a local packaging facility in Iceland to meet this need? Although you know that such local customization could drive revenue about 10% higher in Iceland you have never done this since new machines for such a facility would cost around €3 million. However, it just so happens that the packaging segment of your old production line was recently replaced due to being too inefficient for your current production scale. Since it is very unlikely that it could sell anyway, it could be an option to ship it to Iceland instead and repurpose it for customized packaging that is better aligned to Olaf Asbjørnsson's customer preferences. This option would also save you about €20,000 in disposal costs for the machines.

- **Partnership with Loca-Cola** – Loca-Cola's soft drinks are often sold together with hotdogs or simple meals and King Polo. These combinations are very common in Iceland, and Olaf Asbjørnsson recently informed you that after a very promising meeting with Loca-Cola's local representatives they were planning to intensify this relationship by launching a series of joint marketing activities with them. Initially, you were not amused about this because the executives of Loca-Cola and Mondelex do not see each other as friends. However, because it is very common in Iceland to see King Polo sold together with Loca-Cola, you can imagine how this partnership might be a great growth stimulating opportunity. Indeed, you estimate that this could sustainably increase King Polo revenue by at least 20%. Unfortunately, you are nearly certain that internal approval would never be granted for investing the required €200,000 per year in this joint project with Loca-Cola. Thus, you can only encourage Olaf Asbjørnsson to pursue this opportunity alone and finance it from their own operating cash flow or other sources.

- **Regular marketing campaigns** – the secret behind the steadily rising popularity of SitCat, King Polo's main competitor in Iceland, is its regular and effective marketing campaigns. Ever since it was introduced in the Icelandic market in the 1980s, it has gradually increased in market share to the point that it has almost caught up with King Polo. Your experts suggest that if other King Polo promotional efforts could be supported by annual advertising campaigns, sales and market share would improve and be maintained. According to their analysis, the relationship between the annual advertising budget and its effect on sales is expected to be positive and linear between €300,000 and €500,000. That is, below €300,000 there would be no effect at all. €300,000 would increase sales by 30% whereas €500,000 would drive growth up to 50%. Above €500,000 no additional improvement above 50% would be realized. Indeed, if Olaf Asbjørnsson will agree on a profit-sharing model, you would be pleased to discuss sharing the costs. However, since Olaf Asbjørnsson's controls all marketing activities in Iceland and your role is limited, your expectation is that they take on the bigger share of these costs. Moreover, the smaller your contribution is, the higher your profitability will be. If both sides reach an agreement, you would like to start these regular campaigns next year since you may be very busy this year addressing upcoming product changes.

Joint Venture

Prior to this meeting, Olaf Asbjørnsson has also signaled their willingness to explore the possibility of extending your business relationship further by eventually forming a separate joint venture for King Polo. This would combine their knowledge of the local market with your quality products and financial support and would certainly simplify the potential introduction of other Mondelex products in Iceland. You estimate that the initial financing for such a company should be €5 million. Olaf Asbjørnsson should contribute ca. 80% of it and Mondelex the remaining 20%. This level of financing would help King Polo's realize its full potential in Iceland since it would provide the needed investment to enable sales enhancing projects such as the installation of a €3 million local product packaging facility and important marketing campaigns. Although you have some flexibility on the exact split of financing, you expect the vast majority of it to come from Olaf Asbjørnsson.

The joint venture would be staffed with the sales people from Olaf Asbjørnsson and a general manager and a senior marketing executive from Mondelex. Profits should be reinvested into the core business. Iceland is a rather small market and should these or similar conditions not be acceptable to Olaf Asbjørnsson; then you are fine to just continue this relationship with them as a commercial (non-equity) partnership.

The main objective of the upcoming contract negotiation is to create a fair basis for the sustainable and profitable growth of your King Polo business in Iceland. You have the authority to decide on and commit to any solution you consider beneficial for your company. Negotiate wisely.

Gangi þér vel!

Debriefing

King Polo is a non-scoreable, integrative negotiation roleplay written for The Negotiation Challenge 2014 in Reykjavik. It was used in the final between Bonn University and the Warsaw School of Economics. It is suitable for practicing principle-based negotiation as introduced by Roger Fisher, William Ury, and Bruce Patton in Getting to Yes: Negotiating Agreement Without Giving In in 1981.

King Polo is a chocolate covered wafer that has been manufactured in Poland since 1955. The negotiation described in the roleplay takes place between Mondelex International, its current manufacturer and Olaf Asbjørnsson efh, its Icelandic importer and distributor, and focuses on defining the exact conditions for future cooperation between them.

Olaf Asbjørnsson's King Polo business is very simple. They buy the wafers from Mondelex at a discounted wholesale net price of €5,000 per ton. As the exclusive importer and distributor in Iceland, it then resells King Polo at an average net wholesale price that exceeds €10,000 per ton, averaging nearly €12,000 and sometimes reaching even €14,000. With current sales volumes at about 140-160 tons per year, Olaf Asbjørnsson's annual revenues amount to €1.4-€1.6 million. Olaf Asbjørnsson, however, is also responsible for local marketing and distribution, which generate costs of about 10%-20% of their revenues. These costs are currently covered by Olaf Asbjørnsson alone. Nevertheless, selling King Polo in Iceland is a very lucrative business, which leaves the distributor a gross profit of €420k-640k.

The main issues the parties need to focus on in this negotiation are:

1. **Upcoming package and recipe changes and their potential consequences**
   To improve King Polo's competitive position in Poland, its
   main market, Mondelex is planning to change its recipe and
   redesign the package. This decision has been preceded by
   thorough market research and customer testing. Mondelex
   expects an increase of gross profitability of up to 10 percentage points to nearly 60% without raising the prices. It has also
   reserved a marketing budget of up to €200k for promoting
   these changes in Iceland.

   Olaf Asbjørnsson does not want to change the traditional
   King Polo recipe. They strongly prefer to either restore the old
   package or to stay with the current one. If changed, they expect another wave of customer complaints and negative business impact similar to what occurred when similar changes
   were introduced by Mondelex in the 1990s.

2. **Defining the conditions of the new contract between
   Olaf Asbjørnsson and Mondelex**
   For various reasons, both parties are interested in rene-
   gotiating the conditions of their distribution agreement.
   Mondelex, as a producer, would like to participate more
   in the sales potential of King Polo in Iceland. In turn, Olaf
   Asbjørnsson is interested in collaborating more closely with Mondelex to drive King Polo sales but also wants
   them to contribute to their marketing budget as part of
   this. The main discussion points on this issue are centered
   around the following:

   • **Localizing the package**
     Olaf Asbjørnsson prefers to use the old traditional King
     Polo package, whereas Mondelex wants to change it
     again. Iceland is a small market, which is both an advan-
     tage and a disadvantage for each of the parties.

- **Partnership with Loca-Cola**
  Olaf Asbjørnsson has been offered an opportunity to run a series of joint marketing activities in Iceland with Loca-Cola. Although it is a great opportunity to generate additional sales, it requires an additional marketing budget. However, since Olaf Asbjørnsson does not currently have enough liquidity to finance this alone, it hopes for Mondelex's understanding and support.

- **Regular marketing campaigns**
  Regular marketing campaigns are necessary to strengthen King Polo's competitive position in Iceland and defend its market share against aggressive competitors like SitCat. The positive impact of such campaigns is unquestionable and depends only on the budget the parties can devote to them.

3. **Joint venture**
   The parties can also imagine moving beyond their current commercial cooperation towards an equity-based partnership in the form of a joint venture (JV). Although a JV seems like a good idea for an expansion of the existing business relationship between the parties, multiple issues need to be agreed on before it can be formed. These issues include equity split, governance structure, staffing, cost contribution and profit sharing.

Olaf Asbjørnsson's main objective is to lay a solid foundation for the growth of their King Polo business in Iceland that is based on a participative and profitable relationship with Mondelex. They are interested in purchasing King Polo at a discounted net price of around €5,000 and would like Mondelex to subsidize the largest possible share of their marketing and distribution costs in the form of a distribution fee and a variable bonus based on sales performance.

Olaf Asbjørnsson's strong preference is to return to the old traditional packaging for King Polo and not to change its traditional recipe. However, if Mondelex insists on introducing these changes, a set of **marketing countermeasures** would be necessary. Their marketing experts suggest that to counter the negative effects of the changes and keep revenues at their current level, they would need to invest about €500,000 in a marketing campaign. The relationship between the budget for the marketing campaign and King Polo revenues is expected to be linear. That is, decreasing the marketing budget for this campaign by €100,000 will reduce King Polo revenues by 10%. Taking no marketing actions will cut these revenues by half. If absolutely necessary, Olaf Asbjørnsson could reallocate around €200.000 from other projects, but would prefer to avoid it.

Concerning **localizing the package**, in order of preference, Olaf Asbjørnsson wants Mondelex to either return to King Polo's old traditional wrapping, stick to the existing one or if changes are necessary, make sure that the new design looks similar to the old one. They would also like to convince Mondelex to explore the possibility of customizing the package for the Icelandic market by building a dedicated packaging facility in Iceland. The estimated cost of a local packaging facility would amount to €3 million and would generate an expected revenue increase of 10% (€140k-160k). Unfortunately, Olaf Asbjørnsson does not have the necessary resources to finance this investment and expects Mondelex to do it instead.

Olaf Asbjørnsson perceives a **partnership with Loca-Cola** as a great growth stimulating opportunity. It requires an investment of €200k per year in joint projects and would increase revenues by at least 20% (€280k-320k) per year for the duration of the partnership. Olaf Asbjørnsson could postpone the start of this partnership until next year and finance it from operating cash flow but only at the risk of losing the deal to Nesty's SitCat. Therefore, Olaf Asbjørnsson wants Mondelex to fully finance it for at least the first year and then contribute at least 25% of the investment for subsequent years. Otherwise, they would have to reprioritize other ongoing projects, which they would prefer to avoid.

Olaf Asbjørnsson's experts claim that to regain some of King Polo's lost market share, **regular marketing campaigns** are necessary in addition to the above-mentioned measures. According to their analysis, there is a linear relationship between the budget for such marketing campaign and an uplift in revenues. A budget of €300k-500k would increase revenues by 30%-50% (€420k-800k), respectively. Olaf Asbjørnsson would like Mondelex to subsidize the financing of these campaigns with a distribution fee.

Olaf Asbjørnsson can imagine extending their business relationship with Mondelex by forming a **joint venture**. The initial funding for such a company should be €5 million, in which Mondelex should contribute 80% of the equity and Olaf Asbjørnsson the remaining 20%. This level of funding would allow the ability to invest in a local packaging infrastructure (€3 million) and finance needed marketing campaigns. Olaf Asbjørnsson has some flexibility on the exact split of equity but expects the vast majority of it to come from Mondelex. The joint venture would be staffed with salespeople and a general manager from Olaf Asbjørnsson and a senior marketing executive from Mondelex. Profits could be either reinvested into the core business or distributed equally between the partners. Should these or similar conditions not be acceptable to Mondelex, Olaf Asbjørnsson is fine to continue this relationship with them as a commercial (non-equity) partnership.

Mondelex's main objective is also to lay a solid foundation for the growth of their King Polo business in Iceland through a fair and profitable relationship with Olaf Asbjørnsson. King Polo is estimated to have an average wholesale net price in Iceland of €12.000 or higher. Olaf Asbjørnsson can purchase King Polo at a discounted wholesale net price of €5,000 per ton. The cost of goods sold amounts to around 50% of sales. Despite King Polo's great success in Iceland, the share of sales in the entire King Polo's business have never exceeded 5%, lately oscillating around 2-3%.

Mondelex intends to support the introduction of a new package and a new recipe with a marketing campaign. It has reserved €3 million for this purpose of which no more than €200k should be allocated for Iceland.

The most important issue in the negotiations of the upcoming contract is the **fee structure**. Mondelex estimates that at the moment their gross profit is not even half of Olaf Asbjørnsson's. Therefore, they are planning to base the new contract on a gross profit sharing model and claim around a 30% share of Olaf Asbjørnsson's gross profit. If they agree on this profit sharing model, Mondelex would be ready to cover a part of the marketing and distribution cost. Additionally, Mondelex would also like to receive a licensing fee for sharing their sales and marketing know-how.

Concerning **localizing the package**, Mondelex does not have the ability to produce differentiated packages for different markets due to limitations in their current manufacturing process. However, they do recognize that it might be reasonable to build a local packaging facility in Iceland. Indeed, the packaging part of Modelez's production line has been recently replaced. As it is very unlikely to sell it to someone else, Mondelex sees an option to ship it to Iceland. This option would also save them about €20,000 in disposal costs for the machines. A similar new machine can cost around €3 million, and the expected revenue increase from localizing the packaging is about 10%.

Although a **partnership with Loca-Cola** might be a great growth stimulating opportunity, Mondelex would never get approval for investing the required €200k per year in joint projects with them. Since it is estimated that entering this partnership would sustainably increase revenue by at least 20%, Mondelex has decided to encourage Olaf Asbjørnsson to pursue this opportunity and finance it from their own operating cash flow or through other sources.

Mondelex experts confirm that **regular marketing campaigns** are necessary to regain some of King Polo's market share.

According to their analysis, there is a linear relationship between the budget for such marketing campaign and an uplift in revenues. A budget of €300k-500k would increase revenues by 30%-50% (€420k-800k), respectively. If Olaf Asbjørnsson agrees to divide the gross profit, Mondelex would consider the co-financing of the marketing campaigns. However, they must keep in mind that the smaller their contribution to this campaign, the higher their profitability. Nonetheless, it is important for Mondelex that the agreement is fair and economically justifiable.

Olaf Asbjørnsson signaled their willingness to explore the possibility of extending the current business relationship by forming a **joint venture**. The initial funding for such a company should be €5 million, in which Olaf Asbjørnsson should contribute 80% of the equity and Mondelex the remaining 20%. This level of funding would allow the ability to invest in a local packaging infrastructure (€3 million) and finance needed marketing campaigns. Mondelex has some flexibility on the exact split of equity but expects the vast majority of it to come from Olaf Asbjørnsson. The joint venture would be staffed with the sales people from Olaf Asbjørnsson and a general manager and a senior marketing executive from Mondelex. Profits should be reinvested into the core business. Should these or similar conditions not be acceptable to Olaf Asbjørnsson, Mondelex is content to continue the business relationship as a commercial (non-equity) partnership.

In general, based on the negotiators' ability to recognize each other's interests, as well as to employ necessary negotiation skills, the negotiation might result in one of the following outcomes:

1. **Collaborative solution**
   The main underlying interest that both parties share is to grow their King Polo business in Iceland by defining respective contributions to various growth opportunities in a way they feel is fair and sustainable. Olaf Asbjørnsson needs Mondelex and its resources to regain King Polo's full potential for success in

the Icelandic market. Mondelex is willing to help, so long as the resulting profits are shared in a way it feels is fair.

If the parties share their confidential information, they will quickly realize that with Mondelex's old packaging machine, that otherwise would be recycled at the cost of €20k, it is possible to use it to customize packaging specific for Icelandic customers' tastes. In this situation, no marketing campaign countermeasures would be necessary, and the expected impact of a localized package would generate a 10% increase in revenues without a necessity to spend €500k for marketing.

This increase in available budget could then be spent on the Loca-Cola partnership and/or on regular marketing campaigns, which could drive an additional increase of 20% and 50% respectively. If the negotiators manage to explore these opportunities, they could grow revenues by ca. €1.3-€1.5 million at a cost of only €700k.

However, Mondelex is only willing to explore their contribution to such initiatives if they can participate more fairly in King Polo profits. It is simply not acceptable for them to earn less than half of what the distributor's gross profits are (ca. €400k vs. nearly €1 million). In this regard, the negotiators have full flexibility to agree on what they deem to be fair contributions to costs and fair profit participation. Depending on how fully this potential is explored, a profit redistribution of about 25-30% would equalize their share of the King Polo profits in Iceland. Regardless, an equal distribution is only one of the options, not necessarily the best one.

Lastly, Olaf Asbjørnsson and Mondelex can also tighten their cooperation and form a joint venture. Although it is not critical for continuing their relationship, about 20-30% of the negotiators end up with a joint venture as a part of their agreement. Since each party's expectations are nearly opposing, only negotiators who build a strong and sustainable relationship with their negotiation partners manage to integrate this issue into their agreement. Although there is no clear monetary advantage in doing this, it does send a clear signal from each party on the value they place on a long-term sustainable agreement.

2. **Competitive outcomes**
Growing the King Polo business in Iceland requires contributions from both parties. However, the lower these contributions are, the better it is for each respective party. This creates a competitive tension between the negotiators, which can draw their focus from value creation to value claiming. The effect of this dynamic is that they typically leave a part of the value creation potential unexplored.

There is a vast range of possible competitive outcomes. These include changing the recipe and the packaging and running unnecessary marketing countermeasures, committing to suboptimal total marketing budgets, not running a partnership with Loca-Cola, or building a completely redundant new packaging facility in Iceland.

The pursuit of respective self-interests and a myopic focus on just claiming the biggest share of value often leads to suboptimal outcomes and a bigger piece of a smaller cake.

3. **No agreement**
The differences between the parties and the resulting competitive tension sometimes escalate into a conflict between them. In an attempt to convince each other about the superiority of own arguments, demands and expectations only heat up the debate, make it more emotional and shift the attention away from seeking understanding and problem solving to positional bargaining often resulting in no agreement. In 10-20% of the negotiations based on this simulation, the negotiators either break up the negotiation or end up without an agreement by the end of the designated time.

No agreement between the parties produces a lose-lose outcome. This means that in a best-case scenario, Mondelex changes the recipe and the package and with its limited resources, Olaf Asbjørnsson is unable to neither neutralize the negative impact this has on their King Polo business nor improve its competitive position. This cascades into losing even greater market share to Nesty's SitCat since it is strengthened by their partnership with Loca-Cola. In the worst case, Mondelex, fed up with the situation, pulls their license from Olaf Asbjørnsson's and seeks another way of distributing their products in Iceland.

The key challenges for this roleplay are the large solution space available and a high degree of freedom in determining the outcome. Thus, to reach an agreement so comprehensive that it exhausts the full value potential of the negotiation, negotiators will need to focus on building a quality relationship with each other and applying their respective skills to navigate the complex dynamics of the multiple issues. However, this can be a challenge for even skilled negotiators. During the final negotiation of The Negotiation Challenge 2014, the negotiating teams ran out of time and were not able to reach an agreement. The parties displayed a highly competitive negotiation style and were unlikely to reach a collaborative solution, even if more time had been available.

3.4 Multiparty Negotiation

A team is only as good as the sum of its members. As this is particularly true in negotiation, during at least one round of The Negotiation Challenge, we split the participating teams and setup three-party negotiations involving the participants from different teams.

The negotiators in each triad typically pursue different interests, have different amounts of resources or assets under control and therefore also different amounts of negotiation power. To ensure the fairness of the competition, the participants from each team, e.g., Team 1, 2, 3, etc. are assigned to each of the three roles, (e.g., role A, B, and C) and each of them negotiates in a different triad, (e.g., 1A with 2B and 3C). The rule determining who A is, who is B and who is C is is typically very simple and pragmatic, usually determined by age or alphabetical order of names within a team.

The multiparty round is the only one in which the preparation for the upcoming negotiation takes place individually. Since knowledge of the confidential instructions is critical, we also restrict any possible communication between the members of the same team.

In contrast to general and confidential instructions for the types of negotiations described in previous chapters, instructions for the multiparty rounds are rather short and straightforward. The source of complexity in these rounds lies in the dynamics of the negotiation and the resulting relationships between the parties. Value creation, as well as value claiming, involves all three parties, and in this constellation, coalitions might be built or broken. Also, these are also the most emotional rounds during The Negotiation Challenge being loaded with both positive and negative emotions.

During the early days of the competition, we observed negotiations in which two parties either completely excluded or significantly minimized the share of value assigned to the third. Although this sometimes might be a legitimate outcome during the competition, unfortunately, when it happens, it often leads to an intense emotional reaction from the affected party which creates unnecessary, disruptive tension among the participants. As such, we now try to limit the possibility of explicit exclusions while still giving the negotiators full flexibility in defining the outcome of their negotiations.

During the multiparty negotiation rounds, we have up to 18 negotiations taking place in parallel. Therefore, we decided to base the measurement of the negotiators' performance only on the substantive outcome of their negotiations. Specifically, the final ranking of the participating teams is the sum of individual rankings obtained by the members of each team. Based on the agreements reached by all triads, we compare the results of the negotiators representing each party, (e.g., 1A with 2A and 3A). Each of them had the same instructions and a similar starting position. Based on these results, we compose a ranking for the role A and proceed similarly for roles B and C. Lastly, we assign points for each team member's ranking and add them together, e.g., points of 1A + points of 1B + points of 1C. The sum of points for each team determines its performance for the round.

In the debriefing section for each of the roleplays following, we include actual results from previous TNC competitions for the reader to compare their negotiation outcome with those of the world's best student negotiators.

Schmalkaldic War

Author: **Remigiusz Smolinski**

Number of parties:	Preparation time:	Negotiation time:	Complexity level:
2	**30** minutes	**60** minutes	**intermediate**

Pedagogical focus

information exchange, understanding mutual interests, reservation point, relationship building in multilateral negotiation, coalition building, value claiming strategies in multilateral negotiations, trust creation, objective criteria, fairness, multiparty negotiation

Short description

The Schmalkaldic War is a three-party negotiation that is set within the tumultuous times following the start of the Protestant Reformation in the 16th century. Faced with a military insurrection in what will become known as the Schmalkaldic War, Charles V, the Emperor of the Holy Roman Empire has called a meeting with Pope Paul III and Duke Moritz of Saxony to discuss the formation of a military coalition to defeat this threat and to agree on each member's contribution to the military campaign. However, since their resources are limited, they will need to negotiate shrewdly to ensure they have a coalition strong enough for victory but also one that does not bankrupt their respective treasuries.

General Instructions

When Martin Luther nailed his 95 theses to the church door of Wittenberg castle in 1517, few could have known how quickly that this courageous act of a single man would start unraveling the Catholic-dominated religious, social fabric of Europe, nor of the great bloodshed and war it would lead to across the Holy Roman Empire. However, despite the strong opposition by the ruling family of the Empire, the Catholic House of Habsburg, and its powerful leader, Charles V, within just a few years multiple leaders across the Holy Roman Imperial states were defecting from the established Catholic faith by openly demonstrating their support for this Lutheran Reformation.

Politically, Charles V saw these defections as a serious threat to his central imperial authority. Thus, in an attempt to stop the spread of this movement, in 1521 he banned Martin Luther from the Empire and prohibited the proliferation of his writings. Despite this, it seemed his action was already too late. For it was only eight years later that 14 of the Empire's Free Cities, having joined the Protestant movement, officially petitioned against the ban of Martin Luther and his works. Then just two years after this, in 1531, feeling increasingly persecuted by the Holy Roman Emperor, these Lutheran states established a military alliance, later called the Schmalkaldic League, with an ambitious political goal to replace the Holy Roman Empire.

Alarmed by the inevitable military confrontation that this League threatened, in 1544 Charles V invited his allies, Pope Paul III and Duke Moritz of Saxony, to meet at Duke Moritz's fortress in Leipzig, a key city within the Empire. The goal was to discuss the formation of a military coalition to defeat this threat and to agree on each country's contribution to the military campaign to do so. However, according to the chronicles of the time, these three allies differed from each other in key aspects. The Holy Roman Empire, commanded by Emperor Charles V, possessed the biggest and strongest army in Europe. The Papal States, ruled by Pope Paul III, the religious leader of the mighty Catholic Church, was the most influential and wealthiest country in Europe. The Duchy of Saxony, though the smallest of the three allies, possessed a well-trained battle-hardened army. Moreover, since any battles would probably be fought on their homeland of Saxony, their motivation would be great since they would rather die than lose this war. Despite the great differences between the parties, it remained evident that only by joining forces would they have the necessary means to win this pending war. Therefore, a three-party coalition was the only outcome that could guarantee success.

As the representatives of these three allies, you will now meet to negotiate the best solution to defeat the Schmalkaldic League in this upcoming war. The figures in the table below illustrate your key resources.

	Holy Roman Empire	Papal States	Duchy of Saxony
Population	20 million	2 million	1 million
Total wealth	80 million Gulden	100 million Gulden	10 million Gulden
Military strength	50,000 infantry 10,000 cavalry	20,000 infantry 5,000 cavalry	10,000 infantry 2,000 cavalry

Table 29. Key resources of the allied forces

It is important to note that wealth and military strength represent total figures for the whole country. Thus, the resources that each country is able and/or willing to commit will most likely be smaller. All leaders have asked their advisors to recommend the maximum level of resources they could allocate to the upcoming war. This recommendation is expected to arrive shortly before the negotiations.

At a meeting prior to this summit, the generals of the allied forces have come to the unanimous conclusion that a military operation to defeat the Schmalkaldic League will cost **at least 3 million Gulden and require 60,000 infantry and 11,000 cavalry**. The military strategy drawn up during this meeting relies heavily on all three components. Thus, each of them is a strict requirement which **must be fulfilled** to succeed. Moreover, though it is normally possible to hire mercenaries to fight on one's behalf, usually 50 Gulden for a cavalryman and 20 Gulden for an infantry soldier, due to the war's imminence there is simply not enough time to pursue this option nor is there time to raise more money. They must find a way to meet the minimum collectively required resources with what is currently at their disposal in order to successfully execute their complex strategy.

Although all wars are costly and lead to inevitable material and human losses, they usually result in certain financial and/or non-financial benefits for the victors. The same will probably be true for the Schmalkaldic War. Its potential benefits, however, will not be shared equally by the coalition members. It is believed that the Holy Roman Empire and the Papal States will claim 50% and 40% of the overall benefits respectively, leaving the remaining 10% to the Duchy of Saxony. The distribution of these benefits is not subject to negotiation.

Shortly before the upcoming negotiations, you are expecting a messenger with a detailed report on the resources (money and troops) you can each respectively allocate to the Schmalkaldic War. Considering the various requirements of the three countries' internal and external affairs, this is the absolute maximum you can afford, and you must not exceed the figures recommended by your advisors.

Here is a summary of your objectives for the upcoming negotiations:

- form a **three-party coalition** with your allies; a two-party coalition will lack the necessary political support and/or key resources and is doomed to fail. Therefore, it is not an acceptable outcome.

- **secure the resources** (infantry, cavalry and financing) **necessary to win the Schmalkaldic War**; the strategy drawn up by your generals relies heavily on your ability to secure the requested resources; please note that you must fulfill all of their requirements since failure to do so means the automatic failure of the whole coalition.
- **your contribution must not exceed the amounts recommended by your advisors**; it can be smaller but never larger; this is a wrong time for empty promises since they are likely to result in a fiasco for the entire operation.
- **minimize the total monetary value of your contribution to the military campaign; the smaller your contribution**, the more resources you will have for other purposes.
- **do NOT negotiate the distribution of potential benefits from the war** nor any other issues other than the ones mentioned above (infantry, cavalry and financing).

Confidential Instructions
for the **Holy Roman Empire**

According to your advisors, you can allocate the following resources to the Schmalkaldic War:

- max 40,000 infantry
- max 7,000 cavalry
- max 1.5 million Gulden

This information is **strictly confidential.**

Confidential Instructions
for the **Papal States**

According to your advisors, you can allocate the following resources to the Schmalkaldic War:

- max 15,000 infantry
- max 3,000 cavalry
- max 2 million Gulden

This information is **strictly confidential.**

Confidential Instructions
for the **Duchy of Saxony**

According to your advisors, you can allocate the following resources to the Schmalkaldic War:

- max 10,000 infantry
- max 2,000 cavalry
- max 0.5 million Gulden

This information is **strictly confidential.**

Debriefing

Schmalkaldic War is a distributive, three-party scoreable negotiation roleplay written for The Negotiation Challenge 2011 that took place in Leipzig, Germany in the dungeons of the Moritzbastei, a historic city fortification built around the time of the events described in the roleplay. This roleplay differs from those in previous chapters in that it contains a third party. This significantly increases the intensity of the negotiation process. As such, it is suitable for practicing value claiming skills in a multilateral setting.

The main objective for the three negotiators, Charles V, Holy Roman Emperor, Pope Paul III, ruler of the Papal States and Maurice, the Duke and later Elector of Saxony is to form a military coalition and agree on their individual contributions to the joint military campaign. However, this will be challenging since no one wants to contribute more than they need.

Performance evaluation for this roleplay is based on its substantive outcome. This occurs by placing a common monetary valuation (Gulden) on all various resources so that preferences can be quantified. In this way, each party's success in minimizing their contributions can be evaluated.

Unlike in other multiparty roleplays included in this book, the preparation for Schmalkaldic War can take place in teams before they get split up into separate triads. This preparation involves the reading of general instructions, which are identical for all parties. Following this, they go to their respective triads and receive their confidential instructions, which advises them what their maximum contributions can be.

Table 30 below summarizes confidential instructions for all parties concerning their advised maximal contributions to the joint military campaign. It also includes the minimum required amounts of assets necessary for the success of the campaign.

	Holy Roman Empire	Papal States	Duchy of Saxony	Total	Minimum Required
Infantry	40,000	15,000	10,000	65,000	60,000
Cavalry	7,000	3,000	2,000	12,000	11,000
Financing	1,500,000	2,000,000	500,000	4,000,000	3,000,000

Table 30. The parties' maximum contribution to the joint military campaign.

The specific objectives of the negotiating parties are to form a **three-party coalition** with their allies and **secure the resources** (infantry, cavalry and financing) **necessary to win the Schmalkaldic War** while **minimizing the total monetary value of their contribution.** Such objectives create a tension between collecting the resources necessary to win the war and minimizing the individual contribution of each party. Although all three parties need to work together, they are interested in contributing as little as possible to their military coalition. Despite the amount of resources each party controls, the collective sum of what they can maximally contribute barely exceeds the minimum requirements for the campaign. This leaves little room for saving anything. *Table 31* illustrates this challenge by showing the minimum contributions each party must make to reach their goal even if other partners commit all the resources at their disposal to the common coalition. For example, if Pope Paul III representing the Papal State and Maurice of Saxony offer all of their infantry, 10,000 and 5,000 respectively, Charles V would still have to send at least 35,000 cavalry (88% of the maximum) to fight. His commitment can be higher and include all of his 40,000 infantry but not lower. This same dynamic is the case for all other rulers and all resources.

Minimum required	Holy Roman Empire	Papal States	Duchy of Saxony
Infantry	35,000	10,000	5,000
% of max. infantry	88%	67%	50%
Cavalry	6,000	2,000	1,000
% of max. cavalry	86%	67%	50%
Financing	500,000	1,000,000	0
% of max. financing	33%	50%	0%

Table 31. The parties' minimum contributions to their military coalition.

Since the monetary valuation of resources is the same for all parties: 50 Gulden for a cavalryman and 20 Gulden for an infantry soldier for the entire duration of the military campaign, we are dealing here with a strictly distributive three-party negotiation. This means that the parties cannot create any additional value in their negotiations. They can only distribute what already exists. However, as a side note, it would be easy to convert this into an integrative negotiation if desired, simply by differentiating the costs of the resources between the parties.

Negotiation strategy for this roleplay can be based on various objective criteria. These include population, total wealth, military strength of the army, or if successful, post-campaign division of benefits. The selection of an objective criterion or a combination thereof might be used to justify radically different contributions to the coalition.

For the benefit of reference, the best substantive outcome obtained by a negotiator that represented Charles V during The Negotiation Challenge 2011 was a contribution equivalent to 1,624,000 Guldens. This consisted of 37,200 infantry, 6,600 cavalry, and 550,000 Guldens. On average, however, Charles V negotiators contributed with an equivalent of 2,082,968 Gulden.

The best substantive outcome obtained by a negotiator that represented Pope Paul III was a contribution equivalent to 1,710,000 Gulden. This consisted of 13,500 infantry, 2,900 cavalry, and 1,295,000 Guldens. On average, Pope Paul III negotiators contributed with an equivalent of 2,067,136 Guldens.

Finally, the best substantive outcome of Maurice, the Duke of Saxony was a contribution equivalent to 280,000 Guldens. This consisted of 10,000 infantry and 1,600 cavalry. On average, Maurice negotiators contributed with an equivalent of 590,805 Guldens.

The best team in this round was Aarhus University, and its negotiators managed to top the ranking for two different roles (Charles V and Maurice) and ended up in the fifth place as Pope Paul III.

Interestingly, one of the negotiating triads ended up without an agreement, which was by far the worst possible outcome for all three negotiators. This indicates that in the pursuit of value maximization even the best student negotiators can get carried away by their emotions.

El Dorado

Author: **Remigiusz Smolinski**

Number of parties:	Preparation time:	Negotiation time:	Complexity level:
3	**30** minutes	**60** minutes	**high**

Pedagogical focus

information exchange, understanding mutual interests, relationship building in multilateral negotiation, coalition building, cooperation, value creation and value claiming strategies in multilateral negotiations, trust creation, objective criteria, fairness, multiparty negotiation

Short description

El Dorado is a three-party negotiation. After five years of explora-tion, three acquaintances have finally discovered the lost Muisca treasure of El Dorado in a remote cave in Columbia. Unfortunately, one the explorers has accidentally triggered a hidden destruction mechanism set by the tribe long ago to protect their treasure. Thus, they have only a very short time to negotiate how the trea-sure will be divided between them before the cave and everything in it is destroyed. However, as there is more treasure than they can each physically carry, they must make some difficult choices. Since they all had different motivations in joining the expedition in the first place, this will not be easy.

General Instructions

"Miguel, pinch me!", Tulio said, rubbing his eyes in disbelief. "Do you see what I see?" The twilight of the tiny Andean cave was pierced with brilliant rays of yellow, red and green light reflecting from their flashlights and a mysterious pile of something in the corner in front of them.

Miguel did not respond. He stood there slack-jawed, mesmerized by the view as Chel stepped forward and knelt next to the source of the blinding reflections, closely inspecting their discovery.

Then she stood up, turned around to them and said, "Gentlemen, congratulations! We have just found the lost treasure of El Dorado!" She then walked up to them, gently closed Miguel's mouth and added with a confident smile, "Told you."

Nearly five years ago, in Miguel's cozy mansion, she spent hours convincing them that El Dorado was not a myth. Over the years, Chel became absolutely obsessed with this thought. She knew every legend and every historical account that even vaguely mentioned the Muisca tribe, their history, beliefs, artifacts or rituals. She became an absolute expert on this topic.

The Muisca civilization inhabited the territory of what is today central Colombia, around and north of Bogota. It was a culture as advanced as the Aztecs in central Mexico, the Mayas in southern Mexico, Guatemala, Belize, El Salvador, and Honduras and the Incas in Peru. According to legend, the tribe had vast riches including a culture that revolved around gold. So central was this importance to them that the Muisca chiefs, during their initiation ritual, would be covered in powdered gold and submerge himself in Lake Guatavita. This ritual gave rise to the legend of the golden king or in Spanish, El Rey Dorado, El Hombre Dorado, the golden man or short, El Dorado, the golden one. However, the vast riches that legend says the Muisca possessed were supposedly hidden away by them, fearing it would be stolen by invading Spanish conquistadors. Because this hoard of treasure was never found, the legend of it grew and it has become known as the legend of El Dorado.

Although Lake Guatavita and the surrounding area have been thoroughly explored on countless expeditions by many, no evidence has been found. However, Chel through her extensive research found some obscure old Muisca legend that suggested it was hidden in a previously unexplored area of Andean caves. Having spent her entire adult life looking for El Dorado, Chel's dream came true today.

They quickly inspected their findings and inventoried multiple sacks of gold coins (tejuelos) and gold dust, Muisca jewelry, various precious stones such as diamonds, emeralds, and rubies, golden weapons, ancient artwork, a golden sculpture of El Rey Dorado, and royal insignia of the Muisca chiefs. The table below lists the artifacts discovered together with their estimated weight and divisibility.

Artifact	Weight in kg	Divisibility
Golden coins and dust	50	Fully flexible
Muisca jewelry	25	50 objects
Golden weapons	25	5 objects
Ancient artwork	20	10 objects
Precious stones	10	Fully flexible
El Rey Dorado	10	1 object
Royal insignia	5	1 object

Table 32. The artifacts discovered with their weight and divisibility

145 kilograms of Muisca treasures was certainly much more than they could carry. Even if they tried, they would not be able to take all of it back with them. In addition to their food and equipment, Chel could carry a maximum of 20 kilograms of treasures, Miguel and Tulio could manage a maximum of 40 kilograms each.

In the upcoming negotiation, Chel, Miguel and Tulio will discuss how to divide the Muisca treasures and agree on what to take back with them and what to leave behind. However, while inspecting the findings, Miguel accidentally activated an ancient mechanical mechanism that the Muisca set to protect the treasure from plundering. Since this mechanism triggers the destruction of the cave, all artifacts left behind will be lost forever.

Chel, Miguel and Tulio formed this alliance to seek out El Dorado five years ago. Chel is the mastermind behind the project. She thoroughly studied the history of the Muisca tribe and suggested shifting the focus of their explorations from Lake Guatavita to the neighboring mountains along the tribe's migration routes.

Miguel does not share Chel's passion for the history and culture of the Muisca tribe but has nevertheless financed all five expeditions, hoping only for great financial reward. He took on this risk only in exchange for getting the lion's share of the treasure.

Tulio is the team's adventurer, explorer and survivalist. The idea alone was enough for him to join the expedition. He just loved Chel's idea to search for El Dorado and has enjoyed their expedition. In addition to his extensive survivalist and exploring experience, Chel and Miguel knew that without Tulio's extensive network of artifact and treasure dealers they would never be able to sell their treasures at the prices he could secure for them.

So, regardless of how much they have needed to rely on each other throughout this project and how close they have become, it is now time to divide the treasure of El Dorado.

Confidential Instructions
for **Chel (A)**

So this is the legendary treasure of the Muisca tribe, El Dorado. The mix of gold, jewelry, weapons and artwork created an unforgettable symphony of brilliant and colorful reflections crowning your daring endeavor. Indeed, this breathtaking view has generously compensated you for your years of pain, sweat and tears.

You quickly inspected the findings and roughly estimated their value. The table below summarizes your survey and presents your personal valuation of each of the Muisca treasure categories:

Artifact	Weight in kg	Divisibility	Total personal value
Golden coins and dust	50	Fully flexible	500
Muisca jewelry	25	50 objects	300
Golden weapons	25	5 objects	200
Ancient artwork	20	10 objects	300
Precious stones	10	Fully flexible	80
El Rey Dorado	10	1 object	1,000
Royal insignia	5	1 object	300

Table 33. Chel's valuation of the discovered artifacts

Your main reasons behind this expedition were not greed but your deep passion for the Muisca culture and the urge to prove that you were right concerning the location of the El Dorado treasure. Therefore, in the upcoming negotiation, you will focus your effort on obtaining the artifacts manufactured by the Muisca people with the El Rey Dorado statue and royal insignia being the most important. Should it not be possible, you might have to revise your preferences and insist on obtaining other valuable artifacts.

Time is quickly running out and soon the ancient Muisca mechanism will destroy the cave and with it the artifacts you decide to leave behind. Should you not be able to reach an agreement before the announced deadline, you will perish in the cave and the treasure of El Dorado will be lost forever.

To summarize, your objective in the upcoming negotiation is to:

- **reach a three-party agreement**; not reaching an agreement before the announced deadline means no benefit for anyone
- an agreement is valid only if the proposed distribution is agreed to by all three negotiators, Chel, Miguel and Tulio; two-party agreements are not acceptable
- **maximize the total value of the artifacts** you decide to take with you; you can only keep what you can carry yourself; carrying artifacts for others is not an option;
- make sure you **do not exceed your carrying limit of 20 kilograms**; should you end up with more than you can carry, the value of the least valuable object will be deducted from your score
- focus on what you can carry; **artifacts left behind will be lost forever**, so there is no point in negotiating their distribution

Buena Suerte!

Confidential Instructions
for **Miguel (B)**

So this is the legendary treasure of the Muisca tribe, El Dorado. The mix of gold, jewelry, weapons and artwork created an unforgettable symphony of brilliant and colorful reflections crowning your daring endeavor. Indeed, this breathtaking view has generously compensated you for your years of pain, sweat and tears.

You quickly inspected the findings and roughly estimated their value. The table below summarizes your survey and presents your personal valuation of each of the Muisca treasure categories:

Artifact	Weight in kg	Divisibility	Total personal value
Golden coins and dust	50	Fully flexible	500
Muisca jewelry	25	50 objects	400
Golden weapons	25	5 objects	300
Ancient artwork	20	10 objects	300
Precious stones	10	Fully flexible	200
El Rey Dorado	10	1 object	800
Royal insignia	5	1 object	400

Table 34. Miguel's valuation of the discovered artifacts

Your main reason behind this expedition was not a passion for the Muisca culture but purely financial. You gladly financed the expedition hoping for great reward. Therefore, in the upcoming negotiation, you will focus your efforts on obtaining the most valuable artifacts (El Rey Dorado or royal insignia) and enlarging your collection of precious stones and jewelry. Should it not be possible, you might have to revise your preferences and insist on obtaining other valuable artifacts. A total value of 750 would cover the costs of the expedition and secure a decent profit.

Time is quickly running out and soon the ancient Muisca mechanism will destroy the cave and with it the artifacts you decide to leave behind. Should you not be able to reach an agreement before the announced deadline, you will perish in the cave and the treasure of El Dorado will be lost forever.

To summarize, your objective in the upcoming negotiation is to:

- **reach a three-party agreement**; not reaching an agreement before the announced deadline means no benefit for anyone
- an agreement is valid only if the proposed distribution is agreed to by all three negotiators, Chel, Miguel and Tulio; two-party agreements are not acceptable
- **maximize the total value of the artifacts** you decide to take with you; you can keep only what you can carry yourself; carrying artifacts for other is not an option;
- make sure you **do not exceed your carrying limit of 40 kilograms**; should you end up with more than you can carry, the value of the least valuable object will be deducted from your score
- focus on what you can carry; **artifacts left behind will be lost forever**, so there is no point in negotiating their distribution

Buena Suerte!

Confidential Instructions
for **Tulio (C)**

So this is the legendary treasure of the Muisca tribe, El Dorado. The mix of gold, jewelry, weapons and artwork created an unforgettable symphony of brilliant and colorful reflections crowning your daring endeavor. Indeed, this breathtaking view has generously compensated you for your years of pain, sweat and tears.

You quickly inspected the findings and roughly estimated their value. The table below summarizes your survey and presents your personal valuation of each of the Muisca treasure categories:

Artifact	Weight in kg	Divisibility	Total personal value
Golden coins and dust	50	Fully flexible	500
Muisca jewelry	25	50 objects	200
Golden weapons	25	5 objects	400
Ancient artwork	20	10 objects	400
Precious stones	10	Fully flexible	80
El Rey Dorado	10	1 object	800
Royal insignia	5	1 object	300

Table 35. Tulio's valuation of the discovered artifacts

Your main reason behind this expedition was not a passion for the Muisca culture but the thrill of looking for their treasures. In addition to your extensive explorer and survival experience, which turned out to be very handy during your expedition, you also gladly offered your assistance in selling the treasure if it was found.

You know many ancient treasure connoisseurs around the world who would be willing to pay very well for the Muisca treasure. In the upcoming negotiation, you will focus your effort on obtaining the most valuable artifacts (El Rey Dorado or royal insignia) and enlarging your collection of ancient weapons and artwork. Should it not be possible, you might have to revise your preferences and insist on obtaining other valuable artifacts.

Time is quickly running out and soon the ancient Muisca mechanism will destroy the cave and with it the artifacts you decide to leave behind. Should you not be able to reach an agreement before the announced deadline, you will perish in the cave and the treasure of El Dorado will be lost forever.

To summarize, your objective in the upcoming negotiation is to:

- **reach a three-party agreement**; not reaching an agreement before the announced deadline means no benefit for anyone
- an agreement is valid only if the proposed distribution is agreed to by all three negotiators, Chel, Miguel and Tulio; two-party agreements are not acceptable
- **maximize the total value of the artifacts** you decide to take with you; you can keep only what you can carry yourself; carrying artifacts for other is not an option
- make sure you **do not exceed your carrying limit of 40 kilograms**; should you end up with more than you can carry, the value of the least valuable object will be deducted from your score
- focus on what you can carry; **artifacts left behind will be lost forever**, so there is no point in negotiating their distribution

Buena Suerte!

Debriefing

El Dorado is an integrative three-party scoreable negotiation roleplay written for The Negotiation Challenge 2017 that took place in Bogota, Columbia. It was used during the opening round at Los Andes University. It is suitable for practicing value creation and value claiming skills in a multilateral setting.

The negotiators represent three fictitious characters: Chel (A), Miguel (B) and Tulio (C) and are asked to negotiate the distribution of the El Dorado treasure that they have just discovered. However, due to differences in preferences for each party and in how much weight they can carry, they place different valuations on the objects being negotiated. Understanding and exploiting these differences allow them an opportunity to create value. However, this will not be simple. El Dorado poses a series of challenges for the negotiators. First, as with all multiparty negotiations, an additional party significantly increases the complexity of value engineering processes. For example, the negotiators need to develop enough trust between them to share very sensitive information concerning their preferences with two additional persons. This makes the identification of value-adding options much more complex and less efficient. This is particularly difficult in a highly competitive context, which might draw the negotiators away from value creation and focus them rather on value claiming. Making this mistake would produce suboptimal agreements and leave value on the table.

Performance evaluation for this roleplay is based on its substantive outcome. This is enabled by quantifying each party's preferences for the various artifacts by assigning a preference-specific valuation. Thus, the value for any given artifact may differ between the negotiators based on what their different preferences are for it. In this way, the outcome indicates each party's success in engineering and claiming value.

The confidential instructions for each negotiating party clarify these preferences narratively and give their monetary valuation of each artifact. This also provides an implicit clue that each of them values the artifacts differently. Moreover, each character has a maximum weight limit that they can carry. These maximums are different. This increases pressure on them that they negotiate shrewdly and maximize the value of their carrying capacity. *Table 36* below summarizes what is given in the confidential instructions. This includes the weight of the artifacts, their divisibility and monetary value for each party. It also includes the essential parameter for understanding each party's interest: what the value of 1 kilogram of each artifact is for them.

This allows one to explore more clearly opportunities to arrive at a Pareto efficient distribution. That is, by understanding and allocating all artifacts to the parties that value them the most given the weight carrying limitation more value can be created. This is most evident in the valuations of the two most valuable artifacts. El Rey Dorado is the most valuable artifact for all parties. Although each of them would like to claim it for themselves, giving it to Chel creates the most value for the overall agreement (1,000 > 800 and 100 per 1 kg > 80 per 1 kg). The second most valuable artifact, the royal insignia, shares this characteristic and in the most optimal distribution should be allocated to Miguel (400 > 300 and 80 per 1 kg > 60 per 1 kg).

Artifact	Weight in kg	Divisibility	Total value for Chel (A)	Value per 1 kg (A)	Total value for Miguel (B)	Value per 1 kg (B)	Total value for Tulio (C)	Value per 1 kg (C)
Golden coins and dust	50	Fully flexible	500	10	500	10	500	10
Muisca jewelry	25	50 objects	300	12	400	16	200	8
Golden weapons	25	5 objects	200	8	300	12	400	16
Ancient artwork	20	10 objects	300	15	300	15	400	20
Precious stones	10	Fully flexible	80	8	200	20	80	8
El Rey Dorado	10	1 object	1,000	100	800	80	800	80
Royal insignia	5	1 object	300	60	400	80	300	60

Table 36. El Dorado treasure and its value for the negotiating parties

As shown in *Table 37*, should the parties successfully navigate this path, the maximum value they can generate together adds up to 2,825. It is a sum of the value in which Chel receives 1,125, Miguel receives 1,000 and Tulio gets 700. However, due to the tension between value creation and claiming, this is no easy task. For example, distributing these two most valuable objects to Chel and Miguel creates an imbalance in value distribution to Tulio, which cannot be compensated for by the allocation of other artifacts. This puts him under pressure to claim value in a way that is not Pareto efficient. Thus, it is not surprising that none of the teams participating in The Negotiation Challenge 2017 managed to arrive at this solution, although a couple of them came very close (2,820).

Artifact	Chel (A)	Miguel (B)	Tulio (C)
Golden coins and dust	5	0	0
Muisca jewelry	0	25	0
Golden weapons	0	0	25
Ancient artwork	5	0	15
Precious stones	0	10	0
El Rey Dorado	10	0	0
Royal insignia	0	5	0
Value	1,125	1,000	700

Table 37. Pareto efficient distribution of the El Dorado treasure

For the benefit of reference, the best substantive outcome obtained by the negotiators that represented Chel (A) during The Negotiation Challenge 2017 was a total value of 1,130 and was a result of claiming El Rey Dorado, 6 kg of ancient artwork, and 4 kg of golden coins and dust. On average, however, the Chels claimed a total value of 774, which is the lowest value of all characters.

270

The best substantive outcome obtained by the Miguel (B) negotiators was a total value of 1,110 and was a result of claiming El Rey Dorado, 5 kg of golden weapons and 25 kg of golden coins and dust. On average, the Miguels claimed the highest total value of 886.

Finally, the best substantive outcome of the Tulios (C) was a total value of 1,360 and was a result of claiming El Rey Dorado, 20 kg of artwork and 10 kg of weapons. On average, the Tulios claimed a total value of 818.

Paradoxically, the best overall outcome was obtained by the party that, if it were analyzed by a Pareto efficient outcome, would result in the least total value.

Interestingly, one of the negotiating triads ended up without an agreement, which was by far the worst possible outcome for all three negotiators. This is a clear indication that even the best student negotiators in their pursuit of value maximization can get carried away by their emotions and leave the entire value potential of the negotiation completely untapped.

Energy Turnaround

Authors: **Johannes Grothe, Alexander Ruhland, Manuel Schebel** under the supervision of **Remigiusz Smolinski**

Number of parties:	Preparation time:	Negotiation time:	Complexity level:
3	**30** minutes	**45-60** minutes	**high**

Pedagogical focus

information exchange, understanding mutual interests, relationship building in multilateral negotiation, coalition building, cooperation, value creation and value claiming strategies in multilateral negotiations, ethics in business negotiations, situational conflicts between individual interest and group interests, trust creation, objective criteria, fairness, multiparty negotiation

Short description

Energy Turnaround is a negotiation role simulation for three parties representing three energy providers in Iceland. In response to a governmental call to promote a nationwide clean energy program, they have been asked to meet and discuss various options for their participation. However, each company has different financial resources and strategic motivations that will influence what kind of deal that want to achieve. Moreover, some of the CEOs have some personal issues that may influence the negotiation as well.

General Instructions

"Today, the government of Iceland is pleased to announce that it has set itself a very ambitious goal. Through the initiation of the Energy Turnaround Program, we are taking the first step toward the goal of generating 100% of our energy exclusively from renewable sources. Please join us in supporting this noble and ambitious effort."

S. Trebies, Government Spokesperson

Through its Energy Turnaround Program (ETP), Iceland has a chance to become the first country in the world producing its energy solely from clean and renewable sources. As part of this program, the representatives of Iceland's three major energy companies, which are the exclusive energy producers within their regionally separate distribution networks (Xaver Power, representing Iceland's northwest region, Xynthia Power, its southern region and Kyrill Power, its eastern region) have been invited to a meeting to discuss and agree on their interest in contributing to this goal. Below are the respective company profiles:

	Xaver Power	Kyrill Power	Xynthia Power
Employees	Ca. 5,000	Ca. 1,000	Ca. 1,500
Revenue	5,000 Mio	700-800 Mio	2,000 Mio
Profitability	High positive	Low negative	Low positive

Table 38. The profiles of the Icelandic energy companies

Specifically, since the ETP will be primarily a government-coordinated project, it is anticipated that during the meeting the companies will be asked to discuss their investment interest in **one** of three project options. Table below includes the cumulative investment range needed for each option.

Project	Investment needed
Construction of a **Geothermal Plant**	100-200 Mio
Construction of a **Geothermal Plant** and **Wind Farms**	200-500 Mio
Construction of a **Geothermal Plant**, **Wind Farms** and **Solar Power Plants**	500-1,000 Mio

Table 39. Possible projects and the investments needed

Since the government has already completed much research and made unchangeable commitments to move this program forward, these three options are not flexible. This means other combinations or the construction of Solar Power Plants or Wind Farms alone are not possible. Depending on the investment sum that will be raised, only one of the given projects can be completed. That means if the cumulative investment among the three parties is below 100 million, then no project can be started. Moreover, because the government is trying to encourage the entire nation to support this ambitious project, it will provide incentivizing subsidies only if all three companies invest. However, in the same spirit, the government also wants to avoid that the whole Energy Turnaround Program is completely controlled by just one company. Therefore, no companies will be allowed to complete an option on its own. It must be in at least a two company coalition. Lastly, each company has to contribute **at least 15%** of the total investment budget to benefit from the subsidies.

In preparation for this meeting, the government analysts have determined that all projects can be operated for ten years before they completely depreciate. They have also developed estimates of the return on investment (ROI) for each of the respective project options and how they will subsidize the companies' participation in them. These are provided in the table below.

Project	ROI p.a.	Subsidies p.a.
Geothermal Plant	20%	0
Geothermal Plant and Wind Farms	10%	10 Mio.
Geothermal Plant, Wind Farms and Solar Power Plants	8.5%	20 Mio.

Table 40. Projects' estimated ROIs and the government subsidies

While the returns from the project depend on respective company investment contributions, the subsidies are fixed. **Each company eligible to receive a subsidy will receive a subsidy respective to that outlined in the table above. This subsidy will be paid for five consecutive years.**

The 45-minute meeting to discuss and agree on these issues is scheduled for later today.

Confidential Instructions
for the **CEO of Xaver Power**

You are Sam Graham, the CEO of Xaver Power, a publicly listed company that generates and distributes energy to the northern and western part of Iceland. You have been invited by the government to a meeting with the CEOs of the other two major energy providers in the country. For this meeting, you have been requested to discuss and agree on how Xaver Power will participate in the government's new Energy Turnaround Program (ETP).

In preparation for this meeting, you know that as the biggest and the most profitable energy company in Iceland, with the largest customer base, Xaver Power has both an impressive liquidity position and access to the financial resources necessary to finance even the largest of projects. Indeed, given the government's proposed options for participation in the ETP, you could easily finance up to 500 million krónur all alone. This would secure your company the highest possible subsidies which, according to your experts and based on your experience, are the only reliable figures presented by the government. In your core business, you continuously generate an ROI of 10% or higher and could easily come up with many alternative projects granting similar profitability. Therefore, although you are very interested in getting the subsidies, your plan is to minimize your investment in the project and let the other companies assume as much risk as possible.

You are excited about the negotiation and confident in your ability to conclude it successfully. Having led Xaver Power efficiently and profitably for more than a decade now, you have been one of the most successful managers in Iceland's energy industry. Indeed, you have been instrumental in managing its extensive and highly profitable use of low-cost nuclear energy. However, as you have recently confidentially announced your retirement to the board, you also have some personal issues to consider prior to this negotiation that concern your legacy and retirement finances.

First, despite Xaver's connection to nuclear energy, environmental issues are personally very important to you. With three children, you are particularly sensitive to your responsibility as an energy company to contribute to sustainability in natural resources for the benefit of future generations. As such, you take pride in maintaining an environmentally green image and have been actively engaged in multiple environmental activities.

Secondly, as the day of your retirement is approaching, you look forward to spending more time with your wife after several decades of intense business life. However, unrelated to your professional responsibilities, a personal investment that you made a few years ago with a large portion of your life's savings has failed. As a result, you are concerned that the comfortable retirement that you and your wife have planned is at risk. Although, you have officially shared this information only with a very few highly trusted people, including your wife and the board of directors of Xaver Power, during the last company Christmas party you had a few drinks too many and might have mentioned something about your situation to a group of younger managers. Unfortunately, you do not know exactly what you said and to whom.

With this second issue in mind, you know that the board of directors is planning to honor you for your achievements over the last ten years by working into the upcoming negotiation an outcome-based performance bonus that is also aligned with the interest of the company.

Specifically, since the amount of the investment you ultimately commit to will have a great impact on the company's profitability, the company has provided you with the following bonus payout structure. It clearly is incentivizing you to minimize investment into this project.

Investment (in million krónur)	Bonus (in million krónur)
0-100	5
101-250	3.8
251-330	2.5
331-450	1.7
>450	0

Table 41. The relationship between Xaver's investment and your bonus

This incentive opportunity is encouraging for you since it provides you an opportunity to make up for your recent personal investment disaster. This is especially encouraging because the board has entrusted you with a mandate to negotiate and decide in Xaver's best interests with complete autonomy.

However, to avoid any potential perceived impropriety among anyone outside the company, it is essential that no one else finds out about your personal situation. Indeed, it would be difficult to disassociate yourself from a misperception that a low investment from your side is connected with your personal benefit. Moreover, although you do not have to fear any accusations from people within your own organization, should your negotiation partners find out about your incentive, it might negatively affect the course of the upcoming negotiation. This would be bad for both the company and your bonus.

Moreover, as a CEO of the largest energy company in Iceland you also have a social responsibility to foster the development of renewable energy. Also, investing in power generation from renewable sources can generate nice reputation effects for Xaver Power in the long-term. Both of these are important to you.

Your board of directors trusts that you will effectively represent the company and make an optimal managerial decision. Therefore, despite needing the highest possible bonus, considering your difficult financial situation, try to **balance your bonus** goals with the corporation's interests: **minimizing your contribution while maximizing the subsidies**. These interests are equally important for you. However, although the government initiated the meeting, do not forget that it cannot force you to reach an agreement today.

Lastly, during your long and successful career, you have been involved in numerous memorable negotiations. In one of them, you were tricked by Mr. White, a representative of Xynthia Power. Specifically, he misused your trust for his own benefit. Therefore, you need to be very careful with him. This is your last big negotiation, and this time more than ever before, your performance will be crucial for the future of Xaver Power and yours.

Confidential Instructions
for the **CEO of Kyrill Power**

You are Pamela Martha Ranger, the CEO of Kyrill Power. Kyrill Power is the energy provider in eastern Iceland. In addition to power, the company also supplies the region with water and gas. Compared to Xaver Power, Kyrill has a much smaller distribution area, fewer employees and much lower financial resources. Moreover, unlike Xaver Power, Kyrill Power is partly owned by the municipality in which it is headquartered. Therefore, its local authorities have a considerable impact on the company's business decisions. The rest of its shareholders are widely diversified, including mainly foreign financial investors and energy companies from other countries. Although these smaller shareholders have relatively little influence on Kyrill Power's business decisions, the municipality requires heavy investments in sustainable and green energy.

Toward this goal and despite its limited investment budget, over the last five years, Kyrill has invested 150 million krónur in converting its power generation to what was perceived to be a more efficient and eco-friendly biogas technology. Unfortunately, during the early part of this conversion process it became clear to company experts that due to technological problems, the anticipated efficiencies this technology promised would not be achieved. Indeed, the extent of this problem was so grave that they predicted production would not even cover operating costs. They recommended stopping the conversion process and replacing with an alternative technology.

Despite this, the former CEO of Kyrill Power, Mr. Greenhorn, ignored this advice, completed the project anyway and whitewashed the issue by presenting it as a central element of the company's eco-friendly public image campaign.

However, shortly thereafter an internal audit discovered and disclosed these facts. As a result, Mr. Greenhorn was asked to resign from his post. In addition, a source within the company leaked the details of the audit to the local paper, the Eastern Iceland Daily Mirror, which wrote a scathing and critical article about the whole affair. They described Kyrill Power as pseudo-green and half-hearted in their alleged pursuit of sustainability and that the biogas project was only an attempt to improve Kyrill's deteriorating image.

Even though many people in Eastern Iceland believe that the Eastern Iceland Daily Mirror has a reputation for tabloid journalism, the company's board knew that the credibility of Kyrill Power was seriously damaged and that this damage needed to be quickly repaired. This was the main reason why it engaged you five months ago.

This is the first CEO position in your career. You are highly ambitious and very committed to your job. Known to many as an "Eco-Leader," you are personally dedicated to raising the environmental standards in the energy industry. Consistent with this dedication, for this new role you have communicated a clear growth strategy that is strongly focused on sustainable green energy.

Prior to this engagement, you have worked for several environmental organizations as a senior project manager and have built excellent skills in managing strategic energy projects. As a result, the municipality has high expectations of you including that you will introduce and drive the necessary changes to restore Kyrill's reputation. However, you are aware that you also face some criticism from within the company due to your lack of specific leadership experience in the energy industry. Indeed, there are rumors that you were not hired due to your knowledge and experience but because of your green image reputation. Therefore, you are eager to convince these skeptics.

In this regard, your specific mission is to transform Kyrill Power into an innovative energy company focusing only on renewable energy. However, this will be a tough challenge since making this transition will require enormous investments. Indeed, it is running at a sustained operating loss and because the company currently can barely cover its current liabilities it needs to borrow more to stay liquid. The following table includes a selection of Kyrill's financial data and key performance indicators:

	Equity Ratio[28]	Cash Ratio[29]	Acid Test Ratio[30]	Revenue	Profit
Last Year	9.90%	60%	125%	830 Mio	-2 Mio
Current Year (expected)	4.90%	25%	101%	740 Mio	-13 Mio

Table 42. Kyrill's financial date and KPIs

Lastly, the majority of cash flows that the company is generating are based on traditional carbon-based energy resources like coal and gas. Thus, achieving profitability with sustainable energy will also require very high investments to transition away from the very production infrastructure on which it currently depends, very risky endeavor.

---

[28] The equity ratio measures the proportion of the total assets that are financed by stockholders, as opposed to creditors. A low equity ratio produces good results for stockholders as long as the company earns a rate of return on assets that is greater than the interest rate paid to creditors. Source: https://en.wikipedia.org/wiki/Equity_ratio

[29] The cash ratio is the proportion of a company's total cash and cash equivalents to its current liabilities. It measures a company's ability to repay its short-term debt. Source: http://www.investopedia.com/terms/c/cash-ratio.asp.

[30] The acid-test ratio shows whether a firm has sufficient short-term assets to cover its immediate liabilities. An acid-test ratio of less than 1 indicates that the liquid assets are insufficient to pay the current liabilities. Source: http://www.investopedia.com/terms/a/acidtest.asp.

However, if you are going to accomplish this, you know that the only chance will be through a joint project with one or two other big power producers in the country. That is why you see the upcoming Energy Turnaround Program (ETP) to which you have been invited with the other two major energy producers as a particularly exciting opportunity. Indeed, you speculate that if Xynthia Power and Xaver Power were also to decide to invest in green energy, it could lead to a strong coalition with significant synergy effects. By entering into a strong partnership with other providers, Kyrill could also gain a significantly better credit standing at the banks, which it needs since it has lately been increasingly more difficult to obtain needed credit. In fact, you happen to know that others share this problem.

In preparation for this meeting, as it is most likely to generate the largest reputational effects for Kyrill Power, your goal is to persuade the other parties to agree on committing to the **largest investment project** proposed by the government. However, your contribution, if any, has to be limited to a **maximum 100 million krónur**.

If all parties agree to finance the project, it will boost the bank's confidence in Kyrill's credit standing to such a degree that it will extend to you a much-needed new credit line. In such a case your contribution could then be **increased to 150 million krónur**. Remember, that in your current financial situation you need to **restrict your contribution to the absolute minimum** and make your investment **as profitable as possible**.

However, this may not be easy. You are relatively new in your position and you do not know the other parties that well. You have heard that Xaver Power's CEO, Mr. Graham, is very well known as an experienced leader who enjoys taking responsibility and ownership. He also has a moderate environmentally friendly image and is interested in driving sustainable growth through renewable energy.

You actually have met Walter White from Xynthia Power. He seems to be a very analytical and pragmatic manager. However, your impression is that he is more interested in profitability and risk prevention than sustainable energy. Moreover, after you came into your CEO role, the relationship between Kyrill and Xynthia Power slightly deteriorated due to your response to an offer they made. Specifically, two months ago, they made a financially interesting offer to buy your existing rights to build a dam in an area of your distribution territory. However, because the area is rich in rivers and lakes, you rejected the offer and responded publicly that Kyrill does not support serious interventions in nature. However, despite your strong position against the dam, a re-launch of negotiations with Xynthia Power on this subject may be helpful for the energy turnaround negotiation.

In summary, despite your financial situation and limited budget for this meeting, try to get **all parties** to agree to the **largest investment project, minimizing your contribution** to it and making it **as profitable as** possible for Kyrill Power. Your Board of Directors expects you to reach an agreement that provides **the highest government subsidies possible**. It is critical for the company's survival. Although the government initiated the meeting, it cannot force you to reach an agreement today. However, not reaching an agreement could cost you your job.

Confidential Instructions
for the **CEO of Xynthia Power**

You are Walter White, the CEO of mid-sized Xynthia Power, which generates and distributes energy to all households in southern Iceland. You are well known in the industry since you have been managing Xynthia Power for several years now. You have been invited by the government of Iceland to a meeting with the CEOs of the other two major energy providers in the country. You were requested by the Government to discuss and agree with them on the energy sector's contribution to the Energy Turnaround Program.

Established in 1912, Xynthia Power has a long tradition of serving customers living in the southern regions of Iceland. Moreover, despite having witnessed many economic changes in the energy industry, it has managed to remain the only large energy provider that is still majority privately owned. This majority share is held by the powerful and very influential Quendt family. The remaining shares are owned by small local investors and an association of regional municipalities.

Hence, the company has always represented the interests of the local region, its inhabitants and taxpayers. As a consequence, the company is focused on long-term stable and sustainable growth instead of short-term share price maximizing. This philosophy is also embedded in the company's major investment decisions, which are carefully analyzed and approved by the Quendt family and the supervisory board. As such, this group is keenly aware of the importance of the Energy Turnaround Program for the future of Xynthia Power and its business philosophy. Thus, they have already approved an investment of **up to 200 million krónur**. However, a commitment to this budget strongly depends on the behavior of the other two large providers and their willingness to invest in a way that Xynthia Power plays only a supporting investor role. Xynthia will not be the main investor in the project.

The investment decision has been analyzed in depth by both your local government experts and your strategy and finance departments. According to their predictions, the total benefits that can be expected from your investment depends primarily on the amount of money invested in the Energy Turnaround Program. However, you know that Xynthia Power cannot afford to invest such a large amount of money into a project that proves unsuccessful. Thus, you will not invest at all in a project this big unless the risks can be shared.

Another issue is your rather strained relationship with Mr. Graham from Xaver Power. In the last three years, you have conducted several similar negotiations with Mr. Graham. However, following the last one you heard that Mr. Graham felt very upset with the outcome. You found this surprising since you felt all was negotiated in a fair manner with you simply looking for the optimal outcome for your company. Despite how he may feel, you would be happy to improve your relationship with Mr. Graham again.

Lastly, there is also an open issue with Kyrill Power. Their distribution territory includes an area with rivers and lakes which is considered suitable for building a dam. This would be a very interesting project for Xynthia Power since your company has the skills necessary to complete it. However, since you do not have the building rights to complete such a project, you would need to acquire them from Kyrill Power. Though you always wondered why Kyrill did not build the dam themselves, their last CEO, Mr. Greenhorn, who also promoted a close business relationship between Kyrill and Xynthia was willing to negotiate selling these rights to Xynthia. Unfortunately, Mr. Greenhorn was fired five months ago due to a scandal. His successor, Pamela Martha Ranger, as a strict eco-leader, very publically abandoned the offer for the reason that a dam would cause environmental damage. However, since this project still remains a high priority for Xynthia Power, you may use the energy turnaround meeting to re-launch the negotiations for building rights of the dam. Your finance department assessed the value of these building rights at 80 million krónur.

Your objective is now to agree on the most suitable solution for your company. Therefore, weighing **initial investment**, **expected returns** and **possible subsidies**, take all parameters into account and negotiate the best deal for your company. Remember, although the government initiated the meeting, it cannot force you to reach an agreement today.

Confidential Instructions
for the **CEO of Kyrill Power**

To be distributed 10 minutes after the start of the negotiation

Sender: **Betty Smith (Assistant to Pamela Martha Ranger)**

Hi Pamela,

Tim, the new department manager who came from Xaver Power last month, told me that he has heard that Sam Graham is going to retire soon and has even already bought a beach house on an island. Tim seems to be sure about this. Is that helpful?

Good luck!

Betty.

Debriefing

Energy Turnaround is a three-party scoreable negotiation role-play written for The Negotiation Challenge 2014 that took place in Reykjavik, Iceland. It was used during the opening round at Reykjavik University. It is suitable for practicing value creation and value claiming skills in a multilateral setting. Moreover, it provides an opportunity to address the relevance of ethics within business negotiations, the importance of trust in social cooperation, and in addressing situational conflicts between individual interest and group interests.

The negotiation takes place between three CEOs of fictitious Icelandic energy producers. They are Sam Graham, the CEO of Xaver Power, Martha Ranger, the CEO of Kyrill Power and Walter White, the CEO of Xynthia Power. Their main objective is to agree on a joint investment for a government-sponsored green energy project including their respective company's contribution to it. To incentivize their participation, the government has promised project size-dependent subsidies. The general instructions, which are the same and distributed to all parties, include the necessary investment for each project type, profitability and attributable government subsidies. *Table 43* below summarizes them.

Projects	Investment needed	ROI p.a.	Subsidies p.a.
Geothermal Plant	100-200 million	20%	0
Geothermal Plant and Wind Farms	200-500 million	10%	10 Mio.
Geothermal Plant, Wind Farms and Solar Power Plants	500-1,000 million	8.5%	20 Mio.

Table 43. Characteristics of the project options proposed by the government

290

The confidential instructions indicate the maximum investment each party is willing to contribute to the Energy Turnaround Program:

- Xaver Power – up to 500 million,
- Kyrill Power – 100 million and if all parties agree to finance the project, it can be increased to 150 million,
- Xynthia Power – up to 200 million as a supporting investor only but not a main investor

Each of the parties knows their own maximum contribution but does not know the potential contribution of his/her negotiation partners.

The energy companies collectively have enough resources to commit even to the largest project, which due to the highest government subsidies, is clearly the most beneficial for all of them and the Energy Turnaround Program. However, their strategic objective to minimize their contribution might lead to a situation in which the sum of their committed resources is sufficient only for one of the smaller projects. This creates a tension between the necessity to collect the resources needed to create value for all and the desire for each party to minimize their individual contributions.

The structure of this roleplay combines value creation, which occurs through project selection based on varying levels of returns and subsidies and value claiming, which occurs through minimizing contributions.

This simulation also addresses ethical behavior, an important aspect of negotiation ethics. Ethical behavior means acting in accordance with socially acceptable rules or standards for conduct fitting a situation (the rules of the game). In contrast to conduct governed by laws (e.g., antitrust laws, cartel laws), some situations are not subject to clear legal governance. In these situations, what is regarded as ethically correct and what is not, often remains a matter of subjective judgment. As such, ethics in negotiations can be a sensitive topic since it can be a factor that influences both negotiation tactics and conduct.

In an effort to address this ambiguity, many authors have addressed the subject. Key among these are the concepts introduced by Fisher, Ury, and Patton in their book *Getting to Yes: Negotiating Agreement Without Giving In in 1981*. These authors propose that a negotiator should do the right thing, not because of the potential for better negotiation results, (even though it often results in better outcomes), but simply because the other party deserves to be treated with respect. In this regard, an ethical negotiation can be considered generally successful when an outcome is found that satisfies all parties, is defendable and sustainable according to an informed and neutral third party, and can be justified by universal principles.

Yet, for many negotiators, ethical behavior during a negotiation is considered dangerous. They feel that such behavior weakens their negotiation power as it, among other perceived disadvantages, encourages unnecessary information disclosure as part of the trust development process. This runs contrary to the adversarial stance common in traditional positional bargaining. Indeed, one often sees evidence of this lingering belief in the hard-tactic negotiations that continue to be displayed in the business world today. Unfortunately, when this is the case, the opportunity for mutual benefit is often lost due to the allure of self-gain.

This simulation introduces this subject through various sub-issues in the narrative of the roleplay. First, the personal objectives of the CEOs are such that they could influence the negotiation in a way that causes an ethical dilemma for the participants. This is especially the case for the negotiators representing the CEO of Xaver Power in which the role requires his personal, corporate and social objectives to be juggled in such a way that can be perceived to be controversial. Furthermore, Kyrill negotiators are provided with confidential information that, if used, could constitute a turning point in the negotiation. Since Kyrill Power's CEO is under pressure to reach an agreement, the negotiators might be tempted to use this information. Secondly, Xynthia Power's CEOs may use this negotiation to benefit from another business opportunity with Kyrill Power, who in turn may use the approach from Xynthia Power to its own advantage during the negotiation.

As it is inextricably intertwined with ethics, this roleplay also addresses the importance of trust by including a previous issue that negatively affected the relationship between Mr. Graham and Mr. White. Because of this, Mr. Graham feels that he was treated unfairly by Mr. White. As a result, he currently retains a negative and restrained attitude towards him. This tense relationship has the potential to complicate the negotiations significantly.

With these issues in the background, negotiators should remain focused on the dual importance of ethics and trust and how it can be leveraged as the basis for value creation. Acting ethically and being trustworthy should not be seen as a luxury but rather as a reasonable investment into future relationships. One method to achieve this is to maintain a value-based consistency in words and actions as well as sending positive signals on commitment to these values. It is essential to give the other side a good feeling about one's ability to fulfill legitimate trust expectations.

Now, returning to the issue of possible outcomes of the negotiation, *Table 44* discusses various possibilities with a brief description of a potential negotiation dynamic for each. Most frequently observed are commitments made for the largest and the mid-sized projects since they return greater benefits. Committing to a total investment of higher than 500 million is rather unlikely since it will only worsen the economics of the opportunity.

Performance evaluation for this roleplay is based on its substantive outcome. This occurs by using a common valuation of all resources so that preferences can be quantified. Thus, the final outcome is indicated by the parties' success in driving their returns of investment (ROIs). In calculating ROIs, we considered the cumulative combined returns of the project selected given the amount invested, five years of corresponding government subsidies, and additional value from buying/selling the building rights to a dam. For Xaver, negotiators we also need to combine the ROI of the project with their personal bonus. To do so, we calculated z-scores for both, added them together and composed a ranking based on their sum.

For the benefit of reference, the best substantive outcome obtained by a negotiator that represented Xaver Power during The Negotiation Challenge 2014 was a contribution of 60 million to the mid-sized project combined with a personal bonus of 5 million. Including subsidies, this result granted an ROI of 83%. On average, however, Xaver Power negotiators contributed with 205 million, achieved an ROI of 32%, and an average bonus of 3.8 million.

The best substantive outcome obtained by a negotiator that represented Kyrill Power was a contribution of 80 million to the largest project, which granted an ROI of 156% including the subsidies and the 75 million revenues from selling the building rights of the dam. On average, however, Xaver Power negotiators contributed with 101 million and achieved an ROI of 93%.

The best substantive outcome obtained by a negotiator that represented Xynthia Power was a contribution of 40 million to the mid-sized project, which granted an ROI of 306% including the subsidies and purchasing the building rights worth 80 million for only 7.5 million. On average, however, Xaver Power negotiators contributed with 153 million and achieved an ROI of 64%.

All negotiating teams managed to reach an agreement.

Outcome	Description	Negotiation dynamic
Maximum investment (850k million)	Each party fully invests the budget and Kyrill receives the extended credit line. All three companies receive the benefits and contribute to sustainable energy production for future generations.	The parties are completely convinced about the energy turnaround. They strive to receive the expected returns and the highest subsidy level. They trust each other and are focused on sustainability for future generations. The CEO of Xaver gives up his personal benefits or gives in to the pressure of the others.
High investment – construction of a wind farm, a hydroelectric facility and a solar power plant	All parties invest in the energy turnaround. Kyrill and Xynthia invest a significant part of their budget and Xaver offers the rest. All parties benefit from the most lucrative project.	Kyrill gets its credit line extended. Xaver can be convinced to invest a considerable amount, preferring cooperation instead of personal interests. Benefit from the cooperation helps the parties achieve their secondary objectives (Xynthia). All parties receive the highest level of subsidy.
Medium investment – construction of a wind farm and a hydroelectric facility	All parties commit a certain investment budget, Kyrill might have to invest the maximum. Some mutual benefits and the lowest subsidy level can be achieved.	At least two parties reach an agreement. They strive to reach a certain level of return and subsidy. They balance their costs and benefits and their personal interests. Xynthia and Xaver want to benefit from returns and subsidies, but do not want to invest too much.
Small investment – construction of a wind farm	Each party only invests a small part of their budgets. Even more likely, only two parties agree to an investment. No mutual benefits.	Opportunity costs or personal interests are higher than the benefits of the energy turnaround to some parties. Trust basis might not be sufficient.
No investment	Parties do not reach an agreement.	Opportunity costs too high for the three companies. Mistrust and pursuit of personal interests and goals. Mr. Graham aspires to receive the highest possible gratuity. Kyrill does not find an investment partner.

Table 44. Possible outcomes of Energy Turnaround

Connor Paradise

Authors: **Heiko Hinrichs, Dominik Kanbach, Benjamin Müller, Timon Überschär**
under the supervision of **Remigiusz Smolinski**

Number of parties:	Preparation time:	Negotiation time:	Complexity level:
3	**30** minutes	**45-60** minutes	**high**

Pedagogical focus

information exchange, understanding mutual interests, relationship building in multilateral negotiation, coalition building, cooperation, value creation and value claiming strategies in multilateral negotiations, trust creation, objective criteria, fairness, multiparty negotiation

Short description

Connor Paradise is a multi-party negotiation simulation between three relatively isolated tribes living on a fictitious Mediterranean island. Due to an unforeseen and highly destructive tsunami, their previously prosperous and tranquil lives have been upended causing widespread social demand for the construction of various infrastructure projects to protect them better in the future. However, since their respective resources are limited, only through cooperation and combining their resources can they successfully complete these projects. However, with little previous contact between them, mistrust abounds. The negotiators must therefore skillfully navigate their self-interests and the need for cooperation in an effort to gain the best outcome for their respective tribe.

General Instructions

Three tribes, A, B and C, live together on the wonderful island of Connor Paradise. The island is located in the Mediterranean Sea and its 300 inhabitants are called the Connors. 45% of the Connors belong to tribe C that lives in the south, 35% belong to tribe B that inhabits the north and the remaining 20% belong to tribe A which populates the eastern part of Connor Paradise.

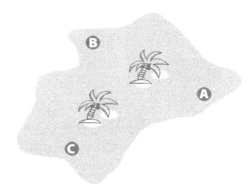

Life is very good and peaceful on the island. Moreover, because there is an abundance of food due to the ideal agricultural climate, the three Connor tribes live rather independently of each other. Because of this, there has been only very limited interaction between the three tribes over the past decades. The members of all tribes love their island and cannot imagine leaving it under any circumstances.

However, last week a very powerful storm, the worst in history, ravaged the island and severely damaged the infrastructure of every tribe. With so many houses destroyed and much of their crops lost, all are distraught and worried about their future. They fear the next storm and urgently demand significant improvements to the island's infrastructure, especially relating to disaster warning and response. These demands have been collected by the leaders of all three tribes and summarily categorized into the following eight critical projects:

1. Observation point – to watch out for storms and tsunamis
2. Wave breaker – to protect the coast of Connor Paradise
3. Astronomical observatory – to improve their weather forecasting knowledge
4. Temple – to worship the god Connor
5. Storm shelter – to establish a refuge for any future storms
6. Repair and improve homes – to repair the storm damage
7. Warehouse – to store food
8. Improve crop yield – to increase agricultural productivity

The construction of each project requires ten units of mutually distinct resources. That is, the resources needed for any particular project cannot be substituted by resources from other projects.

Project	Resource	Amount needed
Observation point	Wood	10
Wave breaker	Stones	10
Astronomical observatory	Lenses	10
Temple	Gold	10
Shelter	Steel	10
Repair and improve homes	Clay	10
Warehouse	Insulation	10
Improve crop yield	Fertilizer	10

Table 45. Resources necessary to construct the critical projects

The leaders of each tribe have counted their remaining resources after the storm. After doing so, each has realized that not enough resources exist to construct any of these projects independently. Therefore, they know that they need to find a way to consolidate their resources with the other tribes. Complicating matters is that each of the tribes has differing capacities, expectations and requirements concerning the projects. Moreover, due to the lack of resources, each project can be constructed only once among the three tribes. Therefore, they need to agree on the specific distribution of responsibility among them to successfully complete as many projects as possible.

Although they have agreed to share resources, only one tribe can be responsible for each respective project's construction. Indeed, because of the control that this responsibility gives (i.e., locating the project on their territory, customizing the project to their own needs, etc.), being responsible for constructing a project brings the highest payoff. As such, the goal of every leader is to maximize their tribe's benefits (score) by gaining collective agreement to construct as many projects as possible. However, in the event that a tribe does not gain agreement to construct a project, other factors need to be considered in the negotiation. These include issues such as whether a project constructed by another tribe can have beneficial or detrimental effects on them.[31]

The overview below illustrates the scores the tribes can achieve depending on the agreement reached for each project:

- **10 points** for the tribe that gains agreement from the others to construct a project
- **5 points** for the tribe that benefits from the construction of a project by another tribe
- **0 points** for the tribe in which the construction of a project by another yields no benefit or penalty.
- **-5 points** for the tribe that suffers from the project being constructed by another tribe

---

[31] More details concerning the benefits your tribe can generate depending on which tribe ultimately completes which project can be found in the confidential instructions.

Lastly, it is possible that the three tribes do not reach an agreement or have insufficient resources to construct every project. If for any reason a particular project cannot be constructed, then all three tribes receive a score of **-3 points** for that project. The resources left unused cannot be used for other projects and are in effect worthless.

In the upcoming meeting, the tribe leaders come together to discuss the sharing of resources and to define which tribe will construct which project. The goal of each leader is to maximize the score for their tribe.

Confidential Instructions
for **Tribe A**

You are the elected leader of tribe A. Your tribe lives in the eastern part of Connor Paradise and is known for its delicious seafood specialties. The people in your tribe are very religious. They devoutly worship the god Connor and follow his teachings called Connorism. One of the most important religious norms that your tribe follows is living close to nature and learning to recognize its signs. Moreover, your tribe has intense pride in its knowledge of astronomy.

You, the elders' council and all members of your tribe, have discussed the eight projects in great detail and have developed a detailed perspective for each. Naturally, you want to be responsible to construct as many of the eight projects as possible in order to guarantee that your perspectives are incorporated. Here is the summary of your perspectives for each project:

Observation point – Although the last storm was not accompanied by a tsunami, Connor Paradise has been affected by them in the past. Therefore, you would like to be prepared before the next tsunami hits the island. Since the biggest tsunamis typically come from the east, your tribe finds it very important that it is the one to construct this observation point. An observation point constructed by tribe B would undoubtedly be bad since your tribe believes that they do not have the necessary knowledge and experience to identify tsunamis correctly. At worst, this could lead to catastrophe for all and at best, lead to them raising numerous irritating false alarms. Although tribe C is more reliable, they live on the south side of the island and could only observe a part of your coast.

Wave breaker – You agree that a wave breaker system would be very useful for your island, especially if it is constructed by your tribe and protects your houses. Since tribe B is planning a wave breaker protecting only their own territory, it is not beneficial for you if they build it. However, as tribe C offered to build a wave breaker, which would also protect some of your houses, you would partially benefit from them constructing it.

Astronomical observatory – You believe that an astronomical observatory would help forecast upcoming changes in weather conditions by analyzing the position and movement of major astronomical bodies. You also know that your tribe has the necessary knowledge and experience to construct it. Although you suspect that astronomy is not the top priority for tribe B at the moment, you know that some of its members have dealt with it in the past. As far as you know, tribe C has shown very little interest in astronomy.

Temple – As religion is a very important part of your culture, you believe that a temple would help improve the spiritual connection with the god Connor, which could decrease the frequency of natural disasters. You have heard that tribe B is also religious and practices a similar form of Connorism. You have no information whether tribe C shares your religious beliefs and whether they would even be interested in building a temple.

Shelter – Due to the disasters caused by last week's storm, it is imperative to build a shelter for the entire population of Connor Paradise as a refuge for any future events. As you expect the other tribes to build a shelter near their own territory, you would prefer to build it yourselves. Indeed, not constructing this project yourself will most likely not bring you any benefits.

Repair and improve homes – Housing is fundamental to the future wealth and happiness of each tribe. Your tribe has solid technical and construction skills, and therefore, you strongly prefer and expect to gain agreement from the other tribes to construct this project. You believe that only your tribe can guarantee that the houses are repaired and improved properly. You fear that if tribe C is assigned to this project, they might use it to improve only their own housing situation. You do not see this risk with tribe B, but at the same time, you do not expect to benefit from the project in that case either.

Warehouse – Your tribe currently has sufficient food supplies. However, this is only the case because each member of your tribe routinely fasts for religious reasons and thus consumes less food. Despite this, you believe that you need to be better prepared for possible future storms by ensuring there is enough food when needed. Ideally, you would like your tribe to build and control the warehouse. Indeed, because you have no trading history with the other tribes, you are unsure that you can trust them with your own food supplies. However, tribe B has unofficially promised that, should they construct the project, they would share all food supplies gathered. Letting tribe C construct the warehouse would probably lead to it being located close to your territory. This would allow you to access your food supplies quickly.

Improve crop yield – You believe that to replenish the lost food supplies from the storm and to prepare for future population growth, you urgently need to improve crop yield. Your tribe's elders have pointed out that letting the other tribes construct this project would not generate any additional benefits for your tribe.

Your strategic preferences concerning the projects are summarized in the scoring table below. Most likely, they are not known to the other two tribes' leaders. Because you are not certain how compatible your preferences are with the preferences of the other tribes, you are prepared for a long and intensive negotiation. Regardless of what is discussed or agreed to during this negotiation, it **cannot change** your preferences described in the scoring table.

Project	Score of A if a project assigned to:		
	A	B	C
Observation point	10	-5	5
Wave breaker	10	0	5
Astronomical observatory	10	5	0
Temple	10	5	0
Shelter	10	0	0
Repair and improve homes	10	0	-5
Warehouse	10	5	5
Improve crop yield	10	0	0

Table 46. Strategic preferences of Tribe A

An overview of your resources is illustrated in the table below.

Project	Resource	Amount owned
Observation point	Wood	6
Wave breaker	Stones	2
Astronomical observatory	Lenses	6
Temple	Gold	6
Shelter	Steel	2
Repair and improve homes	Clay	1
Warehouse	Insulation	0
Improve crop yield	Fertilizer	2

Table 47. Resources available to Tribe A

The resources not used in any particular project cannot be used for completing other projects.

You are about to meet the leaders of tribes B and C. It is clear to you that the damage from the storm has left you with insufficient resources to construct any of these projects alone. Thus, you need to consolidate your resources with the other tribes, verify which projects can be constructed and jointly decide which tribe is best positioned to construct each project.

Therefore, your objectives and evaluation criteria for the upcoming negotiation are:

- **Discover which projects can be constructed** based on the amount of resources committed by all tribe leaders.
- For each project, **negotiate which tribe will construct it.** Remember, each project can be constructed by only one tribe.
- Your performance will be measured **only by the scores** in the scoring table above.
- Remember, your only objective for the upcoming negotiation is to negotiate **the best possible outcome** (the highest possible score) **for your tribe.**

Good luck!

Confidential Instructions
for **Tribe B**

You are the elected leader of tribe B. Your tribe lives in the northern part of Connor Paradise and is known for your outstanding technical skills. The people in your tribe are great logical thinkers and excellent construction workers.

You, the elders' council and all members of your tribe, have discussed the eight projects in great detail and have developed a detailed perspective for each. Naturally, you want to be responsible for constructing as many of the eight projects as possible in order to guarantee that these perspectives are incorporated. Here is the summary of perspectives for each project:

Observation point – Although the last storm was not accompanied by a tsunami, Connor Paradise has been affected by them in the past. Therefore, you would like to be prepared before the next tsunami hits the island. Consequently, your tribe has demanded the construction of an observation point. Although they believe that your tribe's tsunami experts could probably do it much better, they acknowledge that tribe C is also capable of identifying tsunamis correctly. Due to the island's topography, however, an observation point constructed by tribe A would not result in any benefits for you.

Wave breaker – You agree that a wave breaker system would be very useful for your island, especially if it is constructed by your tribe and protects your houses. Since your tribe is located in the northern part of Connor Paradise, it is not beneficial for you if tribe A or C builds it.

Astronomical observatory – An astronomical observatory would help forecast upcoming changes in weather conditions by analyzing the position and movement of astronomical bodies. You feel that your tribe has sufficient knowledge and experience to construct this project. The elders remember an old story that tribe A, based on their astronomical observation, once made a disastrous weather forecast and caused severe panic on the island. Although tribe A still regard themselves as astronomy experts, your tribe and tribe C no longer believe that tribe A is competent in astronomy. As far as you know, tribe C has shown very little interest in astronomy.

Temple – As religion is an important part of your culture, you believe that a temple would help improve the spiritual connection with the god Connor and decrease the frequency of natural disasters. You have heard that tribe A is also religious and practices a similar form of Connorism. Tribe C, however, worships Connor in a completely different way, which Connor might not enjoy. Instead of pleasing Connor, letting tribe C build the temple may actually anger Connor. This you fear.

Shelter – Due to the disasters caused by last week's storm, it is imperative to build a shelter for the whole population of Connor Paradise so that all can find refuge during such disasters in the future. Since you expect that tribe A would build a shelter just for themselves, you would not benefit from it if they construct the project. The leader of tribe C has informed you that they are thinking about sharing the shelter with you in case of an emergency. However, since it would take some time for your people to reach the tribe constructed shelter before a storm, the benefits from this would be smaller than were it to be your own construction.

Repair and improve homes – Housing is fundamental to the future wealth and happiness of each tribe. Your tribe has solid technical and construction skills, and therefore you strongly prefer and expect to gain agreement from the other tribes to construct this project. You believe that only your tribe can guarantee that the houses are repaired and improved properly. You fear that if tribe C is assigned to this project, they might use it to improve only their own housing situation. You do not see this risk with tribe A. Tribe A is very likely to help you repair and improve your homes quickly and efficiently.

Warehouse – Your tribe currently has sufficient food supplies. However, this is only the case because each member of your tribe routinely fasts for religious reasons and thus consumes less food. Despite this, you believe that you need to be better prepared for possible future storms by ensuring there is enough food when needed. Ideally, you would like your tribe to build and control the warehouse. Indeed, because you have no trading history with the other tribes, you are unsure that you can trust them with your own food supplies. However, tribe A has unofficially promised that, should they construct the project, they would share all food supplies gathered.

Improve crop yield – You believe that to replenish the lost food supplies from the storm and to prepare for future population growth, you urgently need to improve crop yield. Your tribe's elders have pointed out that letting the other tribes construct this project would not generate any additional benefits for your tribe.

Your strategic preferences concerning the projects are summarized in the scoring table below. Most likely, they are not known to the other two tribes' leaders. Because you are not certain how compatible your preferences are with the preferences of the other tribes, you are prepared for a long and intensive negotiation. Regardless of what is discussed or agreed on during this negotiation, it **cannot change** your preferences described in the scoring table.

Project	Score of B if a project assigned to:		
	A	B	C
Observation point	0	10	5
Wave breaker	0	10	0
Astronomical observatory	-5	10	0
Temple	5	10	-5
Shelter	0	10	5
Repair and improve homes	5	10	-5
Warehouse	5	10	0
Improve crop yield	0	10	0

Table 48. Strategic preferences of Tribe B

An overview of your resources is illustrated in the table below.

Project	Resource	Amount owned
Observation point	Wood	4
Wave breaker	Stones	6
Astronomical observatory	Lenses	2
Temple	Gold	5
Shelter	Steel	5
Repair and improve homes	Clay	4
Warehouse	Insulation	3
Improve crop yield	Fertilizer	3

Table 49. Resources available to Tribe B

The resources not used in any particular project cannot be used for completing other projects.

You are about to meet the leaders of tribes A and C. It is clear to you that the damage from the storm has left you with insufficient resources to construct any of these projects alone. Thus, you need to consolidate your resources with the other tribes, verify which projects can be constructed and jointly decide which tribe is best positioned to construct each project.

Therefore, your objectives and evaluation criteria for the upcoming negotiation are:

- **Discover which projects can be constructed** based on the amount of resources committed by all tribe leaders.
- For each project, **negotiate which tribe will construct it.** Remember, each project can be constructed by only one tribe.
- Your performance will be measured **only by the scores** in the scoring table above.
- Remember, your only objective for the upcoming negotiation is to negotiate **the best possible outcome** (the highest possible score) **for your tribe.**

Good luck!

Confidential Instructions
for **Tribe C**

You are the elected leader of tribe C. Your tribe lives in the southern part of Connor Paradise and is known for its excellent cuisine and high food consumption. The people in your tribe possess a profound knowledge of storing and preparing food. Many are excellent cooks who highly value the quality of the ingredients. Therefore, over the years, your tribe has developed a mastery of agriculture.

You, the elders' council and all members of your tribe, have discussed the eight projects in great detail and have developed a detailed perspective for each. Naturally, you want to be responsible for constructing as many of the eight projects as possible in order to guarantee that these perspectives are incorporated. Here is the summary of perspectives for each project:

Observation point – Although the last storm was not accompanied by a tsunami, Connor Paradise has been affected by them in the past. Therefore, you would like to be prepared before the next tsunami hits the island. Consequently, your tribe has demanded the construction of an observation point. An observation point constructed by tribe B would undoubtedly be bad since your tribe believes that they do not have the necessary knowledge and experience to identify tsunamis correctly. At worst, this could lead to catastrophe for all and at best, lead to them raising numerous irritating false alarms. Due to the island's topography, an observation point constructed by tribe A would not result in any benefits for you.

Wave breaker – You agree that a wave breaker system would be very useful for your island, especially if it is constructed by your tribe and protects your houses. As tribe A is planning a wave breaker protecting only their own territory, it is not beneficial for you if they build it. However, as tribe B offered to build a wave breaker, which would also protect some of your houses, you would partially benefit from it.

Astronomical observatory – An astronomical observatory would help forecast upcoming changes in the weather conditions by analyzing the position and movement of major astronomical bodies. You feel that your tribe has sufficient knowledge and experience to construct this project. Although you suspect that astronomy is not the top priority for tribe B at the moment, you know that some of its members have dealt with it in the past. Concerning tribe A, the elders remember an old story that they once made a disastrous astronomical-based weather forecast and caused severe panic on the island. Although tribe A still re-gard themselves as astronomy experts, this belief is not shared by your tribe or by tribe B.

Temple – As religion is an important part of your culture, you be-lieve that a temple would help improve the spiritual connection with the god Connor and decrease the frequency of natural disas-ters. You have no information whether tribes A and B share your religious beliefs and whether they would even be interested in building a temple.

Shelter – Due to the disasters caused by last week's storm, it is imperative to build a shelter for the whole population of Connor Paradise so that all can find refuge during such disasters in the fu-ture. Since you expect that tribe B would build a shelter just for themselves, you would not benefit from it if they construct it. You suspect that tribe A is still using an old and inefficient steel-making technology. Letting them construct the shelter could result in the waste of valuable resources and cause damage to the environment.

Repair and improve homes – Housing is fundamental to the future wealth and happiness of each tribe. Your tribe has solid technical and construction skills, and therefore you strongly prefer and expect to gain agreement from the other tribes to construct this project. You believe that only your tribe can guarantee that the houses are repaired and improved properly. Should this project get assigned to tribe A, they are very likely to help you repair and improve your homes quickly and efficiently. Although you do not see these benefits if tribe B constructs this project, you also do not expect any disadvantages either.

Warehouse – Your tribe currently has sufficient food supplies. However, this is only the case because each member of your tribe routinely fasts for religious reasons and thus consumes less food. Despite this, you believe you need to be better prepared for possible future storms by ensuring there is enough food when needed. Ideally, you would like your tribe to build and control the warehouse. Indeed, because you have no trading history with the other tribes, you are unsure that you can trust them with your own food supplies. Moreover, you are concerned that letting tribe B construct the warehouse would lead to it being located at the farthest end of the island from your tribe. This would increase the distance and time it would take you to access your food supplies.

Improve crop yield – You believe that to replenish the lost food supplies from the storm and to prepare for future population growth, you urgently need to improve crop yield. Your tribe's elders have pointed out that letting the other tribes construct this project would not generate any additional benefits for your tribe.

Your strategic preferences concerning the projects are summarized in the scoring table below. Most likely, they are not known to the other two tribes' leaders. Because you are not certain how compatible your preferences are with the preferences of the other tribes, you are prepared for a long and intensive negotiation. Regardless of what is discussed or agreed on during this negotiation, it cannot change your preferences described in the scoring table.

Project	Score of C if a project assigned to:		
	A	B	C
Observation point	0	-5	10
Wave breaker	0	5	10
Astronomical obser-vatory	-5	5	10
Temple	0	0	10
Shelter	-5	0	10
Repair and improve homes	5	0	10
Warehouse	0	-5	10
Improve crop yield	0	0	10

Table 50. Strategic preferences of Tribe C

An overview of your resources is illustrated in the table below.

Project	Resource	Amount owned
Observation point	Wood	1
Wave breaker	Stones	5
Astronomical observatory	Lenses	2
Temple	Gold	1
Shelter	Steel	4
Repair and improve homes	Clay	6
Warehouse	Insulation	7
Improve crop yield	Fertilizer	4

Table 51. Resources available to Tribe C

The resources not used in any particular project cannot be used for completing other projects.

You are about to meet the leaders of tribes A and B. It is clear to you that the damage from the storm has left you with insufficient resources to construct any of these projects alone. Thus, you need to consolidate your resources with the other tribes, verify which projects can be constructed and jointly decide which tribe is best positioned to construct each project.

- Therefore, your objectives and evaluation criteria for the upcoming negotiation are:
- **Discover which projects can be constructed** based on the amount of resources committed by all tribe leaders.
- For each project, **negotiate which tribe will construct it.** Remember, each project can be constructed by only one tribe.
- Your performance will be measured **only by the scores** in the scoring table above.
- Remember, your only objective for the upcoming negotiation is to negotiate the best **possible outcome** (the highest possible score) **for your tribe.**

Good luck!

Debriefing

Connor Paradise is an integrative three-party scoreable negotiation roleplay written for The Negotiation Challenge 2013 that took place in Athens, Greece. It was used during the opening round at ALBA Graduate Business School at the American College of Greece. It is suitable for practicing value creation and value claiming skills in a multilateral setting.

The negotiators represent three fictitious tribes (A, B and C) that are the sole inhabitants of the island. They were asked to negotiate the distribution of responsibility to construct eight critical infrastructure projects. These projects include:

1. Observation point – to watch out for storms and tsunamis
2. Wave breaker – to protect the coast of Connor Paradise
3. Astronomical observatory – to improve their weather forecasting knowledge
4. Temple – to worship the god Connor
5. Storm shelter – to establish a place of refuge during for any future storms
6. Repair and improve homes – to repair the storm damage
7. Warehouse – to store food
8. Improve crop yield – to increase the agricultural productivity

However, due to differences in preferences for each party, they place different valuations on the objects being negotiated. Understanding and exploiting these differences allow them a collective opportunity to create value. However, this will not be simple. Connor Paradise poses a series of challenges for the negotiators. First, as with all multiparty negotiations, an additional party significantly increases the complexity of the value engineering processes. For example, the negotiators need to develop enough trust between themselves to share very sensitive information concerning their preferences with two additional persons. This makes the identification of value-adding options much more complex and less efficient. This is particularly difficult due to the highly competitive context, which might draw the negotiators away from value creation and focus rather on value claiming. Making this mistake would produce suboptimal agreements and leave value unclaimed.

Each project will require ten units of specific resources for successful completion. The confidential instructions for each respective tribe disclose the resources that only they possess. They are summarized for all tribes in *Table 52*.

Project	Resource	A	B	C
Observation point	Wood	6	4	1
Wave breaker	Stones	2	6	5
Astronomical observatory	Lenses	6	2	2
Temple	Gold	6	5	1
Shelter	Steel	2	5	4
Repair and improve homes	Clay	1	4	6
Warehouse	Warehouse	0	3	7
Improve crop yield	Fertilizer	2	3	4

Table 52. Resources necessary to complete the projects and their distribution among the tribes.

A look at the table quickly reveals that all projects except the last one, improving crop yield, can be completed. Here, the tribes have only nine units of fertilizer in total, which is less than the required 10. In all other cases, they must commit nearly all of their resources to complete the construction projects successfully. None of the parties has sufficient resources to complete a project on its own. Thus, cooperation is necessary to create value for all tribes.

Although the resources are shared, each project can be constructed by only one tribe. Thus, each of the tribes has vested strategic interests in winning responsibility for constructing as many projects as possible since self-constructed projects have the highest benefit. Should a project be constructed by another tribe, the benefits will vary. These benefits are quantified by the following scoring system:

- **10 points** for the tribe that constructs a project
- **5 points** for the tribe that benefits from the construction of a project by another tribe
- **0 points** for the tribe in which the construction of a project by another yields no benefit.
- **-5 points** for the tribe that suffers from the project constructed by another tribe
- **-3 points** for all tribes, if a particular project cannot be constructed.

The confidential instructions for each negotiating party include the exact scores that it will receive depending on how the projects are distributed. *Table 53* below summarizes these for all three parties and allows us to determine the scores of all parties, given a particular project assignment.

Not surprisingly, a Pareto efficient outcome can be achieved if every project is constructed by the tribe which most benefits all three tribes collectively. This information is summarized in *Table 54*, which allows us to easily identify a Pareto efficient allocation of projects (marked in bold for convenience):

1. Observation point – needs to be allocated to tribe C which will generate 20 points for all tribes. This is more than the 10 or 0 that would result from allocating it to tribe A and B respectively.
2. Wave breaker – needs to be allocated either to tribe B or C which will generate 15 points.
3. Astronomical observatory – needs to be allocated to tribe B which will generate 20 points.

4. Temple – needs to be allocated either to tribe A or B which will generate 15 points.
5. Storm shelter – needs to be allocated to tribe C which will generate 15 points.
6. Repair and improve homes – needs to be allocated to tribe A which will generate 20 points.
7. Warehouse – needs to be allocated to either tribe A or C which will generate 15 points.
8. Improve crop yield – not enough resources to complete the project, which means -9 points.

In this allocation, the parties can collectively obtain 111 points. However, what is challenging for this roleplay is that to reach Pareto efficiency, each participant will have to cooperate with the other parties, retain a holistic perspective that maximizes benefits for all three teams by staying conscious of the connections between the issues and lastly, be flexible on the issues for which they feel they are particularly adept or have a natural advantage. For example, as illustrated in *Table 54*, the optimal allocation for any single project typically involves allocating it to a party that has very few resources necessary to complete it. However, intuition and ego can blind one from seeing this. Giving up a rather strong negotiation position to complete a project by agreeing to allocate it to a party with fewer resources seems like a poor decision. This is not always the case. To counter this risk, the negotiators must adopt a more open cooperative attitude and address the problem with a focus on how all can benefit. Indeed, this is especially important in this roleplay due to the strong mutual dependence on resources among the tribes and lack of an attractive BATNA (Best Alternative To a Negotiated Agreement).

Initially, this roleplay appears to be a distributive negotiation. This might incline the negotiators to apply positional bargaining strategies in order to claim the biggest share of a supposedly fixed amount of resources. Indeed, it is certainly possible to conduct this negotiation with such a strategy, but it would result in leaving a significant amount of value on the table. Such negotiations would certainly result in lower scores than those achieved by negotiators exploring the integrative potential of this roleplay.

Therefore, more advisable would be to follow an integrative approach by first exploring the interests of the other negotiators followed by a joint search for value-maximizing options. By doing so, negotiators would discover that the allocation of the projects can be linked and that mutual gain can be created by being flexible on initial positions. A necessary dynamic needed for this is each party's ability to build relationships and create trust.

However, in relationship building and trust development, one must remain conscious of the risk of deception. In negotiations like Connor Paradise, imperfect knowledge of each other's preferences and resources poses a temptation to manipulate information as a mean to claim additional value. This adds additional complexity to an already complex (multi-party and multi-issue) scenario. Should this occur and be uncovered, relationships would most certainly be damaged. Moreover, not only would it have profound negative consequences in real life negotiation, but it might also produce a suboptimal outcome in this roleplay.

Despite the importance of value creation as a driving force behind maximizing the Pareto efficiency, one cannot ignore the equal importance that value claiming plays on a strong points outcome for each team. That is, depending on the combination of the parties' value creation and claiming skills, a Pareto efficient outcome can lead tribe A to a score between 27 and 42 points, tribe B to 27-47 points, and tribe C to 32-42 points. In other words, Pareto efficiency itself does not guarantee a great outcome for each negotiator. As the sum of benefits increases for all three teams, each negotiator should insist on getting their fair share. That is, because the ultimate goal in multilateral negotiations is to maximize one's own benefits, teams differentiate themselves by augmenting value creation with that of value claiming. It is the combination of both skills that makes the winner.

For the benefit of reference, during The Negotiation Challenge 2013 four teams managed to identify and agree to a Pareto optimal allocation but only in two cases was the distribution of points among the negotiators the same. All negotiators ended this round with an agreement.

The best substantive outcome obtained by the negotiators that represented tribe A was 42 points (two separate teams), but the final project allocations were not Pareto efficient (total score of 96 and 101). On average, tribe A negotiators claimed 33 points and the lowest score was 22 points.

The best substantive outcome obtained by the negotiators that represented tribe B was 47 points, and the final project allocation was Pareto efficient. On average, tribe B negotiators claimed 34 points and the lowest score was 27 points.

Finally, the best substantive outcome obtained by the negotiators that represented tribe C was 42 points (two separate teams), and the final project allocations were Pareto efficient (111 points). On average, tribe C negotiators claimed 31 points and the lowest score was 22 points

As an endnote to this debriefing, it is now evident that the performance evaluation for this roleplay is based on a substantive outcome. This occurs by using a common valuation (benefit points) that quantifies preferences based on construction project allocation. Unfortunately, the substantive basis of this evaluation partly biases the roleplay toward a short-term perspective. However, since the tribes need to continue to live in peace together on their little island indefinitely and future cooperation might turn out necessary, a longer-term perspective would be more realistic. In this case, it would be instrumental also to measure the relational outcome for each party.

Although for administrative reasons we decided not to do this during The Negotiation Challenge 2013, it would be possible to do so by using a simplified version of the Subjective Value Inventory questionnaire to capture each party's relational outcome. However, in this case, each party would need to evaluate each of their negotiation partners separately. However, since these relational variables are expressed in different units than those of the substantive variables, they would need to be normalized (z-scores) and added together to obtain each party's overall score summarizing their performance (substantive and relational outcome).

Project	Score of A if a project assigned to:			Score of B if a project assigned to:			Score of C if a project assigned to:		
	A	B	C	A	B	C	A	B	C
Observation point	10	-5	5	0	10	5	0	-5	10
Wave breaker	10	0	5	0	10	0	0	5	10
Astronomical observatory	10	5	0	-5	10	0	-5	5	10
Temple	10	5	0	5	10	-5	0	0	10
Shelter	10	0	0	0	10	5	-5	0	10
Repair and improve homes	10	0	-5	5	10	-5	5	0	10
Warehouse	10	5	5	5	10	0	0	-5	10
Improve crop yield	10	0	0	0	10	0	0	0	10

Table 53. Scores for each party, based on different project allocations.

Project	Score of A, B, and C if a project assigned to A:			Score of A, B, and C if a project assigned to B:			Score of A, B, and C if a project assigned to C:		
	A	B	C	A	B	C	A	B	C
Observation point	10	0	0	-5	10	-5	**5**	**5**	**10**
Wave breaker	10	0	0	**0**	**10**	5	5	0	10
Astronomical observatory	10	-5	-5	**5**	**10**	5	0	0	10
Temple	**10**	**5**	0	5	10	0	0	-5	10
Shelter	10	0	-5	0	10	0	**0**	**5**	**10**
Repair and improve homes	**10**	**5**	**5**	0	10	0	-5	-5	10
Warehouse	**10**	**5**	0	5	10	-5	5	0	10
Improve crop yield	10	0	0	0	10	0	0	0	10

Table 54. Scores for each party, based on different project allocations with Pareto efficient allocation marked in bold.

4
BEYOND
THE **NEGOTIATION**
SIMULATIONS

By offering a unique opportunity to compare negotiation skills and check their efficiency in an international environment, negotiation competitions have become a valuable part of negotiation pedagogy. As such, they have become attractive events for graduate students from around the world seeking to become the world's best student negotiators.

Since the collection of negotiation simulations included in this book have each been used and vetted in The Negotiation Challenge, exploring them should give potential participants a better feeling of what they can expect during a negotiation competition. We encourage negotiation instructors and coaches to use them in their teaching or while preparing their teams.

However, practicing negotiation skills with our simulations, although essential for successful participation in negotiation competitions, is certainly not everything. Based on our experience in organizing and judging negotiation competitions around the world, we have also put together a series of seven recommendations we hope will help student negotiators during the application process and also in the preparation for and participation in negotiation competitions.

Involve your professor or get a coach

Over the years of conducting The Negotiation Challenge competition, we have observed that an increasing number of participating teams are accompanied by their professors or coaches. We are very pleased to see this and highly support their involvement since their guidance plays an invaluable role on multiple levels. For their own team, these benefits include assisting with optimizing pre-competition team selection and helping to structure preparation activities. It also includes advising them during the competition. With their external and objective perspective, they can assist their teams with valuable insights that help them tweak their performance. Professors and coaches also accumulate the experience their teams develop during the consecutive competitions and incorporate this into their teaching. However, the value that coaches bring is not just specific to their own team. They also enrich the quality of the competition as they share their experience and feedback with other participating teams and event organizers. Directly before the start of each competition, we organize a special event for the accompanying professors and coaches. We are very pleased to see a growing community of negotiation scholars and practitioners attend The Negotiation Challenge.

Select a strong team, organize an internal negotiation competition

The organizers of The Negotiation Challenge have a tangible interest in increasing the quality of the competition by inviting only the best possible teams. Thus, toward the goal of increasing competitiveness, one of the criteria that influences our admission decision is whether an applying team has been endorsed by their home institution and selected through an internal competition. This is driven by our experience that selecting teams through internal selection procedures, mostly small internal negotiation competitions, is a better assessment filter for skills than selecting teams based just on their applications. Past performance statistics for the TNC support this. Therefore, we encourage potential applicants and their professors or coaches to use the negotiation simulations like those included in this book to set up internal negotiation competitions to determine the best team to apply to The Negotiation Challenge.

Many negotiation competitions also include individual rounds during which the teams are split up, and each team member negotiates on his/her own. Therefore, apart from building strong functional teams, it is important that each negotiator can also master the challenge alone. As demonstrated in one of the previous chapters, individual rounds include negotiation simulations that test a participant's ability to combine both value creation and value claiming skills. Although some specialization within the teams might be helpful during the competition, a team's performance in the individual rounds is the sum of the individual scores of its members. In summary, a school's internal negotiation competition might turn out to be a very helpful tool by which to select the members of the team to represent it during The Negotiation Challenge.

Impress us with your passion

When we started The Negotiation Challenge back in 2007, our goal was for it to become a platform for sharing and comparing negotiation skills for students passionate about negotiation. Ten years of exciting and fun competitions later, this goal has most certainly been achieved. However, what we now have is what some would call a "good problem." That is, because of the competition's growth in popularity in attracting passionate and skilled teams, the admission process has become very competitive. The challenge now is in choosing the best teams among the many applicants so that we can continue to raise the level and quality of the competition. Unfortunately, the TNC admission's committee does not have the direct possibility to test applicants' overall suitability before the competition. Therefore, they must rely on the key proxy criteria outlined at the beginning of this book that are evident within the application packet to help us determine top candidates.

However, there is one thing that we find particularly important. That is a passion for negotiation. This means that to stand out, although applications should certainly demonstrate a combination of knowledge and experience in negotiation, we filter this knowledge and experience through a lens of whether it demonstrates a passion for negotiation. Evidence of this may include any negotiation or conflict resolution courses or seminars taken, or it could also be demonstrated through participation in negotiation competitions or any other extracurricular activities such as student interest groups that focus on negotiation relevant topics. Lastly, it may also include any practical business and legal negotiations made during internships or full-time employment. What is important is to demonstrate that negotiation is the participants' passion.

Work on your negotiation intelligence

As we have discovered from our countless discussions with participants, proper preparation is critical to performing well in The Negotiation Challenge. For many, this preparation begins with enrollment in a negotiation course in the October following the beginning of the winter semester. Such courses are a very good starting point for developing negotiators to develop and practice their negotiation intelligence since they learn both a wide spectrum of negotiation techniques as well as the context in which to apply them.

However, as important as these courses are, they will probably be insufficient by themselves to fully prepare a potential participant for the level of competition that exists in an international negotiation competition like The Negotiation Challenge. Therefore, we also recommend using the roleplay simulations included in this book to extend the learning process and further develop the participants' negotiation intelligence. A repetitive practice regime built on using these competition-tested roleplays will help develop a greater sensitivity and intuition in correctly recognizing the type of negotiation situation one faces and in how to address it most effectively. To support this process, the book provides debriefings at the end of each roleplay that offer important learning insights such as discussions on optimal roleplay solutions. These debriefings also provide benchmarking results from previously held TNC competitions. This provides an ability to compare and calibrate a team's performance against those obtained in an actual competitive environment.

Be prepared for an intense and emotional competition

Compared with the level of emotions typically displayed in our negotiation courses and executive seminars, it is sometimes astonishing to observe how much more intense emotions are during The Negotiation Challenge. This is certainly understandable since, although no one is winning a million dollars, what they are winning is prestige and respect. For competitors as passionate about negotiation as those in the TNC this emotionalism seems magnified.

Therefore, although the overall atmosphere of the competition and the relationships between the teams has always remained friendly, one must be prepared for such an exciting, emotional environment, especially on the potential relational outcome of the negotiations. From a positive perspective, such emotionalism can be interpreted as a sign of honesty if displayed in a way that is perceived by others as positive or in a way that supports a non-confrontational or non-aggressive negotiation style. Indeed, teams displaying high levels of emotions are very popular with other participants. As such, it can strengthen one's abilities. However, emotion can also be a detriment. During past competitions, we have observed that highly emotional teams generally end up with poorer substantive outcomes. They often get deadlocked in arguments about who is right and who is wrong or unproductively clash so long on differences that negotiation time expires without an agreement.

For both reasons, we recommend that teams include in their preparations, methods by which to manage both their emotions and the emotions of their negotiation partners.

Build a positive reputation and do not compromise your moral standards

A previous winner of The Negotiation Challenge once told us that besides the pride that comes from winning the competition and from the ensuing congratulations from the other teams, she was most proud of her team being recognized as having won using a cooperative, considerate and inclusive negotiation style. Indeed, for that competition, upon being pronounced the winner, her team received a standing ovation, not only for winning the competition but for their highly ethical negotiating style.

Over the course of the TNC, participating teams have demonstrated a wide spectrum of negotiation approaches, attitudes, strategies, and tactics, which are built on various philosophies from a principle-based "win-win" approach to something more Machiavellian, pursuing victory by all means. In all cases, whether it is built on integrity, fairness and cooperation, like that described above, or on distrust and deceit, it is interesting to observe how quickly a team acquires a reputation from other participants.

Notably, both types can influence the dynamics of negotiations taking place during the competition and as a consequence a team's performance. Not surprisingly, a negative reputation seems to be stronger and more persistent as teams affected by this behavior inform other teams about it and warn them to take caution not to repeat their mistakes.

As the organizers and judges of The Negotiation Challenge, we do include ethics in the evaluation of performance since it supports the pedagogical mission of the competition to send a clear message about what expectations should be for negotiation champions.

Share your experience and assure continuity

Participating in The Negotiation Challenge is a special experience. However, it is important to see it as more than just a one-time event. Rather it represents an important continuum of activity focused on improving the teaching of negotiation skills. This continuum starts when inspired and motivated participants share their TNC experience with their fellow students back at their academic institution. This knowledge transfer then gets incorporated in ways that strengthen both an institution's preparation program and The Negotiation Challenge itself.

Naturally, for institutions, the experience gained during the competition plays an invaluable role in strengthening preparations for the following year's event whether it is in the continued participation of a returning team or whether it is in their role as a coach or sparring partner in preparing a new team for that institution. In either case, we have noticed that institutions that embrace this continuity typically perform very well and end up in the top of the rankings.

The Negotiation Challenge benefits as well from its network of prominent alumni, who remain involved in the organization, including the sponsoring and judging of future competitions. In this regard, we explicitly encourage all TNC participants to join our networks on social media, help us recruit great student negotiators for future competitions and support us in any way they can.

As with great negotiations, the writing
of this book has been a collaborative process.
In this spirit of collaboration, we are always
receptive to helpful feedback from readers
on how to improve it.
Thus, from the smallest spelling or grammar
error that we have missed to your thoughts
on improving its structure,
please send your feedback to:

book@thenegotiationchallenge.org.

Printed in the USA
CPSIA information can be obtained
at www.ICGtesting.com
LVHW011610130823
755093LV00001B/24

9 788395 002922